Also by Phillip Lopate

Education

BEING WITH CHILDREN (1975)
JOURNAL OF A LIVING EXPERIMENT (1980)

Poetry

THE EYES DON'T ALWAYS WANT TO STAY OPEN (1972)
THE DAILY ROUND (1976)

Fiction

CONFESSIONS OF SUMMER (1979)

Bachelorhood

Bachelorhood

Tales of the Metropolis

Phillip Lopate

Little, Brown and Company   Boston/Toronto

FIRST EDITION

"Renewing Sodom and Gomorrah" © 1980 by The New
York Times Company, reprinted by permission.

The author is grateful to the following publishers for permission to quote as noted:

Hill & Wang for material from *Roland Barthes* by Roland
Barthes, translated from the French by Richard Howard,
translation © 1977 by Farrar, Straus and Giroux, Inc.

Stanford University Press for material from *Kafū the Scribbler: The Life and Writings of Nagai Kafū,* translated and
annotated by Edward Seidensticker, 1965.

Walker and Company for material from *The Burning
Brand,* by Cesare Pavese, translated by A. E. Murch (with
Jeanne Molli), 1961.

Library of Congress Cataloging in Publication Data
Lopate, Phillip, 1943-
 Bachelorhood: tales of the metropolis.

 1. Bachelors. I. Title.
HQ800.3.L66   305.3   81-11744
ISBN 0-316-53198-7   AACR2

MV
Designed by Susan Windheim
Published simultaneously in Canada
by Little, Brown & Company (Canada) Limited

PRINTED IN THE UNITED STATES OF AMERICA

To My Family

Acknowledgments

I want to thank my editor, William Phillips, for his understanding of the book and his prodding to make it better. I owe a great deal to my agent, Wendy Weil, and to the following people for going over parts of the text and suggesting improvements: Diane Stevenson, Bill Zavatsky, Susan Opotow, Ann Lauterbach, Peter Minichiello, Ted Solataroff, Frances Kiernan, Sally Arteseros, Jane Mankiewicz, Max Apple, Carol Ascher, Marjorie Welish, Colin Greer, Melissa Clemence, and most especially my family — Albert, Frances, Leonard, Bettyann and Joan Lopate.

Part of this book was written with the aid of a National Endowment for the Arts grant in Essays, and I want to thank that institution for its support.

Some of these pieces originally appeared, in more or less the same form, in the following publications: *The American Book Review, The New York Times, Sun, Pequod, The Big House* (an anthology of poets' prose), *Cedar Rock Review, Marxist Perspectives, St. Mark's Poetry Newsletter, Approach, ZZZ,* and *Editor's Choice: Literature and Graphics from the U.S. Small Press, 1965–1977*. Grateful acknowledgment is extended the editors of each.

Contents

Introduction

IN writing this book, I fell under the spell of the personal essay. It is a form that, to me, has charm and suppleness and warmth. I am not sure why it lost its popular appeal for so much of the twentieth century, but I am pleased that it seems to be undergoing the beginning of a revival with such distinguished practitioners as John Graves and Joan Didion. I wanted to add to these married voices an unmarried perspective, because, for all that writers and human beings share, it makes a difference — having a mate — in how one sees or "receives" the world.

A bachelor with a detached watchfulness may function easily as a roving anthropologist in his own society. He has certain advantages as an investigator of social life: he can travel light, he can explore milieus without having to make explanations at home, he is sometimes a welcome extra dinner guest. But there are disadvantages in his perspective as well: his need to preserve his freedom may incline him to make judgments of people that are distorted but that allow him to extricate himself from problematic entanglements. Forewarned is forearmed.

I also do not pretend to be a "pure" bachelor. I was married for five years, and it was, to use a cowardly double negative, not an unhappy experience. This means, I suppose, that I can speak about both sides of the track. But the vast majority of my adult years I have spent single.

I would like to begin to rescue the term *bachelor* from the antiquarian, sardonic air surrounding it at present. The half sneer, half indulgent smile with which most speakers pronounce this word has sent me off to the research library in self-defense. It seems that even a half-century ago, *bachelor* conjured up both a bon vivant and an ass: somebody's unmarried uncle with lecherous proclivities (nevertheless probably celibate),* a small independent income, and an all-thumbs approach to domestic details. He was a frequent figure on the comic stage; such play titles as *The Bachelor's Baby* and *The Bachelor and the Chafing Dish* give a clue to the hilarious possibilities envisioned by the public when this character was brought into contact with certain facts of normal life.

I have been advised by some of my women friends that the female counterpart has even more negative associations. *Spinster*, they say, connotes an out-and-out unattractive creature whose sex has shriveled up, and who tends to be envious and mean. Certainly, women have a good case to make. While the dictionary defines bachelor merely as "an unmarried man," it somewhat more spitefully describes a spinster as "a woman who has remained unmarried beyond the conventional age of marriage." It is interesting that the two words also have different class connotations, stemming from their linguistic roots. *Bachelor* comes out of the Middle English *bacheler*, from Old French, out of Medieval Latin *baccalarius*. The French *bachelier* was "a young man aspiring to be made a knight," or "in the service of another knight." In feudal times, the English term was "bachelor-at-arms." That would still make him a member of the property-

* *Célibataire* — French for bachelor.

owning class. At some later point, the words *baccalaureate* and *bachelor* became intertwined with learning and academic degrees — probably because university students were usually unmarried men.

Let us fix in our minds the image of the bachelor as a chivalric, somewhat scholarly escort leading the horse by the bit. He does not have the heroic part in life; he is not the main knight but attendant upon him. In short, he is *waiting for something to happen.*

In George Jean Nathan's *Bachelor Life,* the frontispiece cartoon shows a man in swallowtails clumsily fixing his black tie before a mirror, no doubt in preparation for some lavish social function or dinner party at the Algonquin. So, even as late as 1941, the word *bachelor* had kept its upper-class veneer. *Spinster,* on the other hand, quite obviously derives from the sewing trades. It was the lot of these respectable, unpaired women (or "odd women," to use George Gissing's phrase) of the working classes to support themselves at the spinning wheel. To me, this argues for the resuscitation of the word *spinster* as a badge of working-class pride.

In any event, both terms have fallen into disrepute these days, replaced by the contemporary neutered *singles.* Now, *singles* makes me think of people with tennis rackets, hot to scare up a game. The very use of the noun in plural form strips the solitary condition of its last dignity. Alone, the bachelor or spinster has at least the solace of a trim border around the self.

It is a curious thing about singles: there must be millions of us in the big cities, and the small towns; suddenly we are a force to be reckoned with, in demographic terms, yet all the singles magazines and ads addressed to us start with the presumption that our first urge is to get rid of that identity. Where are the best ski lodges to meet a mate, the best bars in New Orleans to pick up someone eligible? It is as though one were being recruited for a union whose main benefit was the promise of loss of membership. Singles are addressed as accidental casualties of the love marketplace, like workers temporarily laid off in a recession. There is a decorous avoidance of the idea that one may be living alone at least partly out of choice. "As you make your bed, so you must lie in it" is not a popular theme with the singles press. You are admonished instead to go out and meet someone, talk to strangers, keep talking, learn openers. And in fact, most people who find themselves solitary are unwilling to accept the identity from any long-term perspective, but view it as a kind of limbo on the way to becoming coupled.

This is understandable, since the culture regards those who remain single as pathetic figures. The Talmud tells us: "He who weds a good wife, it is as if he has fulfilled all the precepts of the Torah." On the other hand, "He who has no wife abides without good, help, joy, blessing or atonement. He who has no wife cannot be considered a whole man." Further examples could be taken from Christian, Moslem and atheistic writers, all making the same point: if you are not married and raising a family, you are not whole, you are pitiful.

Not that I would argue that we bachelors are *not* pathetic. I would merely extend the category of pathos. Most of us are pretty sorry creatures, regardless of marital status. I have no desire to modishly reaffirm such a message as "It's all right to be single," since, whether it is or is not all right in the final analysis, one may still have to play it out.

Only let me add: I have sympathy for anyone who is trying to live alone with strength. Since there is so little training in the culture for nourishing oneself singly, how does one go about building up a world to support oneself in that state? I hate "how-to" books. What I am trying to do here is rather to describe the many facets of a life, my own, as an example of this process. The leap of faith that Kierkegaard faced was whether or not to marry Regina. The leap of faith addressed here is whether or not it is possible to accept one's life in its persistent ordinary and confused dailiness, knowing that one may and could easily be alone for the rest of it. Can I marry the world, instead of one person?

These pieces (although several have been published individually) were all written expressly for the book in hand, to arrive at something like a portrait in aggregate of the bachelor temperament and a bachelor's life. The book is concerned with four themes, roughly paralleling four aspects of the bachelor sensibility, which I'll label in shorthand as women and love; the bachelor as stroller, observer, voyeur of the urban scene; the bachelor and his friends, married and otherwise; the bachelor as artist and thinker, or controlled procreator. Running through all these aspects, and perhaps the overriding issue of bachelorhood, is the notion of freedom. There is a kind of creative ambivalence about freedom that permeates the bachelor sensibility and gives a twist and tension to the whole perspective. On the one hand, there is a romantic longing for the ties that bind one to a wife, children, a cause. On the other hand, there is the prevailing need to be in the world but not of it. The bachelor wants to be left alone, or at least to schedule encounters with others on his own turf and own time. He wants to be disengaged, not in the sense of wanting not to feel, but in being able to harness and control feeling for some higher clarity. At least that forms the ideal behind the rationalizations.

To say more about the book's plan would be to pretend to a grander thematic structure than exists, since this is, after all, still basically a *collection* of essays, memoirs, nostalgic diatribes, vignettes and poems. If order is to be found here, I would ask the reader to help a little by jostling the pieces against each other into patterns of meaning, like crystals of a kaleidoscope given a knowing tap.

Part

One

My Drawer

I AM looking through the top drawer of my bedroom dresser this morning — something I almost never do. I have a reticence about examining these articles, which I don't quite understand; it's as though the Puritan side of me said it was a waste of time, if not faintly indecent. Since I have moved my socks to another drawer there is even less reason to visit these redundant objects. Six months go by without my doing any more than feeling around blindly for a cuff link. My top drawer is a *way station* in which I keep the miscellanea that I cannot bear to throw away just yet, but that I fully intend to, the moment things get out of hand. So far the drawer can take it. It is too early for triage. But this morning I have an urge to make an inventory of the drawer, in a last attempt to understand the symbolic underpinnings of my character.

In it I find a pair of 3-D movie glasses. A silver whistle. A combination lock in good repair but whose combination has long been lost. A strip of extra cuff material for the legs of my white linen suit — should I ever grow an inch or two I can sew it on. One plastic and one aluminum shoehorn. A button that says BOYCOTT LETTUCE. Keys to old houses and offices. My last pair of glasses before the prescription changed — who can throw out a pair of eyeglasses? Two nail clippers. Cuff links. A pair of rusty unusable children's scissors. A windproof lighter I won at an amusement park; too bad I don't smoke. Oh, and lots more, much more. But before I go on, shouldn't I try to approach this mess more systematically — to categorize, to make generalizations?

One category that suggests itself is gifts I have no particular affection for, but am too superstitious to chuck out. (If you throw away a gift, something terrible will happen: the wastebasket will explode, or you'll never get another.) They include this pair of cloth finger puppets that I suppose were meant to give me endless hours of delight while sitting on my bed pretending to be Punch and Judy with myself. Because I work with children, people keep bringing me juvenile toys — magic sets, mazes with ball bearings, paddle-balls — confusing the profession with the profession's clients. Over the years I have been given a whole collection of oddities that do not really amuse me or match my sense of perversity. Nothing is trickier than bringing someone a novelty gift, since each person's definition of cute or campy is such a private affair.

Now we come to my "jewelry." Most of these items wandered into my possession toward the middle of the sixties, during those few seconds in American history when it was considered progressive for men to wear medallions and layers of necklaces. In my top drawer I find an imitation-elephant-tusk necklace, a multicolored string of Amerindian beads, and a hodgepodge of what I can only call spiritual amulets — tangled-up chains and rings that are supposed to contain special powers or that symbolize the third eye. Usually these ornaments were given to me with the explanation that most men the donor knew would be too uptight to wear jewelry like this in public, but that I was free enough to be at peace with my feminine side. Little did they know. Each and every one has landed in my top drawer, enough for me to open my own jewelry stall at a street fair.

Other mementos of hipper days include a large brown-velvet King's Road bow tie, a pack of moldering Bambu cigarette papers, and both DUMP LBJ and IMPEACH NIXON buttons. I find it hard to throw away political buttons — as hard as it was in those days actually to wear them. There is also a badge from a conference, with the words "Hi! I'm —" and my name on it. Toward the back of the drawer are my war medals: my high-school American history award, with its pea green / navy blue / red tricolor; my yellow-and-white-ribboned English award; the silver badge from the Fire Department for best fire-prevention essay. Glory days! They do cheer me up when I see them, though they are as useless now as the keys that no longer fit my door.

The keys belong to the category of things I kept to be *on the safe side*. For instance, an official bank card for cashing checks, no good to me now since I no longer go to that bank, but what if it were to fall into the wrong hands? I find also a wristwatch case with midnight-blue lining that seemed too pretty to part with, and that would make an excellent box for safety pins or — whatever. Oh, and a suede-looking drawstring purse that once held a bottle of over-priced shampoo (I seem particularly susceptible to these packages for luxury items). I realize I'm fooling myself when I say I will someday find a use for these containers. How can I when I ignore them for months at a time, and forget that they're there? They live a hidden life in the back street of my consciousness. Perhaps the drawer's purpose is to house objects that arouse only half-digested desires never fantasized all the way through. That is why I must not look into it too often. These are secret fantasies even I am not supposed to understand.

Even more than desire, these objects seem to have the

power of arousing guilt; that is, they have fixed me with the hypnotizing promise not to throw them away. I find myself protecting them with an uneasy conscience, like someone whom I caused to be crippled and who now has the upper hand. I suppose if I were to examine the derivations of each of these keepsakes, many would call up some road not taken, some rejection of possibility. Or perhaps they are secretly connected to each other by surrealist logic, like the objects in a Joseph Cornell box, and if I were to lay them out on top of the dresser I could put together the story of my subconscious mind.

When I consider my peculiar, fitful relation to the drawer as a whole, I have to think back to the original top drawer: the one in my parents' house when I was seven and eight years old. There was nothing I liked better than to sneak into their bedroom when everyone else was out of the house, and to approach their large, dark mahogany dresser, with its altar top composed of the round reversible mirror, the wedding photograph, the stray hair-curlers, and the Chinese black-lacquered music box where my mother kept her Woolworth jewelry. Then, taking my time, I would pull open the three-sectioned top drawer by its brass handles. What was so fascinating about rifling through their drawer? I used to find nothing very unusual: some objects of obscure masculine power, like my father's leather traveling case, a shaving brush, a pair of suspenders, a wallet with photos of us, the children. Then I would go over to my mother's side of the drawer, and visit her bloomers and her gypsy scarves. I would pick up each item and smell the perfume: Arabia! Then back to my father's side, for some clues into his stolid, remote, Stakhanovite personality. In the middle section was no-man's-land, with elastic bands, garters, pipe cleaners. Once, it seems to me, I found a deck of pornographic playing cards. Am I imagining this? Isn't this rather what I kept looking for and *not* finding? I know I came across the rumored box of prophylactics, which my older brother had assured me would be there. Yet these balloons did not thrill me much, or as much as they might have if I had only been seeking "dirty things." I was searching for, not clarification, but a mystery, the mystery of masculine and feminine. Certainly I was looking for the tools of sexuality that held together the household, but this went further than mere rude instruments; it included everything that made my mother so different from my father, and that still enabled them to share the same life, as they shared this drawer. The drawer recorded without explanation the ordinariness of this miracle that had given birth to me.

And now I live alone — Oedipal child that I am. The contradictions of my top drawer stem from my own idiosyncrasies and not from any uneasy cohabitation of two creatures of the opposite sex. To pry through their things, I see now, was a kind of premasturbation. Where better to indulge than in the bedroom of one's parents? Even now I must be affected by that old taboo against self-abuse — in going through drawers, at least — which explains why I go through my own top drawer with embarrassed haste.

My drawer has its secrets as well. To honor the old prying and bring it down to earth, so to speak, I keep a box of prophylactics. Also, toward the back, I am ashamed to admit, are a few of those ads handed to me in the street for massage parlors: "Beautiful Girls — Complete Privacy — One Price. . . . Tahitia — Gives You Just What You Expect!" and an awful color photo of two women in a bubble bath with a grinning curly-headed man. These are also kept just in case, to be on the safe side. Here is a squashed-up tube of diaphragm cream, with just enough in it for one more go. Kay must have left it behind, as she did this frayed pair of panties. Do you know we almost moved in together, before we broke up for the very last time? And finally, the most forbidden object of all: the five-and-ten I.D. heart with Kay's name on it. Since I have forbidden myself to brood about her anymore, I must open and shut the drawer very quickly to skip seeing it, and inevitably I do catch sight of that heart-shaped button, the sort that high-school sweethearts wear. She gave it to me in our first year, and thinking I didn't love her enough, she accused me of being ashamed to wear it in front of my friends. She was right, of course — I have always been wary about advertising my heart on my sleeve, whether political or amorous. Kay was right, too, that in the beginning I did not love her enough. And now that I do, and she loves me not, I faithfully continue to wear her pin, in my top drawer. It has the place of honor in that reliquary, in my museum of useless and obsolete things that stand ready to testify at any moment to all that is never lost.

Willy

M Y mother was seeing another man. His name was
Willy. It may have been childish confusion — I
was eight years old at the time — or a trick memory plays on us, but I seem to remember the jeep he drove
was also a Willys. This car has disappeared from modern
life. I am unable even to picture it. But at the time it
colored all my thinking about the affair. First, it was described to me as rugged, able to handle rough terrain, and
so I came to picture the man himself. Second, the Willys
had military associations, like my toy jeeps with green GI
Joe soldiers jolted out of the wheel seat as the car went
over the wooden runners separating one room from another.

My mother and Willy both worked in a war plant near
the Brooklyn Navy Yard, manufacturing radio parts for the
troops in Korea. My mother admired Willy for having been
in the army, and even reenlisting for a second tour of duty.
I come from a long line of draft dodgers. My paternal grandparents fled Russia around 1900 to escape military conscrip-
tion. My father was excused from World War II because he
had four small children. But Willy was not afraid of the
service. Willy's only mistake, my mother said, was to marry

a woman who was a complete bitch and only wanted his paycheck.

But now Willy was talking about leaving his wife and taking Mom and us kids to California, driving across the country in his jeep to the land of fruit trees and big defense factories.

And what about my father? Were we just supposed to leave him behind?

All that I understood about the Willy situation came to me from far away, and I kept forgetting what little I knew as quickly as possible, so that each time I heard about the affair, it seemed to be a novel, improbable rumor. I was still suffering from that childhood dreaminess that allowed me to ponder, for minutes on end, the order of dealing with socks and shoes, and even resulted once in my forgetting, when I had been sent out in a snow to bring back crumb buns and onion rolls, what I was supposed to buy, where the bakery was, and finally, as I looked about and saw everything covered with white, where my house had disappeared to! Not that I was stupid, but my attention was extremely selective. Car fins fascinated me. I was good out of vagueness rather than will. When it finally came to family matters, I relied on my older brother, Hal, to let me know if something important was starting to happen.

The girls had already met Willy and seen his jeep. One day after work, Mom had introduced them to her boyfriend and they went for a ride around Brooklyn, all the way to Coney Island. It seemed as though Mom was buying off the girls with this spin in a real automobile, saying: This is what our life could be like every day with your new "fun" father.

Somehow Hal and I had not been included in this pleasure jaunt. One more reason to detest our sisters when they came back with excited reports about Willy. What did girls know? Hal said. Their heads could be turned so easily by flashy things like cars. But in a way you couldn't blame them. Molly was just a kid — seven — hair still in ringlets, happy, goofy, a daredevil. And the baby, Leah, was three. She went where she was told, had no real mind of her own yet. A cute kid who liked to run around without panties and climb up the piano.

We lived on the top floor of a five-story tenement in Williamsburgh, facing the BMT elevated train, or as everyone called it, the El. Our floors and windows would vibrate from the El, which shook the house like a giant, roaring as his eyes were being poked out. When we went down into the street we played on a checkerboard of sunspots and shadows, which rhymed the railroad ties above our heads. Even the brightest summer day could not lift the darkness and burnt-rubber smell of our street. I would hold my breath when I passed under the El's long shadow. It was the spinal column of my childhood, both oppressor and liberator, the monster who had taken away all our daylight, but on whose back alone one could ride out of the neighborhood into the big broad world.

My father usually took us somewhere on Saturdays — not because he especially wanted to, but because my mother hounded him to get us out of the house. She said she would go crazy if she didn't have a few hours of privacy. In the years when they were still getting along, Father and Mother used to send us to the movies on Saturday afternoons at the Commodore Theater when they wanted time alone together. But once the trouble started, my mother wanted my father out of the house as well. She nagged him and we ganged up too, like wild wolves smelling blood, until about noontime he would put down his book, and take us someplace on the train.

But first, however, he would show his resentment by an uncomfortable little ritual. When we reached the stairway to the elevated train, Father would line us up for inspection. He would find something dirty on our faces, and, wetting a finger, he would correct the offending smudge with his rough laborer's hands till our eyes watered from the pain. Or he would straighten our collar, grumbling aloud, "Your mother lets you go around like ragamuffins!" Never mind that his own fingernails were streaked by green ridges of dirt. His dissatisfaction with our appearance signaled to us that for the moment at least we were our mother's children, he wanted nothing to do with us, perhaps had never wanted us.

Strange, but I would feel a twinge of sympathy for him then. That he should be trapped into working like a dog to clothe and feed us useless kids.

Sometimes he would take us to his factory, which he referred to simply as "the Place." I have to go to the Place, he would announce, and everyone would know he meant his job. It was a ribbon-dyeing plant, with vats and troughs of ink — a business that trafficked only in color, scarlet and indigo. I thought of it also, because of the word *dyeing*, as a place connected to death, a dying factory, where my father gave up his life each day. But it was at work alone he seemed fully alive, lifting enormous spools of ribbons with his knotted arms onto a high shelf, moving through bins with purpose and direction, as he never seemed to move at home.

When he came home he wanted nothing except to eat, fall asleep, or read. Difficult, moody books — Faulkner, Schopenhauer, Dostoevski, James T. Farrell — were his favorites, and when he read it was the same as when he was sleeping. If you woke him accidentally from his nap, he would look at you with harsh nearsighted eyes, his glasses still on the sofa arm, like a boarder who didn't know where these children came from. Sometimes he made us laugh, tickling us with his long simian arms, or letting the girls comb his hair into bangs. Tall and gaunt, he reminded us of Abraham Lincoln. When he was in a joking mood, he would say strange things like "You are being inordinately obstreperous," using words we didn't understand for their humorous effect. It was our mother who would say the really important things, like "I want a quart of milk and some bread and bring back change" — statements to which you had to pay attention. My father drifted from ornamental language into silence. He would slip so far into himself that at the dinner table he would point, as if he had forgotten the words for sugar, knife, meat. "What's the matter?" my mother would say sarcastically. "You don't have a tongue?" We kids, hating her for humiliating our father in front of us, would nevertheless snicker at his strangeness; and he would frown at us with a ferocious look of being betrayed by the mob, that *Et tu Brute* stare.

My attempts to please him, and his to please me, always seemed to misfire. His tender moments had a self-defeating fragility, as though he expected to be rejected for having done something foolish. Since at home he was always under attack for his absentminded clumsiness, he developed an apologetic, apathetic manner, a humility that infuriated my mother even more. It was hard to reconcile in a single notion of "father" both the dread and the pathos he inspired — the first because he was still king of the household, meted out the disciplinary beatings and had a scary temper, the second because he seemed the butt of everyone's ridicule, almost an untouchable.

I remember, for instance, the incident of the marble cake.

We're sitting at the dinner table and eating marble cake. I love marble cake. My father is wearing glasses. He has a serious look, like a monkey concentrating on a metal puzzle.

Suddenly he picks his nose, rubs the boogie into a green ball, and, in an absentminded manner, rolls it against his forehead.

"Stop that, you're such a slob!" my mother says.

At first he doesn't know what she's talking about. Then he realizes what he has been doing and his hand descends. We children look away.

"Is there any more marble cake?" I ask.

"No, that's all," says my mother.

My father pushes his portion toward me. "Here, you can take mine."

I stare at the plate, wishing I could eat it, but disgusted because he has already put part of it in his mouth. "No, thank you."

"Go ahead," he offers, "I'm not hungry anymore."

Still, I can't bring myself to eat it. I stare at the soggy end with regret; my father doesn't understand what's wrong. Finally a look of discouragement comes over his face and he leaves the table.

The particular Saturday morning I remember, we did not go to my father's factory. No, it was the Brooklyn Museum. As usual, my mother called to us out the window, remembering at the last moment some food to pick up on the way back. This time, though, at the El's entrance, there was no inspection. My father just took us by the hand, Hal on one side, me on the other, and swung our arms as though we were great friends. The girls ran ahead. Molly was the adventurous one in the family. She ducked under the turnstile with Leah in tow, pretending to be underage herself. On the platform, Molly started leaning over to watch the first sight of the train coming round the curve from Manhattan. Ordinarily, Father would have scolded her, but this time he gently took her hand, moving a safe step backward, and smiled at us boys. What in the heck was going on?

We got on the last car for Molly's sake. The girls raced over to the rear window to look out. Pop, Hal and I took two cane benches facing each other. I loved those old tan wicker seats, loved to run my hand in the weave and pick out the loose ends. I sat by the window, my legs rocking in excitement. To be inside the train while it was making one of those wide whooshing turns like a roller coaster that could easily jump the track and spill us down into the streets but never did, to look into *other people's* windows and fire escapes, to scrape past the moldy warehouses with their flaking olive walls, to stare down at the public square below every other El stop, with its pizza and delicatessen signs — all this was too marvelous to sit still for. Of course there were no elegant neighborhoods — wherever the El went it looked on or created blight, as who with money would want to live next door to it? — but poverty worse than ours was fun to watch from this height, and sometimes in the distance there would be blocks of trim private homes.

Father pulled out a pad of lined paper, and began writing. Usually he worked the crossword puzzle on the train, but today he was doing a poem. I remember having to memorize a poem for school: "In winter I get up at night / And dress by yellow candlelight." I asked Father what a poem really was. He said it was an expression of feeling, with certain rules that you had to follow. I sat quietly beside him and watched him composing. At one point, he took a pocket thesaurus from his coat and looked up a word.

"Who are you writing this for?" I asked timidly.

"It's for your mother."

"But it's not her birthday. Why are you writing a poem to Mom?"

"To get her love back. Shhh. . . ."

Hal gave me a brief nod, as if to say he understood everything and approved. Hal was like a wise old man sometimes; not a serene old man, but one who had seen too much pain and was afflicted with a permanent wince of understanding.

Looking over my father's shoulder, I read the first stanza:

Once in an antique time you seemed to love me,
Your quivering flesh I circled in my arms;
You panted out your gratitude — remember?
Such amorousness was but a false alarm.

I do not fear your look of proud contempt,
Albeit your motives seem so recondite;
I will not bore you with my sad laments
For disillusionment has banished spite.

"That's good, Pop," I said, not knowing what it meant. He accepted the compliment silently, continuing to work. I was fascinated by the way he kept crossing out words and moving lines around. Writing seemed suddenly sculptural, like modeling clay.

After a while I went to see what the girls were doing. Molly and I fought for the window; then we shared it. There was nothing I liked better than to stare out the back window of a train and watch the world be taken away. Later I turned around and saw Father and Hal in serious conversation, leaning toward one another.

Museums were something to be gotten through; room after room of early American portraits, men in blue uniforms with white socks and wigs, women in salmon-pink satin gowns, the George Washingtons and Mrs. Martin Van

Burens. But we'd come here for Hal's sake. Hal was good at art in school. Though only eleven, he knew he wanted to be a painter. Hal would go right up to the canvas and study the brush strokes. And I would be proud of him studying the brush strokes, being influenced.

But after a while it was not so interesting, with the Egyptian jewelry and the Colonial bedrooms, and the corny French carpets on the wall; running after Molly, who was getting mischievous, and quieting Leah, whimpering with tiredness; and that burning sinus headache I always got behind the eyebrows in museums from the pearl-grey light diffused by the skylights on an overcast day.

Coming home on the train, Pop was still being so loving toward us boys that I decided to test him by curling up across him with my head on his lap. Who knows, maybe what I had wished for had finally arrived. Maybe a whole new feeling-life would spring up between us. I would no longer be afraid of him, and he would play ball with me in Prospect Park like the other boys' fathers, and he would be good to Hal from now on instead of yelling at him. He would be a whole new father. I cuddled against his arm, pretending to be asleep.

2.

A train had stopped outside our living room. It was level with our windows, so the passengers could look in on us, and we at them. Intensely real for a second, these strangers presented their solitude in the dim rushing light, leaving behind a single detail: the memory of crossed legs, a grey creased hat.

"Which is better, Hal, a Studebaker or a Hudson?" I asked.

"A Studebaker."

"Which is better, a Studebaker or a . . . Chrysler?"

"Chrysler," said Hal, unenthusiastically.

"Isn't it true, that a Russian MiG is better than a Sabre-jet?"

"How should I know?"

He knew. He knew everything, my brother. "You do too know."

"I *don't* know. Why are you asking me all these stupid questions? And hold still."

"Am I allowed to look out the window?"

"No."

"Can I talk? I can talk at least."

"Only if I'm not working on your lips." My brother frowned and smudged the charcoal with his finger. He was trying to learn shading. Before, he had always done Battle-ships — dramatic murky black watercolors of storm clouds and aircraft carriers like those in the Brooklyn Navy Yard. But lately he had become interested in drawing people.

"Are you working on my lips now?"

"I'll tell you when I do."

"What did Daddy say to you? On the train yesterday?" I tried to sound casual, but I had been waiting for the moment to ask this question.

"I don't know if I should tell you."

"Why not?"

"Because. You might be too young."

"Oh, I'm not too young to model for you and I'm not too young when we go to the library. I'm not too young to play ball when you need someone to play with, but suddenly I'm too young. I hate that!"

My brother shrugged. "I tell you almost everything."

It was true. In spite of our three-year age difference, he treated me like an equal, his best friend — except when his friends were around. But those betrayals were rare. "Then why can't you tell me what Daddy said?" I persisted.

He looked up at me and looked down at the pad, without answering. Either he was turning it over in his mind, or he was too engrossed in drawing and forgot the question, or he was teasing me.

"I'm not going to stay still if you don't tell me what Daddy said."

"Okay, okay. You're the one who kept pestering me to draw you."

"You said you needed people to draw."

"Just let me finish this." He worked for a minute longer. When he looked up I sensed a change in him. "Daddy said Mommy wants to leave him because she loves somebody else. She wants to get a divorce." Hal's voice cracked, the way it did when he was close to tears.

"Why would she do that?"

He thought for a while, trying to gain control of himself, then answered with feigned calmness: "Because she's a bitch. I hate her. She wants to take us all to California with this stupid guy *Willy*." He pronounced the name with disgust. "I don't want to go to California."

"*I* don't want to go to California."

"Sunshine — big deal! I'd rather stay behind in New York with the cold and snow. We can live here with Daddy."

"Yeah, we can live with Daddy," I said, not really sure what was going on.

"What Mom's doing isn't right."

"What else did Daddy say?"

"He said the men in the family should stick together. Like the Three Musketeers: all for one and one for all. Are you in on it?"

I nodded, but unsurely. I knew enough to stand in line

with the men if we were dividing up that way. The only problem was, how could a little kid like me affect anything? "But did Daddy say what we should do?"

"No, not yet. But he said that if we men were *unified* — you know, that means if we stick together — that we could change Mommy's mind. She would never want to lose her children, because she loves us too much. So if we keep insisting and insisting that we won't go, she would have to give up all this stuff about Willy."

"I don't understand. Why couldn't she just take us, even if we didn't want to go?"

"Because, jerk, she doesn't want us to hate her! Anyway, I have a plan."

My neck was stiff; I got up and stretched. Then I wandered over for a peek at Hal's drawing. "It doesn't look like me but it's nice."

"I still have trouble with noses. So do you want to hear my plan?"

"Sure."

"We don't talk to Mommy. Just ignore her. Pretend she's dead."

"What if she yells at us?"

"So? Let her scream away."

"All right, but . . . what if she beats us with the ironing cord for not answering her?"

"Then she'll beat us," Hal said grimly. "Are you in on it?"

"I'm in. But, why don't we try to get the girls too?"

"Forget the girls. They're undependable."

"Yeah, I guess."

"Besides, we don't need everyone. All we need is to keep the plan and not give in. Come on, I need you in on it."

"I'm in on it. But the only thing is — won't it hurt Mommy's feelings?"

"So what if it hurts her feelings!" Hal said fiercely. "That's the whole idea, isn't it?"

Hal had everything figured out, but it still baffled me. For instance, I was puzzled about his taking Father's side, because Hal had never seemed to like our father very much. Hal was always arguing with him and trying to get in the last word, with Mom quieting them both. It had even come to blows between them recently. Hal brought home a report card with low marks in arithmetic, and Father punished him with a beating, and Hal actually had the nerve to punch him back! Mommy had had to tear Daddy off him. And now we were all allies against her, trying our hardest to hurt her feelings.

Well, it was time I stopped being such a baby. I was a soldier in Hal's regiment, and if the order came down to ignore her, then that was what I would do.

When Mom came home from work, around four as usual, she asked us what kind of day we had had at school. Hal caught my eye, shook his head no, and walked out of the kitchen. I followed him.

"I'm talking to you," said my mother. "Don't I deserve an answer?" We heard her rattling pots around. "What is this, a pigsty? Doesn't anybody wash a dish? I'm supposed to do everything around here? I'm speaking to you boys! Come in here."

I felt my body strain to obey but Hal signaled no.

"You hear me? If you don't get in here in five seconds I'm going to smack your bottoms with an ironing cord. And I mean it. You know I don't kid around. One . . . two . . ."

"We don't have to talk to her," I whispered.

"Three . . . Ah! so you decided to make an appearance. What do you call this? The table's a mess, the sink's full of dishes, the stove has — soup stains all over it. Whose idea was it to make tomato soup? Don't you know that when you make something you have to clean up after yourselves?"

I almost started to say, Hal was drawing me and we didn't get to it yet. Since Mom was partial to our artistic efforts, that would have been a good enough excuse. But Hal's bashful, demoniacal grin reminded me to keep silence.

"What's the matter, you two got lockjaw? You'll answer me good when I whack your fannies. You don't want to talk to me? So go take a flying leap. *Ich hub dir.* See if I care," she said, her eyes watering. "See if I answer when it's: Mommy, I need money for this, I love you, Mommy, I need a quarter —"

Hal squared his shoulders and walked out of the apartment. He had guts! Behind him I flew down the steps as fast as my feet would take me, and Mom stood at the top of the banister, yelling like the witch in *Hansel and Gretel,* "Boys, where are you going? Boys, come back here!" There was a new tone in her voice. For the first time it sounded as though she was begging us.

We ran past the Spanish family that lived underneath; the young mother who had long black braids and made strong Bustello coffee opened her door in her slip to see what was the matter. She looked up at my mother screaming to us. We raced down the third floor, and past the second-floor apartment of our landlady, mean old Mrs. Einstein. We were still running, out the front door, past old miser Einstein's sweatshop on the first floor where the elderly foreign women bent over their sewing machines, when we realized we had nowhere to go.

We hid in the cellar for an hour. Then we came up reluctantly for dinner. But Hal and I snubbed Mother all that night. During the next few days, though she pretended to be indifferent, we could tell the routine was getting to her. You could see her will crumbling.

By myself I would have given in long ago, but I stayed close to Hal, because Hal alone had the vision to defy this all-powerful Empress of our childhood. It was not so much that we were afraid of her. No, what took vision was to defy someone who had been so good to us. Mama had wrapped us in our snowsuits when we were small, and pulled us to market in a sled (lashed together so that we would not fall out). She had protected us the time an ugly grey rat got into my bunk bed, by chasing him with a broom; she had set the mousetraps and thrown out the poor filthy beasts with snapped necks when no one else would touch them, not even my father. It was she who got up on cold mornings without steam and lit the stove to warm the room for us, and made us hot cocoa before school; and when we came home and lay on the floor covering page after page with drawings, she was the one who applauded them all and kept us in crayons and pens.

When you depend upon someone for everything, it's not surprising if your helplessness collects hostility. But that resentment alone would not have taken us very far. We needed to fan our imagination, Hal and I, with propaganda about Mother as an evil woman, a Delilah. I had seen enough movies Saturday afternoons to know that there was a type of woman who was "bad." Oversexed. Went from man to man. It was necessary to keep this picture sharply in mind whenever my mother appealed to either of us with her hurt, "human" expression.

In the evenings, Hal would go to Father and they would have a private talk. I gathered that Father approved of what we were doing. Meanwhile, he was trying in the only way he knew how to win back Mother's love: there were more poems, one a day, begging, cajoling, accusing.

I would come across them unexpectedly all over the house, these onionskin sheets with blots of ball-point ink where my father's hand had rested. Mother would read the poems to herself with a half-sneering, half-pleased look.

3.

On the third afternoon of the pact against our mother, I came home from school to an empty house. Hal had stayed after school for Art Club, Leah was at nursery school, and Molly was running through the streets with her band of friends, boys who played hooky from school.

I took out my pack of warplane cards. I slipped the rubber band off and touched their frayed, greasy edges: the B-29, the Shooting Star, the Thunderjet, the Sabre. Olive and khaki, their very drabness signified awesome power. On the back of each bubble-gum card were statistics about speed and bombload, the name of the builder and a little history. I was particularly fascinated by Sikorsky, the renegade count and White Russian who had come over to our side. On the bottom of the pile was my favorite card, the Russian MiG, with its dread butcher's belly, like Stalin himself. I had a secret sympathy for the enemy — not because my parents were pro-Rosenberg and even knew some Communists, but because I believed what they taught me in school, that the Russians *were* treacherous, and I admired them for their villainy, just as I admired the Joker in Batman comics. Children are obsessed with fairness. I envied the Soviets their freedom to be mysteriously unfair, unfair without a qualm, which at the time I wished I could be.

Then, too, the war was like a baseball game, with its own bubble-gum cards: Americans were the Yankees, the "good guys," who always won. I, being a Brooklyn Dodger fan, hated the Yankees. The Russians were the underdogs. The

Americans were bland and righteous and strong — they were like Willy, all wanting to drive to California and take my mother away from this dark Kremlin household under the El.

But the Russian MiG would shoot them down. Ha ha! I was just setting up my cards for a battle in the air when I heard Mom come in. I knew who it was by the sound of her high heels. "Anybody home?" she called. I heard her kick off her shoes and unzip her dress. That was the first thing she did when she came home, got out of her work clothes.

"Oh, it's you," she said as she opened my bedroom door. How I wished Hal was there to direct me! "Why don't you come in the kitchen, I'll make you some cocoa." I followed her into the kitchen.

"Did you have a nice day at school?"

I nodded. A nod didn't count.

"Where's your brother?"

I shrugged.

"I'm worried about him. Are you sure you don't know where he is? It's after four . . . if he doesn't come home soon I'm going to have to call the police."

I bit my lip; that would be awful, to have the police arrive. It would be my fault. Looking at the front door, I prayed that he would come in.

"I saw Molly downstairs playing hopscotch, and I told her she had to be up by five. But I'm worried about that brother of yours. Where could he be? I'm just going to have to call the police, that's all —"

"He had to stay after school!"

My mother smiled. She couldn't control her delight at having tricked me into speaking. Then she put her arms around me and kissed me. "I've missed you, honey. Let's make up."

"Okay."

She poured me the cocoa and watched me drink it. "This is good," I said, feeling weak-willed and embarrassed.

"Come inside my room," she said. "I want us to have a talk. And I have to change my clothes."

I followed her into her bedroom and sat on the mattress beside her. My mother was wearing her black nylon slip, out of which she seemed to burst. There was a large expanse of freckled cleavage, and her skin close up had soft pores and a smell of buttermilk. I did not like to look at her heavy thighs, the insides of which were riddled with purple varicose veins that made me think of blood poisoning — they came from standing on her feet too much at work, she said — but my eyes kept seeking them out nevertheless. Perhaps it was the desire to overcome my pity and repulsion that made me stare at them. I began to wish she would put on her clothes, as she said she was going to, but instead she kept sitting beside me half dressed, sighing and reaching for the right words.

"Tell me, why haven't you and Hal been talking to me? Am I such an ogre? Have I done anything to hurt you?"

"It's not that. We wanted to help Daddy."

"I figured your old man had been talking to you! What did he say?"

"I don't know, he talked mostly to Hal."

"Did he tell you I was going to leave him?"

"Yes," I said in a small voice.

"And that I was 'running around with another man'? . . . I could kill him! What right — what right does he have to use my children against me?"

"He didn't tell us not to talk to you. That was Hal's idea — and my idea," I added scrupulously.

"But you kids are being used."

"But we don't want you to leave Daddy."

"You don't know the whole story," she said, and let out a powerful sigh.

"Well, tell me."

My mother smiled. "I almost think I could explain it all to you, you seem so understanding sometimes. Naw, forget it."

"No, explain it," I said. I put on my most thoughtful "listener's" face, as I had watched adults do, scrunching up my brow — and waited.

"I'm unhappy, baby. You know the old expression, I feel like I'm being torn to pieces? That's me. A piece here, a piece there. I don't know what's right. I met a man. . . . And he makes me happy. I know you think of me as an old lady. But I'm only twenty-eight. I got married young, I was a — teenager, and I started having babies right away. I'm not saying I didn't want to have babies, of course I did. Your father was the one who. . . . But that's beside the point; what I'm trying to say is that I have years and years ahead of me. I don't want to be unhappy for the rest of my life."

"Why can't you be happy with Daddy?"

"Because I can't. He's miserable, and he's dragging me down. It's no use. You think I haven't tried. You know what living with your father is. He doesn't care about anything but the game on the radio and the book in front of his face. He married me because he needed a *mother*, someone to cook for him and wash his socks. He doesn't lift a finger to help me around the house. Oh, it's not all his fault, I know that. Your Pop had it rough when he was your age. His mother died young, and his stepmother made him wash floors. Like Cinderella. His father, Grandpa — well, you know, Grandpa's no bargain either. A real bastard, cold as they come. No one gave Bert much love, and as a result he — never learned how to show affection. But meanwhile, I'm the one who's paying for what his family did to him! It's like I've got five children to take care of instead of four, and your father's the most helpless of all."

"He sometimes helps you clean up."

"Oh, it's more than that," she said. "A woman needs — to be satisfied by a man — needs tenderness." Mom looked at me with hungry blue eyes. "He doesn't go out of his way to — do for me. A woman — likes to have a man who has manners. Who will open a door for her occasionally, make a nice compliment once in a while, be — considerate. That's all; just to show a little consideration. When you grow up, try to remember that."

"I will."

"I know you will, honey; you're already considerate."

I was flattered that Mom thought I would grow up to be the sort of man she admired. At the same time, I had the feeling that I was being sidetracked and was not advancing Dad's case enough. "But he writes poems to you, doesn't he?" I said.

"With sixty-four-dollar words that I don't understand? Where's the heart? Where's the *warmth?* I can't even read them without a dictionary. They make me feel stupid. . . . Who's he trying to impress, me? No, he's showing off his great brain. Sure, he's smart. I married your father because he was the most intelligent man I knew. I wanted to have bright children. That part worked out fine. But did I know he would turn into a zombie? He used to be fun. We would go to nightclubs and he'd explain to me all about art and — and current events. . . . What did I know? I was a dumbbell working in a beauty parlor, I never even finished high school. And here was this guy Bert, who knew everything. I'm grateful to him for improving my mind. But now — he's given up. He's stuck in that lousy factory job and all he ever talks about is the Place. He gets up, goes to work, comes home, sleeps — like a robot! He's *got* a good brain, why can't he use it? I *tried* to get him to go back to college. It's hopeless. And I'm drowning. We're all drowning. You want me to drown? Look, try to see it from my side. I found someone who's crazy about me. So he's not as intelligent as your father. Maybe it's just as important to be kind and — and decent and . . ."

I said nothing, and my silence seemed to force her doubts to surface. Let's face it, in our family intelligence *was* what counted; we weren't about to trade it in for something as insipid as kindness.

"I don't know what your father has told you about Willy," she said. "You've never met him. You've never given him a chance. He's a very sweet man. He loves children. He's willing to take care of all of you, to break his back for us. Don't you want to go to California? It's warm all year round, it's not freezing like this — hellhole!"

"But I like the snow," I said. "And I don't want to leave Daddy."

"Try to understand. See it from my side! I'm not saying we're going to leave Bert. I haven't made up my mind about that. But if this is my only chance, I'd be a fool not to take it. Wouldn't I. . . . I don't *know* what I want to do, that's why I'm telling you this. Nothing is decided, honey. I'm all mixed up." She kept talking in circles and looking beseechingly into my eyes, as if I had the answers for her. It was then I think I learned that if you stay very quiet and listen to the confusion of others and nod from time to time, people will think you understand. They will go away feeling better.

Much of what she said sailed over my head, but I understood the main part: that she was unhappy. In years to come, whenever I've found myself reenacting this scene of listening to someone (usually a woman) in torment between two courses, my mind has gone back to Mother in her black slip. When I was in a mood to rebel against my personality, I would reproach my mother for taking away my childhood by placing me in the position of her judge and pardoner, and by telling me things that perhaps were not suited to my age. But what's the point of blaming, when it is questionable who seduced whom? She needed someone to talk to, and I would have sold out my "golden childhood" a dozen times over for a compliment like the one I received.

She said: "You know, I keep forgetting that I'm talking to an eight-year-old. It's as if I were speaking to someone older and wiser. You've made me feel a lot better."

I blushed. I had found a new way to make my mother love me.

"Baby, promise me you'll forgive me for making such a mess of things? That you won't hate me?"

"I love you," I said.

She squeezed me against her and kissed me, murmuring, "Precious, precious." I stood there accepting her warm, embarrassing kisses. Then she said with sudden impulsiveness: "Let's celebrate! I don't feel like cooking. Why don't we go across the street and buy some specials." (Specials were the fat kosher hot dogs we loved.) "And pastrami and salami and lots of pickles, sour ones, the kind you like."

"Do you have money?" I said. I hated to ask the bald delicatessen man across the street to "put it on my mother's bill."

"Of course we've got money. Here, take a ten-dollar bill, I'll write out a list for you. And if you see anything you like — just for yourself — like a piece of strudel or knish, throw that in, too."

* * *

I dreaded the moment when Hal would come home and see us talking; but he accepted the new situation without a word, and never demanded an explanation, even in private.

I felt optimistic that everything would work out now. Because we had had this heart-to-heart talk, and I had taken Father's side and she seemed chastened, I assumed that the trouble was settled. It was my first instance of placing excessive faith in the medium of confession. Mother continued seeing Willy, she still made herself look pretty when she was about to leave for work, she still hummed to herself.

My father, meanwhile, had become desperate. The poems had stopped; now he made threats, which my mother laughed at. She seemed to be daring him, like Carmen and Don José. One afternoon she kept needling him:

"Come on, Bertram, why don't you get off your bony ass and put down the goddamn book, *As I Lay Dying* or whatever it is, and help with the cleaning. Make like a human being! Who do you think you are — Sitting Bull?"

"All right!" Those were his only words, and they came out in a strangled, tortured voice garbled by phlegm. Then, strangely, he went back to reading.

"No, it's not all right. Why the hell should I slave on the weekends cleaning up when I work all week same as you. You know, if you were half a man, you would bring in enough money so that I could stay home and keep this place decent and look after the kids —"

"All right, all right!" he yelled. It was amazing how a man of his extensive vocabulary could exist inside those two words for days at a time.

"I'm sorry I brought it up, Your Highness. I didn't mean to disturb your train of thought. I don't know why I bother. It's like talking to a stone wall. I feel like putting on my hat and coat and saying goodbye and never coming back."

"Then go! Go to your lover-boy."

"What is that supposed to mean?" she said.

"You know what it means," he muttered.

"I'd rather not discuss it here like this, if you don't mind."

"Then I'll go. If you don't want me around so much, I'll leave you alone."

"Always making promises, never coming through," she said with a bitter laugh.

My father got up without a word and left the house.

4.

One thing we had never expected was for *Father* to run away. By dinner time he had still not returned, and we all felt guilty.

"Where did Daddy go?" Molly asked Mom for the third time.

"Who the hell knows?"

"What is Daddy doing now?"

"Maybe he's hanging himself, maybe he's run off with a blonde. How the hell should I know?" Whenever Mother felt worried, her language became coarser. "Maybe an A-bomb will drop on our heads and we'll all be dead. What am I, a fortune-teller? Come on, get into your pajamas. Hey, September Morn! Put some clothes on."

"I'm taking my bath," Leah said indignantly, with a lisp, stark naked as usual.

"All right, take your bath." Mom turned on the radio and we listened to "The Green Hornet." We were allowed to stay up later than usual because of the family catastrophe.

The next evening, my mother got a phone call; she made me run for a pencil to write down the number. He had moved into a YMCA room. "Oh, for crying out loud!" we heard her say into the receiver. "Why don't you come home? You know we can't afford two rents." It seemed he wanted her to agree to stop seeing Willy before he would promise to return. Mother resisted: "I can't make guarantees! What are you trying to do, force me by running away? That's so childish, Bert." They argued back and forth; but what struck me was that my mother kept saying "Please take care of yourself" and "Don't do anything foolish" and "We'll work it out."

She agreed to meet him alone for dinner, after work Tuesday night.

Five nights later, on Friday night, my father returned home. No one said, "How was the Y, Dad?" We allowed him to sink back into the family routine. He was sheepish and, for the most part, silent, and we had had too-recent evidence of his fragility to risk upsetting him.

As far as I was concerned — as far as I knew — the episode with Willy was closed. I assumed Father would not have returned unless some satisfactory agreement had been reached. But again I assumed wrong. He had merely given in, tired of his protest at the Y. We had underestimated Mother's stubbornness. She went on seeing her lover. That is, until one shocking night, which ended everything to do with Willy.

5.

My father was beating my mother. She had come home after midnight and he had lost no time smacking her; then he threw her into their bedroom. She screamed but did not run away. Strange to think of him shoving her around because she was the larger — we used to call them Fat and Skinny; but he was stronger, of course.

Through the locked door, and from the other end of the five-room apartment, in the girls' room where we all gathered, we could hear our father beating our mother with an open hand. His slaps came down on her plump body, the flat sound of his hand smacking her reverberating flesh. And Mother's cries: "Enough, enough!"

"I'll tell you when it's enough!" I could picture his spittle dripping at his mouth, the way it did when he lost control.

My brother and my sisters and I held hands. We could see nothing, we could only hear the sounds, which made it worse. It seemed like the end of the world. Little Leah began to wail. Molly and I held each other tighter, frightened but excited by the violence as by a fight in the school yard. Hal's fists kept clenching and unclenching. He looked demented. Suddenly his high-pitched voice startled us. "Leave her alone! *You stop hitting my mother!*"

"Don't, Hal, he'll hit you too," I whispered. "He'll murder us all!" I tried to hold Hal by the arm but he pulled away, screaming: "You leave my mother alone or I'll kill you!"

We heard our mother say: "Bert, the kids are listening. Don't shame me in front of them!"

"You should have thought of that sooner," Father said, growling. Remorselessly he continued his beating, like a man with a long day's work ahead of him. He had found a rhythm for the blows. When would it be enough? How would he know when the job was finished?

At the other end of the apartment we saw the crazy elevated train blazoning our ceiling with its orange headlights. Maybe passengers could look right in their bedroom and see the beating. Our whole living room was lit up with the train's lurid glow, like a bonfire. Crackling and flaming, the train pulled out, leaving us again in darkness.

Leah was crying hysterically. Molly and I tried to do something to comfort her. "It's all right," we took turns saying, "it will be over soon" — as much for our own benefit as for hers. Hal gazed fiercely in front of him. Rocking himself back and forth, he seemed to be measuring the strength in his small arms. But what could he do against Father? Besides, it seemed wrong to me that he should get in the middle of their fight. Mother had to take her beating like the rest of us. Something about the way she was moaning and weeping made me sense that they knew what they were doing, that this had to be done, and that they would respect the limits. They were both playing their roles in concert, with more cooperation than was usual between them. "I swear I'll never go back," she pleaded. "I just had to tell him it was over, Bert!" And he: "If you go back I'll kill you!"

He called her every name under the sun, and with each name his hand re-claimed its harsh beating rhythm. He had found the words at last.

Part of me identified absolutely with my mother; another part was experiencing a sort of sweet revenge. But the greatest part of which I now remain aware told me that this is how it is, this is the mystery you must understand.

How different my hypnotized response was from Hal's. The hero of my childhood, he thought he could act to rescue our mother. And in a way he did. He dashed to the other end of the house, through the frightening no-man's-land separating us from them, and pounded on their door. "Stop it! Stop hitting her! I'll call the police!"

In the end that voice must have gotten through to my father. He left off. But my mother continued sobbing for another hour. We heard her through the door, each sob feeding involuntarily on the last, winding down bitterly to a questioning whimper, like that of a crying doll pushed forward at the waist.

6.

And after that they remained together. Whether that was providential or a tragedy depends on whom you talk to; I for one was glad. It seemed to my childish mind that a beating had saved the family, though that was probably not the case. There were beatings all through my childhood, and disturbances between my mother and father were to occur again and again — but none came so close to splitting us up as the Willy episode, and none seemed to end quite so suddenly. I came away from that night with both a heightened respect for power and a nausea for violence. The peculiar part, though, was that it seemed to me my father's will had been broken, not my mother's, that night. Afterward he acted more defeated, as though the beating had smashed up something in him. And she seemed to pity him more.

Some say that life is a blessing; others, that the truth of life is cruelty. The strong have an air of believing both: they celebrate their ability to overcome experiences of a particularly coarse, violent nature with a heady realism; or else they compress their former exposure to horror into a steady stream of gentleness. Myself, I am made uncomfortable by the notion that mankind is, at bottom, brutal. I would prefer to honor the ironies, pleasures and civilities of life. Yet I cannot get beyond certain brutal memories from childhood whose rumble I still hear going on in my head like an inner trembling. And maybe I hold on to them too much, also, out of pride.

Often I have a dream where I have gotten off an elevated train at the end of the line; the tracks curve to a stop above my head like a hanging comma. Where am I? In the distance there seem to be nothing but empty lots, undeveloped property at the edge of the city line. I turn back in the other direction and examine the storefronts under the El, looking for the old corner delicatessen and the Marcy movie house with its familiar marquee. But in this dark crisscrossed world I recognize nothing. This is a part of Brooklyn I have never been to before. Should I walk back under the tracks until they get to Williamsburgh? Should I move on into the rock-filled empty lots? Try something new? The dream always ends there, without my making up my mind.

Clearing the Space

I am clearing the space for a lover
to enter my life, I am clearing off a big space.
Today when I went bicycling I saw
on the grass one lover pair after another.
They were lying on each other, like rugs, or fur coats,
and all you could see was the shag of a redhead
or the lips a boy pressed down on a girl
while their limbs held chastely still.

I walked my bicycle past them, thinking
for a moment of every lover I had ever enjoyed,
and when none of them made my heart sink
and when I experienced no pain,
then I knew I was free of them
and that I was clearing a new space
as big as my life, as big as the pasture
the lovers were linked on.

I am preparing a space for the loved one,
I know what she looks like already.
She looks like the dark-haired girl in blue
I only saw for a second, before her Spanish lover
    smothered her.
Then, when I circled back on my bike, she was on top.

But I rode on, because my time will come
and meanwhile I am preparing a space,
I am cutting the grass, for the loved one to walk on;
I am cleaning my heart, making my thoughts
   unrancorous,
learning to be patient.
And if it should prove not to be in the end
a woman, not to be a human lover entering
after all, but something fuller and sadder, like the
   world,
like God, I will only say, I suspected it all along.

The Scorched Sweater

WE had been going out only a month when she began knitting a sweater. It was bluish-grey flecked, a pretty wool, and Sara was making it for herself, she said, because she was tired of knitting things for other people.

I accepted this with good grace. Whenever I go out with a woman, she tells me, "Oh, if you had only known me in the old days, I would have cooked you a huge breakfast." In the old days they drew baths, they made seven-course meals, they typed for their men; by the time they get to me they are always turning over a new leaf. I'm used to it.

Besides, it was good that Sara was knitting. She wasn't much of a conversationalist, and the knitting gave her something to do with her hands while I was talking. Oh, I tried to get her to talk. She'd stop and start with preliminary apologies like "I'm not saying this right" or "Probably this will sound dumb to you, but . . ." so that I'd get itchy and want to push the fast-forward button.

To be frank, we were mismatched intellectually. She was ten years younger than I, which added to her shyness. But people can't be the same or equal in every department. When you go out looking for love, the point is to find the

Other. *Vive la différence,* right? And she had other adorable qualities. The first time I saw her I thought, This is for me. That inner glow, that open smile. And what a body! She could have been a *Playboy* centerfold (except she didn't have orange skin). The odd thing was, she didn't seem to know she was a beauty. Whenever I complimented her features she brushed it aside as if I were crazy. She would peel off her flannel checkered shirt and jeans and get into bed next to me without the least self-excitement, as though any lumberjack's wife might be expected to look like her. I didn't know where to start. I could have spent a half hour worshiping each portion. But she lay stiff as a board, not really grasping what I was getting so worked up over. I was drooling like a man invited to a feast at a religious household who can't remember the right words to say grace so that everyone can begin to eat. In the end she would accept the entrée, but the soup, the nuts, the fruit cup, the creamed cauliflower, the after-dinner mints, didn't interest her.

At most, her hands feathered my back as a reluctant signal of participation. Deep down, I thought, maybe she just doesn't like me?

A week or so after thinking this, I got an encouraging surprise. She bicycled over to my house at lunchtime (that was not the surprise, she bicycled everywhere) and, frowning, said she had something for me but it was damaged, she was very upset. She pulled out of a brown paper bag the woolen sleeveless sweater.

"For me!" I cried.

"Oh, you *knew* it was for you all along, you must have guessed a long time ago. I'm such a poor liar."

"No, I didn't. I'm totally surprised." I kissed her gratefully, wrapping my arms around her. She was practically crying. "What's the matter?"

"I brought it to the cleaners to be blocked and they burnt it, see?" She showed me two scorch marks, where the bluish grey had been singed brown.

"That's nothing," I said, trying it on. It fit snugly and the wool felt beautiful against my bare chest (as it happened, I was naked at the time), like chain mail. "A dry cleaner'll remove those spots."

"No, they can't, because it's *organic!*" She said the word with a peculiar pungency. "Wool is organic. It's just as if you had burned your skin."

"I'm sure they can do something."

"Will you take it to them? I don't have the heart to ask and find out it's ruined. . . ."

"Silly! Don't you understand how happy I am that you knitted this for me? That's what's important."

"But it's spoiled!"

"But I love you." I took her into my arms. "I love you!"

"I love you too," she whimpered. Then she left to bicycle back to work.

Of course she liked me! How could I think she didn't? And she was an angel! She had even knitted me a sweater.

I took the sweater to the best dry cleaner's in the neighborhood, the Hungarian's. He only confirmed what Sara had suspected: that there was no way to remove the scorch marks. "I'd only be taking your money," he said, with a sort of Old World knowledge of limits. So I brought the sweater back to Sara, because she said she would rip out the rows near the top where it was scorched and do them over again. But not right away. She said she didn't have the heart to go back to it right away.

I didn't want to rush her, but I hoped, after a week or so, that she would return to the sweater soon, because things were not exactly going well between us. Sara seemed withdrawn. I couldn't put my finger on what was wrong, but I began to prepare myself for the romance to collapse in two months' time. Of course once you decide two months it's more like two minutes. I remember the time I was going out with G——. It was the last week in October and my birthday was still two weeks away; she had planned to buy me a beautiful bathrobe. We were having our problems, but I figured we would hold until after New Year's, or at least until after my birthday. We broke up October 29. No robe. This time I was determined to get the sweater.

Friday night we were to get together late, around eleven at my house. Sara had some chores to do first, and I had been sitting around watching the late movie, waiting for her to come by. I was in a contented mood. Sara arrived at 11:45, looking wistful as she wheeled her bicycle into my living room, and announced that she was depressed. She apologized for being depressed. She said she had been unhappy all week.

"How come?" I asked.

"Oh, it's stupid to talk about — mostly because I'm not accomplishing what I set out to accomplish when I moved to New York."

"Like what?"

"The job, my music lessons, everything. I'm sorry, I'm not much fun to be with tonight."

"You don't have to be jolly to spend time with me."

"I know, but — I don't want to talk about myself, it's so boring. I'd rather hear what you've been doing and I'll just listen."

So we did.

After twenty minutes of review-of-the-day, with Sara asking "listener"-type questions and knitting (something else — a cap; she still did not have the heart to redo the sweater), she put away her needles and said she was going home. She was really too depressed; she had to be by herself tonight.

I should have just let her go. But I was beginning to wonder if this was part of a larger pattern to avoid, in general, spending the night with me. Suddenly I sensed that her depression was not only about her job or the "little things" she said upset her so much and shouldn't have — but that it was about us as well. Mostly about us.

"Tell me what's wrong."

"You're so forgiving and kind and patient with me," she said, "and it makes me feel guilty because I'm so selfish and I'm giving you so little in return."

Ominous words. When a woman starts with the kind-and-patient business, it's like handing you your hat and coat.

Let's get to the point, I said to myself.

After a certain amount of tooth-pulling and high-speed drilling, it came out that she was indeed a reluctant partner in this romance. Our worlds were too dissimilar, she said; our paths didn't seem to converge naturally. "It doesn't feel like — me," she kept repeating.

I will do anything for love. I will tie myself to a bicycle wheel, I will beg, I will humiliate myself. But for this shilly-shallying consolation, this nebbishy urban arrangement to dull the pain of loneliness — no. I would rather have the truth and be done with it.

I brought up her reluctance in bed. She said that had given her great pain. "When one person is more sexually attracted to the other than the other . . ." Sara faltered.

"Now I'm insulted."

"Well, I didn't mean to insult you, that wasn't at all why I said that. You told me to be honest."

"You're being honest and that's commendable; and I'm being honest by telling you that I'm insulted."

She thought for a minute before speaking again. "What makes me feel bad is that . . . when you like someone in so many ways, it should be possible to like him in all ways, including the sexual. It seems like a shallowness on my part that I make that separation. . . . I know you think I'm shallow because of it."

This was poppycock. You're either turned on or you're not. Hadn't I learned that hard wisdom in the past, by being in her position enough times when all I wanted to do was run? And yet, the fact that she no longer wanted me to be her lover hurt me more than I had expected. Suddenly it seemed as if everything I had loved was pushing me away. Why, you male chauvinist pig! I can hear the reader say. You got what you deserved! All you wanted was to hold on to a body that gave you constant erections — you didn't care about her, any more than she cared about you. Probably not. And yet — this is no small thing, to love the physical. Besides, I did have a certain sympathy and affection for her above and beyond the carnal. Perhaps I've neglected to describe it. Oh well; too late.

"What should we do?" she asked, in a voice tinged with apprehensiveness.

"I guess," I found myself saying helpfully, "I guess we should stop seeing each other."

Now she began thrashing around in her guilt, the ramifications of her long-kept secret of not being able to love me, enjoying the power of speech more than I had ever heard her. Explanations came easily, now that the pressure was off her. It was 1:30, I was beginning to wish I had watched the rest of the late movie — *Alfie*, appropriately — instead of having to listen to all this. I awoke from my reverie to hear her say:

"But the bottom line is my feelings."

What can you say to a line like that? All you can do is nod. But then, with a sincerity that demanded no less than total honesty from me, Sara paused, to ask the classic question of our times. Liebnitz had his all-consuming conundrum; we have our philosopher's stone. "What are *you* feeling now?"

"I'm waiting for you to leave, so that I can go to bed."

She got up and left without a word. I helped her with the door while she wheeled her bicycle out.

It now occurs to me that she may have wanted to go home earlier in order to avoid this confrontation — in order to prolong, that is, our unnatural life as a couple. It was I who probably forced things to an end. When she had gone, the first thing I thought of, naturally, was my sweater, which I had only gotten to wear for a *minute*. Just like the phantom bathrobe. These things are always happening to me. If only I would learn to lie low, I could have a whole new wardrobe by now!

Getting a Cat

AFTER so many years of living alone, I broke down and got a cat. I really didn't want a cat. Once I was in Jungian therapy and the therapist said to me, "You should get a cat." He was a very decent man, I gained a lot from him, I listened respectfully to everything he said, except when he gave me practical advice like this. "You should try it. You'll learn interesting things about yourself. . . ." And then he slid away into his mysterious smile. One might almost say, a Cheshire cat smile.

You can't imagine how many people have been offering me their superfluous kittens over the years. Why was everyone so eager to give me a cat? I saw them all smiling, rubbing their hands: "Ah, he'll get a cat, very good, it's a good sign, means he's settling down."

By what Darwinian logic was I supposed to graduate from one to the other? Maybe I was to start with a cat, then go to a sheep dog, next a pony, then a monkey, then an ape, then finally a Wife. It was far more likely that, if I got a cat, I would stop there. What annoyed me was this smug assumption that because I lived alone, I was barren; I needed to start making "commitments" to other living creatures, to open my heart to them and take on responsibility. As far as

I can piece it together, the idea seems to be that we should commit ourselves to something in this black hole of a universe. We should make an effort to join the Association of fellow creatures. Now, "commitment" comes into popular discourse when belief in love starts to slide. They're not so sure anymore, the experts, the theologians, that there is such a thing as love. So they tell you you should build up to it — practice. Throw your arms around a tree. Myself, I still believe in love, what do I need commitment for? So this was one reason for my not getting a cat. Plus my apartment is too small — there are no doors between the rooms — and I sometimes have to travel on the spur of the moment. Most important, I didn't feel I needed a cat.

Very well, you might ask, how did it happen that I got a cat?

It was partly a misunderstanding. I was in the country one weekend, where one is always more prone to sentimental longings and feelings of incompleteness. That's why I stay out of the country as much as possible. But I was visiting a friend; and there was an old man also staying at the house, a respected old writer, a lovely man whom I'll call Claude. This old man has beautiful silky white hair. He moves with graceful modesty, slight of build and wearing threadbare sweaters with holes in them, not because he can't afford any better but because he has already stopped caring about making an impression. He lives alone and seems wonderfully self-sufficient, except for his cats. He and I were standing inside the threshold of his bare country room and bending over a box where the mother cat was sleeping with her four kittens. The children were all sleeping head to foot, with their tails in each other's mouths so that together they looked like one big cat.

They made, I had to admit, a cute effect. I was trying to

get a suitably fond expression onto my face and he was explaining about their delivery.

"There was a lot of hard labor involved. Usually she likes me to be around — some cats don't. There has to be a box ready. She knew just what to do. She ate the umbilical cord, and the afterbirth, which is supposed to be good for them. Then she licked off the first kitten and was ready for the next. Each kitten comes in a different sack . . . they're not like humans that way."

"Hm," I said, impressed with his knowledge of nature. Each kitten had a different coloration: one grey, one black, one cinnamon orange, and one whitish. A Mendelian demonstration. I liked the grey cat, because he was so straightforward, your basic alley cat. I was also drawn to the milky-orange one but distrusted her because she was *too* pretty.

Claude's hand, which was large and sensitive, pale veined with brown spots — I shook it every chance I got — descended to stroke each of the cats along its furry back.

"What are you going to do with all the kittens?" I asked idly.

"I'll give away as many as people want, and let her keep one to raise; and the rest will have to be taken to the vet to be killed. That's the difficult part," he said. The fold above his eye twitched as he talked, and he turned his face for a moment deliberately toward me, with a politeness and candor that showed he was not afraid to look me in the eye. "But she isn't willing to do it," he said, "and so I have to. I don't need more than one cat, you see."

I was so taken with this, with his acceptance of the world as it was, that I wanted to have one of his cats. I spoke up like a fool who raises his hand at an auction just to participate, to release the tension, and offered to take a kitten. He looked at me with a kind, piercing gaze, and asked if I was positive I wanted one. I said I was absolutely sure, trembling at what his look of examination might have told him about me. For a while he pretended I hadn't made the offer at all, in order to let me gracefully off the hook. But I kept forcing myself toward a firm statement that I wanted one of his kittens — the grey one probably. Although the cinnamon-orange one was pretty too. And suddenly I became horribly torn between these two animals, as between two ideals.

If I took the grey alley cat, I would be opting for everything that was decent peasant stock, dependable, ordinary and hardworking in myself. The idea pleased me. But I would be turning my back on beauty. I stood over the box, wondering if I should be ruled by a flash of prettiness, mystery, the gamine, the treacherous, as I had been so often in my life, or if, by embarking on this new, "more mature" stage of commitment, I would do better to choose sturdier virtues for companionship. In the end I picked the grey, partly because I was feeling guilty for having wanted to go back on my promise to him, after noticing a new, more fetching piece of fur.

Two or three days later, back in the city, grimly contented, coolheaded, myself again, I realized I had made a terrible mistake. I didn't want a cat! I wanted to be this old man. I wanted to grow up more quickly and be done with my idiotic youth and literary ambitions and sexual drives that bossed me around, and — I wanted to be Claude, gentle, pure. I must have fallen in love with his white beard and his spotted hands; and under his spell, in their charmed propinquity, whatever he had warmed with his glance that moment I probably would have coveted. Fortunately it was only a cat; it might have been worse.

I had to find a way to tell him I was backing out of the

deal. For a long while I did nothing. I sat on my hands. Finally I wrote a card to him saying that I hadn't forgotten, that I hoped he was keeping the grey kitty for me — but maybe it was the orange one I really wanted, I couldn't make up my mind. It was a scatterbrained, sloppy note, and I hoped it would convey the impression of an irresponsible young man who cannot be counted on for anything he says. You may be amazed at this subterfuge, but it was the closest I could get to telling the truth.

In any case he did not get the hint. Like Death coming to call, Claude telephoned me once he was back in New York, and said that it was time for me to stop by and collect my kitty.

With a heavy heart, I rode down in the taxi next to the black metal carrying box that friends had lent me, my Black Maria. I had already provisioned my apartment with the supplies that Claude, in a moment of doubting me, had called to remind me to have ready as soon as the cat should enter its new home. I climbed the stairs to Claude's loft, wondering how the old man managed them every day. He opened the door to me with a peculiarly impish smile.

I wanted to get this over with as quickly as possible. "Hello, kitty," I said, bending down to pet the grey kitten.

"No, that's not your cat. I gave that to someone else. Here's your cat," he said. "There she is — she was under the bed! She's a very timid creature. Not like her brother Waldo, the grey. *There* she is! *There* she is." He held her in his arms, and poignantly gave her over to me.

I need not say how grateful I was that it was the orange one. She was warm in my hands, and gorgeously, obscenely pretty. Old Claude must be some student of the human heart.

The rest was odds and ends, formalities of transfer. She had already had her first distemper shot but I was to take her again in four months. I would be better off not giving her too much milk at first. She liked Purina tuna most of all the brands he'd tried. She was a good jumper — a first-class jumper; but as she had been up to now in the shadow of her brother Waldo, she seemed retiring. That would probably change. He had noticed it sometimes happened with girls, when they had brothers, that the boy kittens would be very active and dominate them. A good thing was to get an empty crushed pack of Winstons, which she liked to play with. Did I smoke? he asked. No, I said. "Well, then get your smoking friends to save them for you. She also likes to play with a little toy ball, and I'll give that to you." He located the ball, and his last empty cigarette pack, and give me a box of dry cat food and would have piled on several cans of tuna if I had not stopped him and said I had plenty at home. "Very well," he said, simply and with loss. "I guess that's it."

We were caught in such an emotional moment that I wanted to throw myself into his arms and comfort him, or be comforted myself. Instead, I shook his hand, which was always a good idea.

"Goodbye, *****," he said, calling her something like Priscilla, or Betsy. I didn't want to hear; I wanted her named existence to begin with me. "You're going off to your new home," he said. "Have a good time."

"Won't she be lonely for her brother and her mother?" I asked.

"Yes . . . but that's life," he replied, smiling at both the threadbareness of the phrase and the truth of it.

He walked me to the door and stood at the top of the stairs with me. "If you have any questions, ask people who have cats for advice. They'll be more than happy to give it to you, and most of it will be wrong — but that's all right, they'll all have dozens of tips. And of course you can call me anytime you want if you're having problems with her. I know very little but I can hold your hand."

2.

And so I settled down to my comfortable married life. After she had overcome her first shyness, the girl began to demonstrate her affectionate nature. She would take my finger in her mouth and lick it, and move on to the next finger, and the next. Her little pink tongue, rough as a washcloth, would sand away at my skin until it became sore. Then I would push her away, and pick up my book.

But a little while later, I would try to entice her back. "Come here, Milena," I would say. She would look uncertainly, mistrustfully up at me. I would wave my hand in the air, a gesture that hypnotized her each time, and wiggle my fingers until she jumped at them. Then I'd *catch* her and clutch her to me and squeeze her. She didn't like to be squeezed, or at first even petted; she would immediately turn around and start licking the hand that tried to stroke her.

In the evening she would curl up on my lap and close her eyes and make that motor-running, steady-breathing sound. I didn't have the heart to move, with her on my lap, purring like that. Moreover, she held her paw on my wrist, as if to detain me. How could I reach for a pencil?

On first arriving, she had investigated every corner of my apartment, going around the perimeters of the living room into the bedroom, the kitchenette, and finally into the bathroom, where she took note of her cat box. I was wondering when she would begin to use the box. The first day passed, and the pebbles were unruffled. Then another day came and went, without commission, and I thought she might be so nervous from the move that she was constipated.

On the third day I sat down on the couch; something was wrong. My nostrils opened. Right next to me on the sofa was the most disgusting pile of shit. I nearly retched. I cleaned it off distastefully and dropped a piece of it in the cat box, so that she would know that was the proper place for it. Then I lowered her into this same cat box and she hopped out of it as quickly as from an electric shock. This was too much. Claude had assured me that she was toilet trained! I sprayed the sofa with Lysol disinfectant. She kept returning to the spot like the criminal she was, and sniffing the upholstery, trying to puzzle out the two different smells, and backing away, bewildered.

That afternoon I called Claude, to get the exact name of the cat litter he'd been using. I told him what she had done. He said, "Oh, dear, that must be disagreeable; I'm so sorry to hear it . . ." Never mind, I thought, just tell me the name of your cat litter. It turned out to be another brand; so, hoping this would make the difference, I went from supermarket to supermarket until I had found the preferred gravel. I lugged twenty pounds of it home with me and poured a deep, cloud-releasing stratum in her box.

That night I couldn't sleep. I was so revulsed by the image of finding that bundle on the couch, I felt as if my house, my sanctuary had been ruined. Why had I gotten a cat? That night my dreams were full of unpleasant surprises.

In the morning I awoke to the smell of a stack of her shit on the white brocade armchair. This could go on for weeks. My work was suffering, I couldn't concentrate, I couldn't do a thing until I had broken in that cat and shown her who was master. I bet she knows that's her box, I thought, but she just prefers taking a crap on a nice comfy armchair or a sofa surrounded by pillows. Wouldn't we all? She must think I'm a total sucker.

I sponged the chair, again sprayed with Lysol, deposited a piece of her droppings in the cat box. Then I grabbed her by the neck, not so gently, and dropped her into the gravel. She jumped out like a shot. I caught her and put her in again. She hopped out, whining. I threw her in again. Romance of education: she was the wild child, Helen Keller, I was the stubborn tutor. I was willing to treat it like a game: you jump out, I'll throw you back. She bounded, I caught her. My arm was stuck out like a fence to grab her as soon as she escaped. Each time she grew a little slower in leaving the box, a little more pensive and frustrated. Staring at me with her big, victimized pussycat eyes. "That look is wasted on me," I told her. She fell in the gravel, defeated. She seemed to chew over the situation for a half minute. Then she sat up in the posture of evacuating, and lowered her bottom ever so gradually. She got off (it was a little pee) and carefully kicked some pebbles over the spot. Hurray!

After that we had no more surprise "bundles." Life fell back to normal, or let us say, my new normal, which seemed to consist of my spending days running to the store for cat food and litter, and buying a vacuum cleaner to swoop up the cat's hairs so that my allergic friends could visit me, or locating the right scratching post before it was too late. Milena had found the underguts of a chair and was taking clumps of stuffing out of it for sport. In fact she was doing nightmarish things to all the furniture. Since I live in a furnished apartment, I was terrified of what would happen if my landlady came snooping around. My landlady is not fond of signs of life in any form. I had been afraid to ask her permission in the first place, and had sneaked in the cat on the *fait accompli* principle. If I had asked her, I knew, she would have said no; this way she would either have to accept it or start costly eviction proceedings.

One afternoon, as I was walking up the stoop of my house, where my landlady lives also, unfortunately, directly beneath me, she told me that "there was someone knocking" at my door. I thought this was odd; but then I noticed the scowling, misanthropic expression on her pudgy face and the two tufts of dirty-blondish hair sticking angrily out of her ears (God, she looked like a bulldog!), and via this animal association I realized that she was referring in her elliptical way to my cat. She followed this "knocking" statement with: "No cats, Mr. Lopate. We can't have cats here. They smell up the place and destroy the rugs and we can't have cats here, you understand?"

I said nothing, and proceeded past her into my apartment and closed the door, trembling with anger. I was ready to fight her to the bitter end. I turned to Milena, all innocent of the threat against her. "Don't worry," I said. "I won't let her throw you out. We'll move first." So our destinies were tied. "But you must," I said, "you must control your destructiveness. We live in this woman's house, don't you see; this is her furniture! If you go tearing large holes in everything it will cost me a fortune. Look, I bought you a scratching pad; can't you bring yourself to use it?"

In the meantime, something had to be done. I consulted friends. Some advocated declawing, others were aghast at the idea, with a foaming passion that made you suspect they were talking about something else. Anyhow, someone said, a kitten her age was too young for the operation. When I learned that it was indeed an "operation," that she would have to go to the hospital for it, I postponed the project indefinitely. Instead, I clipped her toenails and coaxed her to try the new scratching post (I had replaced the cardboard stand with a fabric one). The man in the pet shop said, "If you put some catnip around the base she'll be sure to like it." I bought a container of fresh catnip — anything for my baby girl. I spread the leaves up and down the scratching post. She did love the smell; she licked at the catnip and slept on the fabric base when she needed a rest from her more exhausting vandalisms.

3.

After that, a strange, sullen period began for us. At times I thought I loved her, at other times I would be completely indifferent to her. I would kick her off the bed when she tried to sleep with me, because I wanted to be alone and not worry about rolling onto her. But always when I had almost forgotten she was there, she would crouch into my vision.

She had the annoying habit of trying to stop me when I dialed the phone, as if jealous of my speaking to anyone else. She would smudge the dialing circle with her paw, forcing me to dial the same number several times. We often got in each other's way. She and I competed for the bright red armchair — the one I considered my "writing chair." Milena always seemed to be occupying it just as I was getting ready to lower myself. Sometimes I would come home after work and find her sleeping on that chair, a lazy housewife. She would blink her eyes as I turned on the light.

When I totally ignored her, she began knocking down my knickknacks. She would tear through the house. She seemed to be taking over the living space and squeezing me into a small, meaningless corner. I resented having to smell her all over my apartment. At my typing desk, in the kitchenette, there was that warm, cloying, offensively close odor from her shed hairs. And I got cross at her for not raking under her shits. Cats were supposed to be "fastidious creatures" and do that instinctively. It seemed a violation of the contract.

I was looking for violations, I suppose. In the back of my mind I kept thinking that I could send her away. It was hard for me to grasp the idea that I was going to have to care for her always. Until one of us died.

Claude called from time to time, "to hold my hand," as he put it. He was very sweet. I was delighted to have the chance to talk more often with him, even though our conversations were rather specialized. Once he suggested that I spread baking powder through the cat litter to cut the smell. Not a lot on the top surface — she wouldn't use it if you did — but a little throughout the mixture.

All this lore of cats! It was too much to take in; and it was only the beginning. As Claude had predicted, everyone had instructions for me.

Now, there were four things I could never stand to hear people going on about: one was their dreams, two was their coincidences, three was their favorite restaurants and meals, and four was their pets. And I never did like going over to a friend's house and in the middle of an intense conversation watching the friend's eyes turn senile with fondness as he interrupted to draw my attention to the cute position his cat had gotten herself into.

Now that I had this cat, every visitor started off with fifteen minutes of reaction to her. Women friends, particularly, made much of Milena. One commented that it was rare to find an orange female. Another said the cat was so elegant that she herself felt "underdressed" around her. Kay, my old flame, remarked: "Your cat is so gentle. I can't get over how delicate — how attuned she is! Oh, she's exquisite."

I felt abashed for not having perceived this special "attunedness" in Milena. From my point of view she was doing a kitten's job adequately, she was holding down the role, earning her can a day, but not setting any records. They all seemed to want to find something unique about Milena, whereas I, on the contrary, liked her precisely because she was just a cat. True, she had an appealingly pathetic stare: those black pupils with two concentric circles of olive around them. But I resisted the flattering appraisals, which seemed to me as farfetched as newborn-baby compliments. I had no idea how fond and proud I had grown of her until I came up against a nonbeliever.

My friend Emily remarked, without having seen her: "She's not as nice as my cat, is she?" and assured herself no, as if it were self-evident. I was furious. Not that my cat is so great, but why should hers be better? Emily was my model of the delusional cat owner. She had theories about how her cat knew her moods better than anyone, stayed away from her when that was the right thing to do, comforted her when she was down, intuitively kept her claws in — a miracle of a domestic cat that didn't need to be declawed, spayed or altered or anything else cats usually need to be, because it was so considerate and discreet. Her cat was a Colette novel. Often, people hurt Emily with their rudeness or selfish insensitivity, but her cat — never. Her cat sets the standard, I thought sardonically, that all of us, her friends, must chase after and miss. When Emily shuts the door on her last visitor of the night, she curls up with her kitty cat, the understanding one.

This would never happen to me, I vowed. First of all, I have no fantasies that Milena understands me. How could she, when our interests, our hobbies, our yearnings, are so different?

I don't pretend to guess her secrets. I watch her.

There she is, chasing a fly.

Now she knocks a spoon off the table, a Magic Marker from the desk, and starts kicking it about. Everything is a toy to her. She drags her booty through a square hole she has scratched in the white brocade armchair. I don't know how to stop her from gouging the seat covers. This one tear-hole particularly has a use in her play. What does it mean to her? Someone said to me, "Kittens have such imaginations. They think they're in the jungle!" Is that it? Are you thrashing through the Amazon brush chasing enemies? Milena, you have your toy, you have that rubber ball with chimes inside. But to you, all the world is your plaything.

Milena can do all kinds of tricks. She can tear a paper towel into shreds and strew it over the apartment. She can stand on her hind legs and turn on the lamp. It's the truth.

When I go into the bathroom she likes to come in with me. Even when I shut the door she manages to squeeze inside. She crawls into her cat box and inspects the gravel surface, then sifts through to see if the droppings are still there. They're her property, her valuables in the safe-deposit box. You're like a rich old dowager, Milena, with your orange-and-white mink coat and your jewels.

Then I come out of the bathroom with my robe on and she starts squeaking. She wants to eat! Take your time, you'll get it. She's so eager that she doesn't let me scoop out all her canned food. She gets in the way so that I can't even put the rest on her plate — a clump of it drops on her head. You see that? If you'd only let me . . .

Now the cat is quiet. She has gotten what she wants to eat, her tuna. She sits in a pool of sun. The days are getting shorter and shorter. Winter is coming, Milena, I explain to her.

The Japanophiles

When she was young, in her twenties, she had gone to
*   Japan.*
She had studied Noh dance, and had
a Japanese lover. I can imagine him
with sloping muscles, hairless chest, an earnest face
that squinted when the window shade was opened.
She hungers for that Japanese type now. Something
*   about*
the way they made love, something he taught her
about silences, the engrossment, the going-under
that she tried to take back with her to the States.
Vain about her gift for sexuality,
she let herself be backup love for some well-known
writers, painters, publishers, Powers;
she did it open-eyed, unjealous of their wives,
living off crouton-sized bits of love and free-lance work,
a cultivated stylish woman approaching thirty-eight.
Depressed as she so often is, her head lowered, her neck
resembles a geisha's in an Utamaro print, graceful,
*   waiting*
behind a mosquito net.

I come by her hotel room every so often.
We talk about Japanese things.
I, also Japanophile, claim that it is a very unhappy
   culture,
obsessed with the retrospective glance, the irretrievable,
a fatalism in the prose and brush. Perhaps
permissive childhoods, doting grandparents,
followed by too-strict schooling, conspire to make them
bound, tied in knots, thinking of the past
as a golden age. I may not have the social science right,
but the fact remains that their art is melancholy
which is why I love it. No accident that Kawabata
chose Beauty and Sadness
for the title of his last book.

She disagrees. "No, you don't understand,
you are exaggerating the transience theme,
the cherry blossoms and so on; that's a cliché.
What foreigners tend to overlook in Japanese art,
but what I learned when I was over there," she says,
"is that they treat the moment like a synapse:
all they will speak about is the just-before,
and just-after . . .
but there is no people that take more pleasure
in the moment, no people better able to block out
everything but the immediate, these four walls —
which is why they are so good about sex.
Take Saikaku. They have none of that Western shame
about sexual appetite, that post-coitum *letdown*
(which I have never understood myself,
though I've witnessed it in men often enough).
The Meiji era spoiled some of that, true, with their
Westernizing drive, but if you go back to before the
   Meiji . . ."

We both have our Japan.
Mine is elegiac, hers ecstatic.
I cannot help but think that she pays for that ecstasy:
transfigured by an old ghost of sublimity,
her works are scattered, ambitious but diffuse,
she lacks practical footing in the world,
while in her mind exists, with great clarity and taste,
a room of lust.
She's kept alive her vision of pure sensual space
that paradoxically ties her to depression
and shocks from bruising, ordinary life, to which
she must still present her résumés
with sore availability.

No doubt we are both right. Or wrong.
Long ago I settled for
a workmanlike productive stoic life
in which the concept of bliss is meaningless.
Maybe I fear her capacities.
                              I would almost
step forward and offer myself as a lover,
but I see in her eyes that my body
is all wrong, hairy and soft —
she would prefer a man who knew more silences;
while I too have my exotic fantasies.

Platonics

I HAVE come to a time in life when platonic friendships count as much to me as romances, and sometimes more. They sweeten my bachelor existence. How much drabber and colder my life would be without the supporting friendships of two or three clever, tender and sarcastic women!

By "platonic" I mean merely that we do not and never have slept together; there is nothing otherwise in the relationship, so far as I can tell, that pertains to the philosophy of Platonism. Now, why should it be so important to observe this one restriction? We are reaching an epoch, some might argue, when sex has become a simple courtesy, a way of consoling a friend on a lonely night, no more significant than watching the sun come up together used to be. I don't believe it. Once the deed is done *everything changes*. Possessiveness, fury, jealousy, absolutism, scorn, inability to tolerate the other's weaknesses — all the glories of romantic love, in short, rush in. On the other hand, I have no right to speak authoritatively, since I have never put any of my platonic friendships to the test. It is said of O'Hara, the poet, that he could move in and out of this kind of intimacy easily, take a friend to bed one night out of sheer closeness and drunken good spirits, and then return the thing to a cordial camaraderie the next; and that several dozens of people, when he died, regarded him as their exclusive best friend. Were *my* platonic friends and I to begin shacking up, I have the feeling that the balance we have so tolerantly and religiously built up would suffer a disastrous strain. And we care about what we have too much to risk losing it. (It might be that nothing terrible would happen. That would be terrible in its own way.)

Besides, the presence of formal constraints in friendships and other relationships can become a source of rich understanding. There is an aesthetic pleasure to be enjoyed in observing forms, like the rules for a sonnet or fugue.

Take the incest taboo.

I think, on the whole, it is a good thing that I did not sleep with my two sisters, though they are both very sexy. I would never indict anyone who succumbed to that temptation (both parties consenting), but on the other hand I cannot join the ranks of those who argue that the incest taboo stands in the way of psychic liberation. It would be a pity to see the old fence go.

I can appreciate now that growing up with two beautiful, bossy, doting and clever sisters must have been good practice for the present stage of my life, which seems to be dominated by platonics. However, it took a while for the lessons to cohere. I can't remember having any good female friends when I was in my twenties and married. It was only when I turned thirty that the change began. Jung speaks of the stage when a man stops regarding everyone of the opposite sex as his potential enemy or conquest, and begins to make friends with the Woman (the woman in himself, perhaps). I rather think that the hostility never goes away completely. But a platonic friendship at least offers the chance, or becomes the arena for, intimacy and charity to be played out between a woman and a man — free from the intense unrealistic expectations and disappointments of romances. It may even be a dry run for some serener marital companionship to be undertaken later on.

There are no rules for the making of good platonic friendships, but it helps for one or both parties to be *less than totally physically attracted to the other*. A little plainness is good. I am not saying the friend need be ugly — and in fact, it would be hard to have a friend whom one did not find, on some level, pretty or handsome. But all the same, it creates a problem if the person is so delectable that you keep wanting to pounce on her. That is sure to lead to pouting resentments and forced distancing. Best is to find someone who is certainly attractive in his or her own way, but not your *carnal type*. Then you can appreciate the genre of looks without having to be uncomfortably aroused by it, and can rest easy escorting the friend in public, knowing that he or she is presentable and attractive to others and therefore no discredit to you.

Escort duty is, in fact, one of the most solid uses to which platonic friends put each other.

My friend Emily is the ideal platonic woman friend. Since I knew her first, in the old days, as the wife of an old friend of mine (they are since divorced), the taboo was already set in place; and the fact that she is thinner than the type of woman I go for — and a little plain, God bless her — drove it in further still. There was perhaps a moment or two when it might have turned out differently, when we first started seeing each other after her divorce, and would sit in her car talking before she went upstairs. I even fancied that she was attracted to me, but both of us were too tactful to make a first move, or too engrossed in something else that seemed to be developing between us, and in the end we left it that way. We still talk about spending our old age together, having camper trucks side by side in Florida. That is one thing platonic friends always promise each other: becoming "a number" in old age. Even then, we will not be able to live together. We will have to have separate campers because Emily is so finicky, and I, of course, so used to living alone. One can already see the outlines of a strong-willed old woman, a preview of coming attractions, emerging in Emmy from time to time. She has become an encyclopedia of lore about health, food and safety, and does everything the right way, and in a certain prickly order not to be denied.

A typical Emmy remark is: "I just have to go by the bank and do Y, and then we can do X and Z." Sweetly, but with chin set, and no mistake about it: it will be Y, X and Z in that order! I long ago gave up trying to argue with Emmy about plans, and surrendered to her full arrangements. It is such a comfortably passive holiday for me to go somewhere with her, to put myself in the hands of someone who has precise notions for doing *everything*, like a Montessori kindergarten teacher.

Every year we plan an excursion out of the city, usually during the dog days of August. The first four tentative dates are canceled, because Emmy is taking a course and needs to study harder (Emmy is always taking a course), or because she wants to train to run in a marathon, or because her boyfriend is coming in for a few days, or simply because she won't be able to start till the afternoon and she doesn't want to drive when it's dark. I never listen to the excuses anymore, I just say, All right. Because she has the car. And there is no possibility of getting her to change her mind, once she develops resistance to a plan.

Nevertheless, excursion day does come. I phone her in the morning to ascertain that the weather meets with her standards, deserves a day in the country. I bring my swimming trunks, tennis racket, baseball bat, everything, just in case. "Just in case," says Emmy, "we decide to go to Lake Momo instead of Lake Domo. Lake Momo has clay tennis courts, but I don't like the water there." Whatever you say, Emmy: I am *at your service.*

When we get in the car I am nervous for three seconds. Emmy and I have had only one big fight. This was about my slamming the door of her Volkswagen. She claims I do it too hard and that it will damage the doorframe; the subtext of this fight is that in her view I sometimes act without thinking, without first considering all the consequences — an impetuous physical recklessness for which she forgives me, generally. As I forgive her her thoroughness.

We are ready to take off. But not yet. It is not so easy to leave the city with Emmy. She is having some friends over for dinner, seven hours from now, and she will need to stop off at three stores near the George Washington Bridge. Why not just go to the supermarket? Because one has good bread and not good fruit, and she wants to make a fruit compote, and she might have to buy some fish because she's afraid that the stores will be closed by the time we get back, on the other hand the fish might spoil in the car . . . Pointless to argue that we will probably be back hours before the stores close. "No, they close early in the summer," she says authoritatively. The result is that we make the three shopping stops and drive back to her house to drop off everything in the refrigerator. But then we are free for the rest of the day.

Once out of Manhattan, Emily relaxes. She cracks jokes, observes funny road details, listens, draws me out — a perfect companion. Our favorite conversation is exploring the bad manners and blindnesses of our mutual friends. We are particularly merciless toward married couples. (Why not? Being single, have we not suffered most at their insensitive hands?) I am the more malicious-tongued of the two of us, but Emmy is the more dark-visioned and pessimistic. Perhaps because she places so little hope in people's changing for the better, she usually counsels — when another friend and I are having difficulties — that I go around the problem.

My instinct is always to confront directly; hers, to wait out the storm. Emmy is an adept at what we have come to call, in a private joke, Sneak Therapy. One day we set down some of the rules for Sneak Therapy:

1. Make them think they have the upper hand.
2. Don't trust them but don't let them know it.
3. Lay low; wait them out. Let them provoke the rift. (Especially good when you want to break up with a lover.)
4. Don't bother to be straightforward and honest, it's wasted on them anyway. They'll just misinterpret and twist it to their purposes.
5. Promise the hosts anything but sneak out when they're not looking.
6. When you get a lousy waiter, keep smiling and don't leave a tip.

I often fear Emmy is practicing a little Sneak Therapy on me. Since she understands me so well, though, I suppose it is a small price to pay.

Emmy and I are scampering over rocks, climbing some gradual hiking trail that she found in her topographical maps. We stumble on a natural swimming hole in a rushing stream. She becomes like a child, all curiosity and independence and wide eyes. I find myself sitting on a rock with the waterfall rushing under me, the roaring current tickling my bottom, making me laugh uncontrollably. Emmy smiles at me, waves, then goes around a bend exploring. I love being with her in Nature, because she leaves me alone, doesn't force me to appreciate anything.

Once a month or so, I go uptown to Emmy's house for dinner. If it has been snowing she will say, as soon as she opens the door, "Take off your shoes. I don't want the street salt tracked in, it's toxic" — but in so gentle a voice that one does not mind complying. "Why don't you come into the kitchen, while I fix dinner." We always start off in the kitchen, a tight squeeze of table, cooking range and refrigerator, with a clothesline right outside the window. Emmy gets me a beer (she orders some excellent dark German brand by the case) and I sit at her table watching her cook. "Are you *very* hungry?" she asks. "Medium," I say, already sleepy and quiet in her kitchen. Here it is all right to relax and say nothing. I do not have to sing for my supper, as I feel I do at other households.

While she is cooking, we gossip about the people we have seen recently; about all that is strange and uncanny left over from social situations. Forty minutes later, after parents, friends and relatives have been swept off the stage, the section called "Love Problems" begins. Now it is time to examine from every angle the calculus of indecisions, noncommitments, disappointments, attractions, chagrins. "It's hopeless," Emmy will say. "What shall I do? Put my foot down?" She will laugh, knowing how little this has changed things in the past. I give my cagey male advice. "Men respond to direct commands," et cetera. Or, if it is my turn to complain, she will shake her head at the capriciousness of the woman in question. She has no patience with these silly women. It is one of Emmy's most endearing qualities that she is not forever pestering me to be more sympathetic to the other person's position. She knows that in time I will be sympathetic; meanwhile, I want to complain! Nothing is more obnoxious than a friend who is forever taking the side of one's antagonist-love and identifying with her as the victim, or else always nudging one's vexed account toward the pole of greater compassion. Emmy waits till I have delivered myself of the whole sorry narrative, with all my favorite details and harangues, before inserting her own cautious wisdom. Even then, it is phrased in terms of how I might avoid further pain to myself.

The joke in platonic friendships, especially if both friends are single, is that each complains at great length of the thirst for an enduring love relationship, of the maldistribution and scarcity of decent partners of the opposite sex, while in a sense the solution to the problem is ever present. The opposite sex is pummeled *in toto*, with an exception being made for the listener, whose understanding personality is appealed to, flattered, and made into an ideal. "But you're not a typical woman." "But you're not a typical man!" And by the way, where do my platonic women friends dredge up their crew of male losers? They always seem to get involved with men who are near-catatonic, sleep a lot, won't see them more than once a month, won't go anywhere with them in public, won't leave the house, are at a low point in their careers, defeated, alcoholic, saddled with child-support payments, never buy presents, are violent, withdrawn, compulsively unfaithful, cute and sexy. I think there must be a club where all these sleepy narcissistic men hang out. I can't, I refuse to believe that this is what the male sex has come to. More likely, this is what the female sex is still attracted to. Another platonic friend, the glamorous A., seems to fall in love with nothing but these slugs with drooping bedroom eyelids. According to her, she is turned on by men who operate out of a libidinous energy (and who are often lost and disoriented in the work world), as opposed to men who operate "from the ego," like me. So much the worse for her, for me, for the human race. It seems to me that some sort of prejudice is at work that tends to segregate the clever and ambitious people from one another as sex partners.

None of these speculations ever arrives at very satisfying or profound conclusions, but it is fun to turn them over. The psychology of male-female attraction forms an inevitable subject of interest to platonic friends.

By now we have moved to the dining room, Emmy and I; I have set the table and brought in the Pyrex serving pots and salad bowl, enjoying all the charming duties of couple domesticity without the ennui and risk. We sit at a marble-topped table in front of the window filled with Emmy's hanging plants, and Emmy brings in the Parmesan cheese and wine, and I pretend we are in a good, cheap, cozy, working-class restaurant, in Italy. The sounds of teenage Hispanic kids playing ball in the street, the elevated train rolling by past the tenements with black-tar roofs, with the Bronx projects in the distance, under a rosy dust of late-lingering sunset, are all conducive to good appetite. Sometimes there is even a light rain to listen to. Emily is a fantastic cook, and they used to be even more wonderful, these meals on the marble top, before she became a vegetarian. It is unfortunate. I can't help thinking that something has *gone out* of our banquets. Now I must make do with second helpings of lentils and *groats* and summer squash and African yams. I must admit, she prepares them all deliciously; if only they might prove to be the surroundings for something more.

After the meal a quiet time follows. We retreat to the couch in her living room. Emmy stares at her cat. "Gato! Come here, silly." Gato wanders over to the couch and jumps up on the woolen blanket between us and starts actively licking my armpits. "Enough, Gato." I try to pull my arm away.

Then there are little cups of espresso, with lemon rind.

Afterward, Emmy may show me her latest series of photographs. Or else, if there is no new work to share, some bargains she has picked up in a thrift shop. If I am lucky we get a fashion show and try on all her new *shmattes*: a Chinese turquoise brocade padded robe, a navy pea jacket, some sweaters, scarves.

Then — a yawn, the signal that she is getting tired and I will have to leave soon. She has very precise notions about her bedtime. Though she is a person of immense, enviable stamina, Emmy's energy leaves her, when it leaves her, all in one second. She explains apologetically that she has to get up early tomorrow to drive to her job, and she is no good for anything if she tries to fall asleep past eleven o'clock. Yawning, she has become exactly like her cat; and I lift her face with her short red hair up to my lips and give her a good-night kiss, first on the nose or mouth, then on the top of her head, my platonic friend.

Just to Spoil Everything

For Kay

I won't call up first, I'll just ring your bell
out of left field, and walk in:
just because you told me
we were not supposed to see each other
until you said it was all right to do so,
until you felt less hysterical
(or whatever your crazy excuse was).
But I'm going over to your apartment house
right now, while you're waiting for some old boyfriend
for tea, just to spoil everything.
I'll rush in by surprise,
sit in your rocking chair
and say nothing, don't expect a scene.
Perhaps I won't even take off my overcoat,
with the orange knit scarf
you gave me once for Christmas.
My scarf will glint reproachfully at you.
I'll show you how unworldly I can be!
Because I want to make a mess of things,
of the fond poetic understanding last impressions
you would like to keep of me.

Train Company

Waiting on the platform for the Amtrak train to take me home from a conference in Philadelphia, I looked around as usual to see if I had any striking fellow passengers. Near the escalator was a tall, very tall blonde, pretty in a healthy, conventional way, who was saying her last goodbyes to a man several inches shorter and at least fifteen years older than she. I was intrigued by the way she kissed him goodbye — once, on the lips, and I could actually taste it, it was a good kiss, and then I backed into the train, still looking to see if she would kiss him again. She obliged, bending her head down coolly, without sacrificing sensuality, to the curly-haired man with the shoulder bags, and I wondered if she really cared about the guy.

I took a seat at the end of the car. It gave me more room to stretch out, and it was the only part of the train where the seats faced each other. A man in a blue three-piece business suit entered and sat across from me. He seemed about forty-five, with greying temples and faded Gig Young good looks and a quality of old-time American mercantile decency. Someone who obviously rode the train a lot. He threw his suitcase beside him and unbuttoned the top of his vest. Then the blonde came through the car and stopped at the two seats across the aisle from us. She stretched out her legs in her jeans and cowboy boots on the seat opposite her; I took up my book of philology. But I could barely read, so excited was I that she had come to join us, thinking how rare it is that one gets a second chance to be with a pretty girl spotted in a crowd.

The ruggedly good-looking man in the three-piece suit, his cheeks turning slightly florid (I could watch him above the line of my book, though not the blonde), wasted no time addressing her. "Got enough room there?"

"Yes, thanks."

"I asked because you're pretty tall for a girl. I guess everyone says that to you," he began his train rap, easily and pleasantly. I would not have thought of such a simple opening, and listened with admiration and envy while pretending to read.

"No, not everyone. But they think it," she said with a light southern accent. "I can tell sometimes they want to say it. It's better when they do."

"How tall are you?"

"Six-two."

"Are your folks tall?"

"My father is, but my mother's only five-foot-three."

"That so?"

"When I first came to New York looking for work, all the agencies said I was too tall."

"If you don't mind my asking, what do you do? You a fashion model?"

"Yes."

"I could tell because you still had your makeup on," he said grinning, boyishly proud.

"Yeah. I didn't have time to take it off. I don't like the way it feels on my face."

"You don't need it," he said gallantly.

"Thanks. I do mostly beauty face shots and lingerie. Not whole body shots, because they say I'm too tall. But in a year or two, tall will be in."

"How can you tell?"

"I just know, that's all."

"By intuition?"

"No, it's not intuition, just looking at the fashions, studying the trends."

The man fell silent, as though impressed with the science of it.

"When I first came to New York," she continued, "I was seventeen — that was three years ago, and everyone said, 'Get rid of her, she's too tall!' and I was gettin' real discouraged, but my father had brought me up here, and he started giving those people hell. He said, 'You don't know your own business, this gal's a natural.' My father's a career navy man so people listened. Navy, retired."

"He's used to giving orders, eh?"

"You said it."

I stole a quick look over at her face. Wow, she *was* beautiful — I had underestimated her. Maybe talking about modeling had brought out her glamour and confidence. She had superb cheekbones. I am drawn to women with strong, delicate cheekbones — as though the morbid evidence of bone pushing through flesh had to be there.

"How are you doing now? Able to make a living from it?" asked the businessman.

"I'm doin' all right. I've been self-supporting since —" she counted on her fingers — "March. But sometimes I don't know where the next month's rent is coming from. I may not have enough to pay the rent *this* month," she said laughing.

"Whereabouts do you live?"

"Over on the East Side, Sixty-eighth Street. It's nice there! I share an apartment with two other girls. It sounds real crowded, I know, three girls in a two-room apartment, but you'd be surprised. It isn't. One of them is usually away at her boyfriend's house. The other one's always out on dates. One of my roommates goes out only with rich guys," she volunteered. "I'm not like that. She goes out with Edward Farouk. He's an Arab oil man."

"Does she like him, or is it only for the money?"

"Oh, she likes him well enough, she *says*, but she wouldn't have gone out with him if he didn't have the money. Some of the girls —" she yawned mightily — "are like real gold diggers. Not me. 'Scuse me, I'm so tired. Can't wait to get to bed."

"Must have made some night of it," he said grinning. I looked over at her long legs, which were opened at the pelvis; she moved her leg side to side slightly as she talked, a suggestive parting rhythm. So young, I thought, only twenty; her approach to sex must be pure sport. She took his impertinent remark in stride.

"Well, I was up all night with some friends. They started playing games, like dragging me across the rug. I got a burn on my thigh. I came in to the shoot today for my photographer friend, he looked at that bruise — I said, 'It's not what you think!' "

They laughed.

"It wasn't anything kinky, just pranks. College stuff. I was so tired during the shoot. But I'd gone all the way to Philadelphia just to do this photographer friend a favor. It was for his annual Christmas card. He uses it for business. I didn't even get paid a lot for it, just did it as a kind of favor. I could barely keep my eyes open. But you have to concentrate, pay attention. It's hard! Most people don't know that but it's hard work."

"Oh, I believe you."

"What kind of work do you do?" she asked.

"I'm in Food Delivery Services. You probably don't know what that is . . ."

"Well, tell me."

"It's like seeing that large shipments of frozen food get delivered to hotels, and selling to hotels and institutions. In a way, you might say I'm a salesman. I like my work," he added, sounding defensive. "It's up to me to make sure that the shipment gets there and everybody eats, so I like the responsibility part. I get to travel a lot."

"Sounds interesting," she encouraged him.

"Then I come home and relax. I live on a farm in the country — I raise horses. That's what really gets me going. I would die for my horses. I said goodbye to them this morning, almost didn't want to leave. Now I'm on this three-week sales trip. I don't really like going to New York City."

"Why not?"

"New York's not my place. I'm a — 'country boy,' I guess, deep down. One time I walked for what felt like forever in that downtown part, Forty-second Street. With every disgusting thing I had read about, all those prostitutes and — queers," he said, halting apologetically; I kept reading my book. "Don't get me wrong, I like some things about New York. My idea of a good time in town is to stay over Saturday night at the Saint Regis, and go over to that hotel restaurant near Central Park in the morning for their big Sunday brunch. That brunch is great! Ten dollars and all you can eat. I mean they give you a platter stacked to here. Champagne, the works. Know which one I mean?"

The blonde nodded. "The Plaza has a good one too."

"Oh yes, course, the Plaza, that's a nice brunch. I'll say this for New York: the restaurants, there's no place you can beat 'em. But you've got to have the bucks," he declared with an air of wisdom, and sitting back, unbuttoned his vest still farther.

"Oh, for sure! But I like New York still. Before I came here, when I lived with my folks in Rehoboth Beach, I didn't do anything. Just sat around and ate a lot of junk food. Now I eat foods that are good for my health, and I walk — you walk a lot in New York," she declared. "And before I came to New York I never read a book. Now I like nothing more than to spend a quiet evening at home reading."

Between her elongated thighs was the reading matter she had brought along on the train, Harold Robbins's latest. (In hardcover, which did imply a certain commitment.)

"And I'll admit I miss the beach sometimes, but my mother sends me the fare to come home for Christmas. My birthday's around Christmas, so it's a double celebration. My mother's always offering to fly me home for a couple of days. . . ."

I went back to reading my book. *Common speech has a mixed parentage. It is empirical and formal, mental and behaviorist, physical and sociological, actual and abstract. . . . Its inchoateness is its efficiency. A danger of any definite constructed language, developed abstractly, is that it will impose on and prejudge experience and decide* a priori *what can be said. To prejudge would be disastrous, especially for a language of science, which is hypothetical and probabilistic and thrives on freedom of inquiry; and in his* Logical Syntax *Carnap worries this problem a good deal. . . .* All this seemed to be too obvious. Or was I missing a subtlety? I read on for another fifteen minutes. When my eyes grew tired I started listening again. The salesman was talking about his preference for the train over other transportation. "It's a pleasure to take the train. I feel like I spend too much time behind the wheel."

"I know what you mean. But I like to drive when I get home to Rehoboth Beach. I get in my Mustang and *so long!*"

"It must be a roomy car for your legs to fit in."

"It is."

"But then I'll bet it uses up a lot of gas. With this oil and energy crisis, I'm afraid we're gonna run out eventually."

"I don't think so," said the blonde. "I have confidence in this country. We are not gonna run out."

"That's not what the President says. And from what I hear, the fossil fuel supply is diminishing —"

"I don't think there's a real oil shortage. That's fake."

"Now I don't know," said the man, not willing to concede, but shaken by her confidence and conviction. "How do you figure that?"

"The good ole U.S.A. can take care of any oil demand in the near future. I just think it's a fake. The corporations, they're doing it."

"Well," he laughed uneasily, "we can't tell without the figures before us anyway. We could argue all night and it still wouldn't prove anything."

"Let's ask *him,*" she whispered, meaning me.

"He's probably a professor of economics and is sitting there with all the answers in his head!" The man chuckled.

"Or a scientist, he looks like," she whispered. I was blushing and trying to keep a straight face. "How about it, mister?"

"No, I'm not a scientist or an economist and I don't know a thing about oil. I'm a writer," I couldn't help adding.

"Oh, I go with a writer from time to time." Her eyes

glazed over. "But not too often. He's usually so busy, we hardly ever see each other. Writers are like that, they want their privacy."

"It's true; they do need a lot of solitude," I said, trying to make the profession sound mysterious.

"He lives on the East Side. Not far from me," she added. "Sometimes I'd walk over late at night and visit. You can do that in that neighborhood, it's safe to walk around at night. But I haven't seen him in at least a month. Guess he got tired of me. Do you like Scotch?"

"Not particularly," I laughed.

"Well, you're the first writer I ever met who didn't!"

Whoever this writer is, he must be a swine, I thought. The old drunk, taking advantage of this pretty, scatter-brained novice's unsophisticated interest in everything and then throwing her away (not that I wouldn't like to do the same thing, probably).

When the train pulled into Penn Station, I wondered if she and the food-service man would go off together. I said goodbye to them and took the escalator up to the taxi stand. It was a cold night, with no taxis. I turned around and the tall blonde was coming up the steps alone, dragging her traveling case.

"Hi! Want to share a cab?" I suggested.

"Well, I'm going east and you said you lived on the West Side."

"All right," I said disappointedly, shrugging away the idea.

A yellow cab pulled up and I opened the door for her to take the first one.

"Aren't you going to get in?" she asked from inside.

"Sure!" I hadn't realized it was all right with her. "Thanks!" I gave the two addresses to the driver; he headed west first, toward my house. I was suddenly tongue-tied, wondering how to break the ice with her. "That was fun, that conversation on the train."

"You should have spoken up sooner."

"Yes, well . . . I wanted to listen first, eavesdrop."

"You wanted to hear the man put the make on the girl," she laughed. I was thrown by her shrewdness. Oh well, she's probably bright, just not educated, I thought to myself.

"You hit it right on the head."

"But he didn't," she answered. "He was just a nice friendly man who wanted to talk."

"Yes, he was nice," I agreed, grateful to him now that he had left us alone; he became for me a great American rock of normality and trust. "I liked the way he spoke about his horses — the way they meant so much to him."

"Yes, he was crazy about those horses," she said wearily, with a surprising touch of malice. "And anyway, I don't do that."

It took me several seconds to understand what she meant. The taxi was about to pull up to my corner. I wondered: Should I . . . ?

The cab stopped on Central Park West.

Oh, what the hell, just forget it. Let her remember me as another nice friendly man, the kind one meets on trains and never sees again. "Well, it's been very nice talking to you." I offered her my hand and a few dollars for the ride. "What is your name?"

"Veronica. Just that one name, Veronica." She flashed a brilliant smile.

"I get it: like Verushka. Well, I'm Phillip Lopate. It was very nice to have met you." I climbed out of the cab. After all, I told myself, standing on the street corner, it's not irrevocable. If I ever change my mind, it shouldn't be too hard to find a fashion model with the sole name of Veronica in New York.

Part

TWO

Quiche Blight on
Columbus Avenue

"What expectations have they that they take such good care of themselves?"

— KENKO, *Essays in Idleness*

OVER the last five years I have had the mixed pleasure of watching the avenue near my house, Columbus, go from a sleepy, gently decaying backwater to one of the city's major thoroughfares, a Via Veneto for swells and near-swells. It is no longer possible to carry groceries home without stumbling over the pointy shoe of some magazine-cover type watching the passersby with glass of white wine in hand at an outdoor table, or being nearly run over by a disco–roller skater from one side and a panting runner in Perrier T-shirt from the other. The hurricane of chic that has hit Columbus Avenue has swept away the old life as surely as a storm like Camille on the Mississippi Gulf Coast.

What was it like in the old days, Father? Well, first of all, Columbus Avenue wasn't even a "walking street"; people used Broadway, one or two blocks west (depending on where that rambling White Way cut its path) for their prime thoroughfare. And on Broadway and Seventy-third Street is Verdi Square, or "Needle Park" as it was known then, because of the junkies and dealers that hung out there. You would see them stoned out of their minds, helping each other up to Columbus Avenue, where many of them lived. Or hanging around cheap burger joints like the White Tower (now it's that fancy yogurt-and-quiche store). It was this element, the junkies and the more argumentative transvestites, that some locals refer to when they say, "Now isn't it better than the way it used to be?" Of course they forget to mention that many tenants pushed out by the real-estate boom were quiet working-class and poor families, living in walk-up tenements that have since been gutted, remodeled, and subdivided into smaller units for singles. In any case, there used to be a lot of luncheonettes with counter stools and orange juicers and a ratty, seedy look, where old beaten men and women hung out.

Now, why should these establishments with their griddle-grease reek always have such a calming effect on me? Part of it has to do with the fact that I grew up in poor neighborhoods, and their odors revive a comfortingly maternal presence. But another part, less justifiable perhaps, stems from that sentimental and condescending equation between metropolitan vitality and the lower classes. The struggling immigrant family, the corner bum, the dice players, the pensioned old, and the new reigning queen, the shopping bag lady, have often been written up as symbols of the life-pulse in a big city; and I am as guilty as any of this romantic shorthand. I feel reassured when I walk around the open markets behind the bus terminal and see Filipino fruit stands and owners with thick accents. I like to go into those candy stores with chipped counters that serve malteds to the few regular customers who still bother to come in, and carry slow-moving stationery supplies — years-old flyspecked Cinderella coloring books waiting for Prince Charming behind the glass case. The truth is, I am drawn not only to the thick of crowds, but also to decay: those genially fetid hardware stores and laundromats that, living in the past, have forgotten to raise their prices and are being squeezed to death by inflation. I love the air of failing business. My patronage may be seen both as tribute and omen: I no sooner become attached to one of these places than the owner dies, or the business is sold.

Up and down Columbus Avenue you had businesses like that. And one by one these ma-and-pa outfits caved in, to be replaced by a chic emporium. Quiche blight attacked the neighborhood. Quiche blight is that disease wherein what was once considered fringe delicacy becomes the monopoly. Croissants drive out bagels and rolls; there is no more ordinary cheap bakery bread, but you may get the most exquisite hand-baked loaf with natural grains, bananas, orange rinds, currants and honey, and it is sold for seventy-five cents a slice. A gourmet food dispensary opens on one corner of the avenue; soon there is a second, a fourth, a tenth! How many pieces of brie can you stuff down your mouth at one time? If it is not so easy to find a shoe-repair or a hardware store any longer, no one seems to notice. And suddenly the avenue boasts the most highly specialized storefronts, catering to needs you never knew you had: a shop that sells only Western boots, another that carries only goods with the motif of hearts and valentines, a Japanese *futon*-mattress shop, a store for running shoes, another for coffee, a one-dress boutique, a cosmetics stand, and so on, each with its write-up from *New York* magazine in the window.

Then there are the marts given over to *high theater* — like Bruce's Pleasure Chest, which stocks sexual implements and leather goods. There is the florist whose poignant settings for one or two roses in the window are like opera sets (always the last scene from *La Bohème*). Most curious of all are the decorator-concepts stores where it isn't always clear what they are trying to sell, what their merchandise is. In the window are paper flowers, a teddy bear, and long-stemmed glasses. You enter and look over the pencils with bushy tails, the three boxes of mauve stationery, an inkwell in the shape of a foot, and framed dime-store photos of unknown fifties starlets. Each object is placed carefully in isolation, like a secret leering joke, invoking dizziness. Props for a seduction.

Another code of camp references reigns over the many antique furniture and clothing stores along the avenue. The recycling of associations carries a steep price: no bargains with the past here. Bowling shirts are now the rage in secondhand clothing stores; it used to be Hawaiian shirts, and before that, cowboy outfits. But what a sight it is to see a stunning woman (of which the new Columbus Avenue has more than its share) holding up one blouse after another before the mirror! This season the pretty women are wearing wrinkled men's white shirts. The more wrinkled the better, as though hastily pulled crumpled from the dryer. And blazing lipstick is back. Everything is getting more garish. I think this is a good sign.

The fact is, by no means do I regret the arrival of some artifice and amenities; it is simply a matter of degree. This way of life, once set in motion up and down the avenue, seems to reproduce itself like copies from a Xerox machine out of control.

Take the question of restaurants. At first there were only a few Greek coffee shops. Then came the singles bars, which served the usual hamburger-and-salad at inflated prices. These must have done well, because soon a new restaurant seemed to be opening every week: tandoori restaurants, chili parlors, Mexican cantinas, vegetarian, Czech, Szechuan, French, Hunan, Japanese, Argentine, Turkish, Italian, all right on top of each other, breathing down each other's necks. They are shoehorning them in so fast there won't be room for anything but restaurants. And where will they find enough hungry customers? Doesn't anyone eat at home anymore? The food tastes curiously similar up and down the avenue. It is as though all the dishes were prepared in the same underground kitchen and then shipped to the various restaurants via color-coded subterranean ducts. The spices are similarly bland, the portions about the same (small). Most of the restaurants fall into the "spinach salad syndrome" of catering to people who are worried about their weight; such customers will pay more for the favor of being served less. Despite their expensive, wedding-invitation menus, the legion of cafés along Columbus Avenue are essentially fast-food operations that fool their dull-palated clients with fantasy decor and false promises of ethnic variety, the staple of our middle class's post–melting pot nostalgia.

I give them each a try. One night I walk into the Café Carob, a tiny white-walled boîte with the determined air of a supper club. There are white designer tables, square and severe, with SoHo neon art on the walls: a Kenneth Noland-ish neon bull's-eye, an orange arrow running up the staircase; and in the window the words "Café Carob" glisten like a pink waterfall. I suppose it is the place to go if you have on a backless turquoise evening gown, which one blond woman does. But the illusion barely has a chance to set in because the room is so narrow: two stories of only six paces across. Mirrors on the back wall double the visual space, giving the impression from the street of a much bigger restaurant, while providing a hazard for new waitresses turning the wrong way. The menu tries for New Orleans — jambalaya and gumbo and a fish of the day and pecan pie — but the food tastes more like that from a mediocre health-food restaurant with continental aspirations.

Surely, many of us in the neighborhood thought, a saturation point would be reached, and some of these restaurants go out of business. Which is exactly what happened — although other restaurants took their places instantly, standing in for the fallen soldiers. The Café Carob is now the Yang-Yang. Here also the more prosperous restaurants saw their opportunity: they knocked down the dividing walls and took over their failing neighbor's space, they expanded into the "garden," they set up tables on the sidewalk and covered them over with tinted glass bubbles. Even the Greek coffee shops secreted sidewalk bubbles. Like overweight Casbah merchants, they burst out of their trousers and gave themselves Parisian airs. It was getting out of hand. Each restaurant printed up its own T-shirts and sold them for four bucks apiece to their faithful customers, who strode around wearing their bistro's colors like gang members in feudal China.

The result of all this bubbling and building, stirring and mixing? *Instant café society.* But unlike the café habitués in a small European city, where everyone of a certain class indeed knows everyone else, the people who sit at the tables along Columbus Avenue are strangers to each other. Their air of mutual complicity and joint feasting is pure optical illusion, decorator's craft. If they appear to be a group, it is only because of the homogeneity and complacency of their tastes; but their communal connection is something seen only from the outside, by the envious passerby. Inside the experience, they are as alone and cut off from their neighbors as American urban life has always prepared them to be.

There are exceptions to this anomie. In fact, a form of street-corner society has sprung up to replace the old derelict band along Columbus Avenue. On any given day you see young people with the cutest hairdos and the trimmest bottoms running into each other on street corners, throwing their arms around one another with brisk eroticism and then trading information about their latest jobs. These are the boys and girls of the chorus. They set the tone for the whole avenue, so that, unconsciously or not, strollers from all walks of life find themselves imitating the perkiness, the overfond embraces of distant acquaintances, the hurried step and underfed look of eternal adolescents, the team-players' spunky optimism, the casual quick-change costumes, and the grace under unemployment — turning the whole strip into one big Warner Brothers musical canteen. At any moment Jimmy Cagney could run up and grunt, "All right — you, you and *you*."

The actors loll in the new cafés; the musicians carry or wheel by their somber instrument cases (always something of the dray horse about them, always a bit more domestic than the actors because of their devotion to that attendant creature); the dancers hop off the curb and across the street against traffic, lightly gripping the drawstrings of their dance bags; the opera singers show off in a snowstorm, arm in arm, three abreast, chests out, bellowing arias and Christmas carols; and the writers — the writers look in the bookstore windows, mad with envy.

Joining the show business procession are those professionals with a little extra money — the lawyers, the CPAs, the therapists, the dentists, the counselors, the academics, the fund raisers — who come to Columbus Avenue for the good life. On a hot summer night they may be seen strolling along, usually in couples, in their after-office leisure costumes, licking double-scoop ice cream cones. Here is one pair, these two who look as if they were married forever, but to different mates, and suddenly find themselves going out on dates again — the man with wild grey hair and clinician's glasses and plump little belly, his arm around a dark-haired, confused-looking woman who was once deeply attractive, as they stand in line at the ice cream parlor. And now he grabs her and kisses her "sensuously," which only deepens her confusion before she recoups and smiles, both grinning now — grinning too much, in fact.

But in this whole parade, where are the families? Where are the kids on tricycles, where are the old family restaurants, why is every table occupied by a gang of grinning adults in their prime? This is the bond that unites today's Columbus Avenue. The childless couples and gays and swinging singles have formed a whole new society, a parish of people who live outside traditional family life. They would probably disapprove of the (very un-urban) intolerance of senior-citizen retirees who prohibit children from their planned communities — and yet that is exactly the situation they have brought about. "KEEP IN MIND THE CHILD-LESSNESS WE SHARE," wrote poet James Merrill; "THIS TURNS US / OUTWARD TO THE LESSONS & THE MYSTERIES." He must have been talking about another crew. The only mystery these people seem to have on their minds is where to find the best cheesecake. The collective hedonism at the core of this moving crowd — if one can use so grand a word as "hedonism" to describe such a bland customer itch — is both reward for not having children and substitute for them. It is the influx of this new moneyed childless constituency that has so changed Columbus Avenue, and (it bothers me to say it since I am one of them) their barren situation is exactly mirrored in the avenue's new establishments. These are people who spend all their money in the street — on their backs or in restaurants and taxis. There is no need to put away for the children's college educations. High inflation reduces the incentive to save. Even the classic pattern of middle-class accumulation seems irrelevant here; why buy a new washing machine when there are

half-a-dozen dry cleaners up the street? Apartment life re-
stricts the number of pieces of equipment one can store, in
any case: a TV, a stereo, a car to get away on weekends. The
rest is fun money.

The decision of the middle class to reclaim Manhattan as
its playground meant that any halfway-acceptable neighborhood not far from midtown was doomed to "renaissance."
The construction of the Lincoln Center cultural complex a
few blocks south encouraged restaurants to settle in the
area; then ABC-TV expanded its studio facilities, introduc-
ing a round-the-clock work force; at the same time, a sizable
homosexual community began to develop, with the gay en-
trepreneurs providing much of the commercial savvy and
style for the avenue's development.

Beyond these local factors is a significant larger pattern:
the demographic bulge among singles' households over the
last ten years, together with an acute housing shortage
brought on by recession and a lack of new construction,
made for a landlord's market, in which owners were encouraged to renovate and subdivide once-spacious family
apartments into studio units for singles. Because of the
larger turnover among single renters, such tenants are also
more profitable, as the landlords are allowed by city law to
raise the rent 15 percent each time an apartment falls
vacant.

The housing stock directly on Columbus Avenue, those
grim five-story walk-ups that had once been used for crash
pads, still remained less desirable, being right above the
noise; but even those muddy brown facades have been getting upgraded — often courtesy of the restaurant underneath that wants an eye-catching color scheme to draw
attention to the whole building. Suddenly the tenements
were painted maroon with cream trim, or canary yellow, or

the dirt was sandblasted off them and they were left to stand embarrassed in their original buff. The most mundane, taken-for-granted slum buildings with fire escapes running down their faces were placed, as it were, in the italicized quotes of architectural revivalism. It must have been a shock to the winos, those remnants of the vagrant population who have still not left the area, and who pass the bottle back and forth, calling out ribald remarks to the new denizens of the avenue. Their comments are usually in Spanish or slurred by drink, so that the recipient is never sure how far he or she has been insulted. Fortunately, there is always a cheese-store window to stare into, with its antique tureens in the shapes of turtles and turkeys, its long loaves of French bread, and its quiche.

It must be pointed out that the neighborhood has always had certain ties to epicureanism and glamour. The Ansonia Hotel was a sort of bedroom borough for Carnegie Hall, housing Caruso and Toscanini and Stravinsky; the Dakota has had its share of famous movie stars and theater people; and there were always a good number of rehearsal halls in the area, mostly on Broadway, where sweating ballet dancers were to be seen at the practice bar, one flight above another kind of bar. The tree-lined blocks with rows of brownstones all through the West Seventies and Eighties, which ran from Central Park West to the river and intersected Columbus Avenue, had a pleasantly understated elegance; but it was still something of a secret, or at least had not yet become the height of chic.

No, the East Side was where all the fashionable and social-climbing types seemed to be moving. In fact, the very term "East Side" became synonymous with that self-indulging life-style that was quickly turning streets like First Avenue into a kind of Coney Island strip for *arrivistes*.

The West Siders prided themselves on being funkier, more family oriented and more racially integrated. The East Side was the Republican party and the sexual revolution and duck restaurants; the West Side liked to think of itself as Reform Democrat, social responsibility and lox. So provincial are New Yorkers that they can cling to these ideological-geographical stereotypes to the end without understanding that they are being hit with a homogenizing national phenomenon. When quiche blight struck the West Side, just as it had laid low places as far-flung as Sausalito and Woodstock, Provincetown and Aspen (having sharpened its techniques first in the experimental laboratory of vacation towns), and gone on to devastate city areas such as Denver's Pioneer Square, San Francisco's Ghiradelli Square, and vital chunks of Seattle, Boston and New Orleans, all the West Sider could say was that the neighborhood seemed to be going "a bit East Side." And even this disdainful comment concealed a pride that it could never happen here. Now that Columbus Avenue has sadly overtaken the East Side in *quichisme*, the time has arrived for the white papers, the soul-searching, the blue-ribbon panels. Where did we go wrong?

And yet, dismayed as I am by the bourgeoisification of Columbus Avenue, I have to admit that the new scene amuses me. In the outrageousness of its quest for pleasure and status (here they come to the same), the crowd sends out a throb of life. Maybe I belong here, on Columbus Avenue. As someone who now has a little jack in my pocket and is eager to spend it, I see myself mirrored swinishly and yet touchingly in the passing parade. And street life is not less street life for being middle class. Let's face it, why should I assume that the signs in Spanish advertising delicacies for the ghetto immigrant — "Hay Mavi Fría!" "Hay Mangos!"

— have any more vitality or integrity than the calligraphic logos along Columbus Avenue? Whatever the injustices of one class toward the other, at this moment their pretensions to a better life are astonishingly similar. Both the middle class and the working class mostly want to look good, stuff their mouths, and forget.

The Tender Stranger

I was running to school in fourth grade to get to class before the bell and as I rounded a busy corner I banged into a tall man rushing from the other direction and I was thrown into the air. He weighed so much more than I that I sailed for quite a ways before landing on the sidewalk.

"Are you all right?" The man bent over me. His overcoat was a fine camel's hair, such as I had seen only in the movies. He had on a soft beige scarf and brown woolen gloves and a brown fedora. "I'm so sorry, it was my fault completely. Are you all right?"

I nodded, laughing now at the comic spill I had taken, like a cartoon character. How could I explain to him that it had been a pleasure to fly through the air, that there was something even comforting about a collision with such a manly, yet considerate, adult as this stranger.

I pulled my sticky palms off the sidewalk. The skin was torn up, and bleeding.

"Here, I think I've got a Kleenex," he said. He reached into his pocket, felt around, and came up with a monogrammed handkerchief. I stared at the sharp crease in his pants as he crouched alongside me, brushing off the dirt; I was so in love with him that I felt too embarrassed to look at his face. "Does that hurt much?"

"No, it doesn't hurt at all," I lied.

"I just didn't see you. I was in too big of a hurry, I guess."

"I was also in a hurry."

"This corner is very tricky. People always seem to have accidents here."

I wondered how he knew that.

As though he could read my mind, he went on to explain: "I have a law office nearby, and I see these accident cases all the time."

Suddenly the words *Notary Public* popped into my mind. I had read them on golden decals in store windows and wondered often what they meant. "Are you a Notary Public?" I asked.

"No, just a lawyer," he laughed gently. "My name's Tony, Tony Bauer" (it sounded like). "My office is right across Roebling Street, on the second floor. Why don't you come visit me sometime?"

"Okay."

"Do you think you'll be able to walk now? Maybe we should take you to a drugstore first and get them to put some iodine on your hand."

"I'm all right. Honest."

"You sure now?"

"I'm all right," I said, letting him help me up. He handed me my blue-and-red bookbag. Only now did I realize I felt dizzy from the blow. Everything was whirling with black outlines in the winter snow. I was going to have another of my headaches.

"Well — goodbye for now. It was a pleasure meeting you," he said, and I felt he really meant it. "Too bad it had to come about this way." Then the stranger took off one glove, and was careful not to hurt my bruise in his handshake. I had never seen an adult show a child such tact. As his back turned and he walked away, I had the peculiar urge to yell out, "Daddy!"

Afterward I often tried rounding that same corner at full speed, but no one ever banged into me again.

An Old Old Woman
Asked Me . . .

Aɴ old old woman asked me if I could walk with her to the end of the block. As soon as I said it was all right she latched onto my clean white shirt with collier's hands: filthy palms, black like shoe polish, and her fingers were quite strong too. They dug into my forearm. We began walking up the long block from Columbus Avenue to Central Park West. At first she did no talking. She was quite short, came up to the middle of my shoulders, with blown-up swollen ankles and thick black shoes. I wondered if she might be a derelict, a bag lady; that is, I wondered what I had got myself into. She was a little too well dressed to be a bag lady. She had on a spring coat and a sweater, though the temperature was in the nineties. We were walking so slowly it was more like swimming. Tiny step by tiny step. And the heat waves dancing in the air on this hot June day made it even more like feeling one's way underwater. People swerved around us. She became voluble, and told me that all sorts of good things would happen to me as a direct result of helping her. Things I hadn't even wished for. It had come true with almost everyone who had helped her. I got the impression she was trying to pass herself off as an elf. She began to reminisce. She told me she'd been so

sickly a child in Ireland, who would have believed she
would live so long? While the others all were dead. The
others back in Ireland, and here too. What was the difference between here and the old country? I asked. Oh, the
people in Dublin keep the streets much cleaner than they
do in New York. Looking down at her hands, I thought she
was no one to talk. Suddenly she asked, "Are you married?"

"No, I'm single."

"Just like me!" she replied.

We had gone only three-quarters of the way up the block,
but she told me she could manage all right by herself the
rest of the way. "God bless you," she said, and then, as I
nodded, and started walking away, she added, with a certain
stubbornness, a certain cockiness, "God *will* bless you."

Jumping Beans

I BOUGHT a pack of Mexican jumping beans and put them in my shirt. They clicked inside my pocket like chattering false teeth. I held them up against my heart. They responded well to warmth. I took out the instruction sheet and read: "The restlessness of the caterpillar flinging himself against the walls of his prison is what causes the bean to hop and roll."

In the subway train, I heard them pounding away. If I stood still, the clicks became subdued. I wondered if they might be spelling something out in Morse code, or picking up my signal, like those ring stones that change colors with one's mood.

Later they grew thoughtful and businesslike; their jumps were as the steady clicks of an abacus.

The Warehouse Fire

O N our way to a downtown loft party in Emily's Volkswagen, Emily, Kay and I, we stopped off to see the ruins of a fire in the waterfront district, on Thirtieth Street and Twelfth Avenue. This whole neighborhood, along the western spine of Manhattan, has always been mysterious to me, with its deserted steamship offices that look like flaking Venetian facades, and its imperturbable warehouses where no one ever seems to go in or out. A few blocks east are skyscrapers, but between those skyscrapers and the waterfront lie empty lots where my imagination has more than enough room to turn frightened. Emily parked the car, and we heeled our shoes cautiously on the tractionless ice. The fire had been a week ago. It had been so close to zero the night of the blaze, and ever since, that the water from the fire hoses had frozen. Sheets of white ice hung down the collapsed timbers, which were charred black and leaning diagonally against each other. Looking at the warehouse was like staring into an abandoned Colorado mine shaft, wrapped in an unfinished cathedral of snow. Smoke continued to pour up, apparently from the warehouse basement where the fire smoldered and was still alive, incredibly enough, in all this ice. The smoke burned the eyes so that we didn't dare get any closer to the ruins than across the street. The smoke floated up between the webs of ice and out of the roof and across the street to our side, to some railroad tracks lifted on a raised platform, with iron railings, behind which were stalled maroon-brown freight cars. Everything began to swim together in a delicate chalky light that was uncanny, no matter where I looked. The bones of ice, the boxcars, the ruined warehouse, the half-moon. It was like an overhead shot in a wonderful suspense movie when something horrible is about to happen; the filigree of the train railings had a trembling clarity, a rib of aquamarine seen through the smoke, as though in a grisaille painting. But these comparisons with art only understate the rareness of the spectacle. We all realized we might never see its like again. Emily began taking pictures. The watchmen from the fire department returned, and Emily, who is good at striking up conversations with policemen or museum guards, left us and began talking with them.

Kay and I were shivering; it was too much of a good thing. I wanted to get in the warm car and go to the party. I signaled to Emily with a yank of my head (she ignored me, of course); then I headed for her fire-engine-red Volkswagen to wait by the hood. At this farther distance and angle, the warehouse ruins did not look so special. What if the poetry had already drained from the scene? It was a matter of getting that grey green to line up with the white again.

I was debating whether to clatter back to a closer vantage point, when Emily wandered over to us, explaining as she opened the car door: "I just wanted to find out if the night watchmen felt too jaded to enjoy it."

"Were they?"

"I said to them, 'I find this very beautiful — do you?' and one guy said, 'It's tremendous! I can't get enough of looking at it.' "

We were pleased with his answer, suddenly feeling warm affection, probably condescending, for the watchman who shared our aesthetic excitement. So, apparently everyone thought this was an extraordinary sight. The knowledge of its universal appeal reassured me, even as it spoiled the pleasure slightly.

In any case, we were probably the only people at the party we were going to who had seen it.

Osao

SATURDAYS I try to use for writing. Sometimes the release from everyday work stirs up all I want to say; but sometimes just the opposite happens, and I cling to errands like doing the laundry. It was the second kind of Saturday, and I was looking for excuses so as not to confront my brain, as I walked to the Xerox shop. I know the man who owns the shop, Pak. He is a Korean who came to the United States as an exchange student, got his doctorate, and taught philosophy in midwestern universities for several years, before becoming a New York City shopkeeper.

His choice of the medium of xerography has always seemed to me to have a wry secret connection to his philosophical training. With his waxy skin indoor-pallid, his eyes baggy from serving these insatiable and unreliable machines, his short athletic body making half turns in the constricted space behind the counter, he seems to have become a kind of Xerox ascetic. Actually, I am making him sound more retiring than he really is: the shop does a brisk business. It is not as if he is "burying" himself, in fact he has quite a few entrepreneurial sidelines — used typewriters, offset printing jobs, a half interest in the restaurant upstairs.

All the world seems to come to Pak's shop on Saturday. Most of the steady customers are self-employed, work at home, and hang around the Xerox place as a substitute office. The show people in the neighborhood, the dancers, the choir directors, want reviews and résumés multiplied; the music students have to have their scores duplicated on the folio machine; the nervous organizers of Balkan and Ukrainian support committees need hundreds of copies of their letters of appeal.

Though it purports to be cut-and-dried, a Xerox parlor arouses in some people a craving for special treatment, an undefinable "sweet tooth" to be indulged, like a bakery of the word. That particular Saturday, there was a small old lady with dark lipstick who had income-tax forms she wanted copied. From the excited way she talked, it might have been her first outing in years. When Pak yelled, "Anyone with offset jobs?" she asked in a panic, "What's that?" and a lady next to her said, "It's printing."

The old lady was none too pleased when she got her copies back. "It's so light I can barely read it!"

"That's because you use pencil," said Pak, making it sound "pen-soo" in his soft Korean accent.

"But it usually comes out darker than this!"

"No machine in the world do any better on pencil."

He turned to hand someone else his copies, but she stayed. "It's not in order! I don't see a third page. Couldn't you make this one darker?"

"I'll try, madam." He was remarkably patient (one might say, *philosophical*), even offering to charge her only for the dark sheets. But still she clogged up the counter, turning the pages this way and that, and pulling everyone else into her confusion.

In spite of the fact that I had nothing to do but waste

time, I got carried along with the general impatience and kept staring at my watch, furious that it was taking so long.

Pak nodded at me when I handed him five poems. "How is Poet? You got any more big advances?"

"No, and I never had any in the first place."

"Don't tell me. You must be writing big money-maker."

All this was standard: I was getting rich, I was getting famous, and only my innate stinginess prevented me from buying all the used typewriters in his shop. But this time, as he handed my change back, Pak added something in an undertone, so that the other customers wouldn't hear it:

"I have a Korean friend who needs help translating poems into English. She's very nice. Just few poems."

"I don't know any Korean."

"No, no." He laughed. "She has already translated into English. This is just to give it — 'final poetic polish.' " Pak looked down at the floor, as though shy about asking a favor. "Can she call you? I told her you were 'sensitive young man,' fine 'poet,' " he said, giving the last word a faintly ridiculing, caricatured twist. "All right?"

"Sure, why not." I was hoping this woman would be beautiful and it would lead to an adventure. "Tell her to phone me in the next hour. I'm going straight home from here."

It was a time in my life when I had no love interests. I was between girlfriends and I had not slept with anyone for months. I had vowed to myself that the next passably attractive woman who crossed my path, I would chase.

By the time I got back to my apartment I was already picturing her as one of the Utamaro beauties hanging on my wall calendar, the voluptuous pearl divers, the decorous geishas. What is it about such out-of-the-blue assignations that raises all one's hopes of at least finding the woman of one's life? I prepared myself for disappointment: she was probably homely and wrinkled, or one of those cross matron-auntie types in Ozu movies. I equipped her with a hunchback, a patch over one eye, pock scars and sparse grey hair; I had so fertilely and successfully distorted her in every way that by the time the phone rang that afternoon I was surprised to hear a voice fresh, intelligent, and "pretty." Let me explain what I mean. Generally I can tell just by the phone voice whether someone I have never met is physically attractive. There seems to be a way that people who have received compliments all their lives put themselves forward, or rather, only part of themselves forward.

I began straightening up. She would be over any minute. I had to act professional. Pretend I was a private detective waiting for some client.

I went to answer the doorbell.

"I am Osao," she said with a trace of deprecation, as if apologizing for the fact that she was only this one person, as if she too were in on the joke of the multiple forms to which my imagination had subjected her.

There was about her the maturity of a woman in her mid-thirties, probably a few years older than I was, which was not necessarily a mark against her. From the way she stood at the front door, from her no-nonsense manner, I had a momentary image of her as a nurse, or someone used to making house calls, an impression that I later learned had no basis in fact. She had straight black hair, cropped short, a high-cheeked, pretty face and round black eyes that warned, "I am nobody's fool." I walked in front of her down the hall, and I noticed, turning for an instant, her full figure just at that shadow line between voluptuous and plump.

To be honest, I could not yet make up my mind whether I was or was not attracted to her.

She was not what I had expected, being neither as seductively Oriental as my most dreamy fantasies, nor as homely as my efforts to preempt and contain disappointment. I had to deal with a solid professional woman of the kind I met often in my teaching rounds: clearheaded, with no wish to appear glamorous (a wrap denim skirt seemed to signify preference for practical uniforms); yet there were faint touches of a will to beauty if one wanted to notice them.

She sat down on the couch, and I offered her tea, both of us smiling, perhaps at the comedy of my making this Asiatic gesture. From the stove, I noticed her looking around my apartment; perhaps she was doing her own kind of anthropology. What generalization and conclusion she was coming to I would have loved to know.

She got up to look at a poster of a celadon statuette from a museum exhibition. "Is that Korean?"

"Yes," I said.

She sat down, contented. I brought over the teacups.

"Did my friend explain to you what the job was?" she asked, getting down to business the moment I sat beside her, as though aware of the romantic interpretations to which her entering this strange man's house might be put, and wishing to steer far away from that level.

"You said something on the phone about your father and a calligraphy show."

"My father is having his first exhibition of calligraphy in America, at the Korea Society. You know the Korea Society?"

"Oh yes. I think I've been there once."

She looked at me doubtfully. "His show is in two weeks. Maybe you will be able to come?"

"I'd love to come. When is it?"

"Friday, July twenty-first, is the opening. Two weeks from

yesterday," she said, and then added, "He is staying in my house in the meantime." From her tone I inferred that her father's visit was not an unmixed blessing.

"Do you not get along?" I asked.

"Oh, yes. This is the first time he is in New York so he is happy to see the sights. He walks around all day. But when I was younger we always used to fight."

"What about?"

She blushed. I wondered if I was going too quickly. But her explanation was ready: "My father is a difficult man. He is very — old-fashioned in his thinking. He is very proud to be old-fashioned. He has the typical Korean 'male chauvinist' attitude toward women."

"In what way?"

"Oh, you don't want to hear about that. I think I should discuss the price with you. How much do you usually get for work like this?"

"I don't know, I've never helped translate Korean poems before."

"These are Chinese. My father would never bother with Korean poems." She smiled. "He considers them not — *refined*, is that the right way to say it?"

"Unrefined, yes."

"You must forgive me, my English is very bad."

"It sounds perfectly fluent to me."

"Hardly fluent." Osao made a face. "Shall we discuss a fee?"

"Let me see what it is first, then I'll have a better idea."

She took out a sheaf of folded papers from her black plastic pocketbook. First, she had translated the original Chinese into Korean, then she had translated the Korean into English — but she would not let me see these until she had apologized for how awful they were. Each time I reached over to take the papers from her hand, she pulled them back, explaining that she had no instinct for poetry, she was completely "uncreative," her grasp of English was shameful, after living here fifteen years; I was not to worry about hurting her feelings, she knew she had done a terrible job, that was why she had sought professional help. At last she handed over the poems.

"But these are not bad," I said, reading the translations. "They're almost there." I saw that merely by quickening a phrase here and moving a line-break there, by finding a plainer diction, taking out the archaisms — by "de-poeticizing" them, in a word — they could be made into classical Chinese poetry to suit modern taste; that is, the kind that is currently being translated and imitated by American deep-image pastoral poets. The style was not my own, but it amused me to take up the challenge of mimicking that limpid, reverent surface.

We set to work. Going through the poems line by line, we tested, rewrote, crossed out. Again and again she asked me the reasons behind my suggestions, until I began giving them automatically. I much preferred this sitting alongside each other, addressing a common task, to the earlier clumsy probing — I always prefer getting to know someone by our working together. And we were making headway, through the waterfalls and winding streams that always seemed to separate friends, the mournful bird cries that reminded the poet of his native province to which he would never return, the flower that peeped up through the snow; we were zipping right through the Confucian sayings, the advice on how to live a well-ordered life, the nonresistance teachings of the Tao. Meanwhile, Osao made sardonic sideswipes at the ideas, which she thought outrageous (much more so than I did).

"What does 'I make my spirit supine' mean?" I asked.

"Oh, that is more of that same junk," she said bitterly. "The Chinese scholar gentleman is supposed to do nothing. He just 'contemplates nature.' And sends his wife and children out to work! It is so passive, it makes me crazy. That is their idea of the good life: 'Do nothing'!"

"Yes, but what is the exact literal meaning behind 'I make my spirit supine'? That doesn't sound right. . . . Can we go back and look at the original character?"

She frowned and turned over the pages. Several times I had made her put the strict literal translation of the Chinese character back into the text, and I saw now she thought there was something lazy or dishonest about this. "It says, 'stand-soul-against-wall.' "

That sounded good to me; but on the other hand, it had associations with a firing squad. "We need a more 'American' way of saying it. How about just 'I *loaf* . . .' " I suggested, thinking of Whitman's "I loaf and invite my soul."

"What does that mean?"

"It's sort of like wasting time, idling your life away. And 'loaf' can also be like a loaf of bread," I said enthusiastically, if irrelevantly. The more I thought of it, the more I loved sneaking in this tribute to Whitman that no one else would notice.

Osao agreed to the change. We had half-a-dozen more short poems to get through. Sitting next to her, I began to feel a dry warmth rise between us, as though we had been riding together on a dusty road inside a stagecoach. I had to stop myself from acting on the impulse to clutch her hand in her lap. There was that sexual current that exists between different races, and something else, the amorous gratitude I often feel toward a woman colleague working well with me. I wondered what she did for a living. When we were finally through, I asked her, and she said, "I teach high school," as though she were absolving me of any need to show further interest in her.

"What's wrong with teaching?" I said. "I work in public schools, and I find it very stimulating."

"You teach, too?"

"As a visiting poet. But there's something I like about the atmosphere of public schools."

"Oh, I love it!" She did a turnabout. "Especially I like my students. But . . ."

"What subject?" I asked, glossing over her *but*; anyone who worked in the schools did not have to have that *but* explained.

"Bookkeeping. Algebra. My father has all the creativity; I have a good mind for the practical. I told you I was not artistic!"

"But I can't believe you've never done anything artistic. Your translations are sensitive. You must have written at some time."

"When I was younger I wrote poetry," she confessed. "But not for many years. Oh, I wish I could. I have tried many times. I envy people who express themselves in writing. Like you." She blushed.

"I'll teach you how to write," I said.

Osao laughed. "You don't know how hard it would be, that's why you say that."

"No, I mean it."

"Come, let's talk about the fee."

"Nothing." I smiled.

"Please, you must let me pay you something," she said as though it were a cultural insult even to consider accepting my offer. She took out her checkbook.

"Why? It was fun for me. How can I take money for this? It was just an hour of work and I wanted to do it."

"But you should still be paid for your work, even if you enjoy doing it."

"That's true, but in this case, the fact is — I refuse. I can be very stubborn."

"Well, all right," she said, "then perhaps you will at least let me invite you to dinner?"

I could not have planned it to work out better if I had tried. "I would love that."

"Sometime soon? Next week maybe. While my father is still here. That way it will be more interesting for you."

I didn't know why she had to pretend that she needed an added attraction to engage my interest. And I was a little put out to hear that the father would be around; but the more I thought about it, the chaperon aspect seemed to add spice to the evening ahead. We agreed to make it next Friday, at Osao's.

I kept thinking of the way she moved down the hall after we said goodbye, her walk centered in the haunches, confidently sensual. Would I be able to win such a mature woman? What would our first dates be like? And afterward? Would she put up much resistance — or would her experience make everything fall into place? I imagined being sucked into one of those strange "realm of the senses" undertows of sexual obsession: the older woman and the younger man; the inescapableness of flesh. And, on the other hand, if it all worked out, I would propose marriage (I had always toyed with the dream of marrying an Oriental woman); we would go to Korea and live there for a while, then come back here. I could see us taking a summer house together on Martha's Vineyard; our children were all beautiful, our youngest daughter in her neat shirtwaist dress and hair ribbon was a famous child violinist. How she looked at me, my Eurasian daughter, with her wistful, slightly crossed almond eyes.

Osao lived on a down-at-the-heels-looking block between Broadway and Amsterdam Avenue, in the shadow of the Cathedral of St. John the Divine. Crumbling, pre-Depression apartment buildings muscled out the last moment of sun. A boy went by me on a skateboard, yelling a warning that hung suspended like a screech pasted on mid-air. It gave me a shudder to walk on this block, reminding me of my student days at Columbia, the grim, malnourished, overcast quality of life then. I fished out Osao's address. Hers would be that dejected grey stone structure with a courtyard, a dry fountain and a right and left entrance. Mothers talking in Spanish stood in front with baby carriages, and I passed by them in my white suit as quickly as possible. I was afraid they would know where I was going, could read on my face my seducer's intention, and would gossip about Osao behind her back.

The hall was so ill lit that I had to feel my way up the staircase. Why was she living in such a squalid place? Teachers made good enough salaries to afford better. Was she banking her money? Perhaps she was politically committed, a Maoist, wanted to "live with the people." I tried to see the lodgings through her eyes, as reassuring, the warm fried-onion smells of family life reminding her in her homesick moments of dense parts of Seoul. All this as I was searching the dark green doors for her number.

I knocked at the door, and Osao let me in. "You're early," she said. She had on a white blouse and brown skirt, and her eyes were shining.

"I hope not too early."

The small room was an obstacle course of papers and books, with a few throw pillows on the floor. "Excuse me, the couch didn't arrive from Macy's. It was supposed to come Wednesday and I stayed home to receive it but the delivery took it to the wrong place. I'm so embarrassed."

"That's all right; I'm used to sitting on floor pillows."

"Can you make it?" She offered me a hand. "I don't want you to get your beautiful white suit dirty. You look so elegant, I feel ashamed."

"Oh, but you look very nice," I said, annoyed at myself for not getting this in sooner. Because her compliment had come first, mine sounded forced.

"I don't. I look horrible." Which was not true at all. Either she was very modest, or very vain. "I had no time to get ready. You're early!" she said again, though in strict fact I wasn't. "Can I get you some Scotch, or a beer?"

I told her a beer would be fine. She disappeared into the kitchen.

The apartment was a chain of tiny doorless chambers: kitchen, living room, dining room, and bedroom. I looked around the living room. In addition to stacks of what appeared to be manuscripts (was she taking in typing on the side?), there was a small black upright piano, the kind my mother used to play, with sheet music composed by — if I squinted my eyes I could see — Bloch. Next to it stood an ebony-and-gold screen; on the wall was a framed calligraphy scroll, and above my head a mounted advertisement from the thirties of a couple silhouetted in violet before a round moon, and the slogan "Don't Get Caught Unprotected!," which I took to be evidence of Osao's sense of humor. There were signs in the decor of a certain level of cultivation, which reassured me; or, to put it more bluntly, there was nothing of such appalling vulgarity as would have made me pause before considering an involvement with this woman. Still, the surroundings gave little information about her personality — except, perhaps, that they reinforced an earlier impression of downward mobility. This seemed too cramped a cage for her.

I thought of all the times I had been to apartments like this, paying a first visit to a woman I was interested in — seen pinched rooms and cracked walls only partly disguised by visual reminders of a past family ease, or a largesse of soul uncontained by present hardships — and I tried to figure out to what degree it was proper to equate the person with the box drawn tightly around her. So connected seemed the fit of fate, personality and decor, however temporary or unfair the match may have been, that I wondered if it was even possible to see someone as distinct from his or her surroundings.

"Where is your father?" I called out.

"He is resting. He will get up for dinner. He is looking forward to meeting you!"

I started to pull myself up to join Osao, when she came in with a tray: "No, no, sit. Sit! I will bring you what you want." Apparently I was to be served like a sultan. Along with the beer, she brought a salad of shrimps and radishes, and there were unfamiliar stuffed delicacies handsomely arranged by color on the plate. "As you can see I am not used to this sort of thing," she said self-consciously, by which I took her to mean being a hostess, or waiting on men. But, all her nods toward Women's Lib to the contrary, the impression I received was that she had been perfectly well trained to serve the man, almost like a geisha. And I noticed for the first time, in the lamplight, as she bent down to replace a plate, that her cheeks had a thick layer of whitish-pink powder, and she had done something to her eyebrows, blacking them in sharply.

"Sit down, please, Osao," I bid her.

"I am not finished yet," she said, hesitating between staying and going.

"But you can talk for a minute?"

"Yes . . . I am afraid this will be a boring evening for you."

"I'm expecting just the opposite. What makes you think so?"

"I am not very talkative tonight. I am not good at making conversation. My language skills are so poor!"

"Why do you say that? You speak perfect English, from what I can gather."

"Don't you find me —" she paused, almost coquettishly searching for the right word — "don't you find me 'verbally underdeveloped,' to use the jargon of our trade?"

I laughed, first because the complexity of her diction so belied her assertion, and second because the word *underdeveloped* had made me think of her opulent figure. "Hardly. Your speech is not my idea of verbally underdeveloped," I said.

"You are just trying to be nice to me."

"No, I assure you." I was puzzled by this insistence on "deficits" that seemed to go beyond modesty. Or was her self-disparagement only a routine Korean expression of good manners? To change the subject I said, "You play the piano?"

"I — used to. I have given it up. I don't have the time. The school day takes everything out of me. Don't you find?"

"Sometimes. I don't teach every day, so it's not as wearing for me."

"You are lucky! You can keep your enthusiasm up. I need to find my enthusiasm again. . . . I used to love teaching. You must be a wonderful teacher."

"I have my good days, and my bad days. What are all these stacks of papers?"

"My thesis," she said perfunctorily.

"You're writing a doctoral thesis too?" I was surprised by

this wider ambition, which made her even more desirable. "What field?"

"In sociology." She wrinkled up her nose.

"Why do you make a face when you say 'sociology'?" I asked.

"No, not sociology — it's the thesis. It is taking so long! I have no time to do it. I have finished all my research and statistics but I have such a hard time to write it up. That is why I envy writers!"

"I'm sure you'll find a way to write it when you give yourself some time."

"No — it is a real problem for me. I would ask you for some advice, but I know that must be horrible for you. Besides, I have to cook! I didn't know if you are vegetarian or meat eater, so I made both!" she laughed. I followed Osao into the kitchen so we could continue talking, though I sensed she was uncomfortable about my going in there.

Sweat blistered across her forehead, and she had fallen silent, turning all her attention to a head of lettuce in the sink. At first I thought that she was merely concentrating very hard on the cooking, but then I realized that she was averting her eyes, embarrassed for some reason. The customs here were strange, and I had better tread lightly. "Would you rather I went inside?" I asked finally.

"No, no," she protested.

"What's the matter?"

"I am ashamed to have people over here. Because of the *****!" Her nervous giggle drowned out the word.

"Because of *what?*"

"Because of the bugs, the roaches! *You* know. I'm so ashamed for people to see them. If I see one I start screaming! You must think I'm a crazy woman."

"But everyone has them in New York."

"I will never get used to them." She shuddered. "Please, promise me if you see one you will close your eyes!"

"I promise," I said, smiling.

Osao, relieved, went back to her cooking. Everywhere there seemed to be pots spitting froth from under their lids, vegetables waiting to be diced on the wooden cutting board, meat dumplings steaming, fish broiling, and Osao controlling it all, checking, chopping, spooning.

"Can't I help?"

"No, please. My father would be shocked if he even saw you in the kitchen! He is old-fashioned and thinks the woman should do everything. A typical Korean male, like your friend Pak."

"Pak thinks that way too?" This was a new insight into my Xerox man. "How long have you known Pak?"

"I know him well enough," Osao said, with an ironic smile. "He is a strange man."

"Yes, he is a strange man," I said eagerly. "But in what way do you find him strange?"

"It is really not fair to talk about him."

"Why not?"

"I went out with him once a long time ago."

"For how long?"

"It was nothing serious, believe me. But lately, every time I run into him I get the feeling he does not approve of me." She stopped short, regretful at having said even this much.

"Why wouldn't he approve of you? . . . Go on, you can tell me. Do you think I'll think badly of you? I assure you I won't."

"It's not that," she said meditatively. "It's just I don't like to talk about these gossip things, do you?"

"What things?"

"*You* know: 'affairs of the heart.' "

"What else is there of any interest to talk about?" I said.

"It's just that . . . Pak does not approve because he knows I have a friend. I live with a man friend." She turned away to wash the broccoli.

This was bad news. Still, there was the possibility that the man was nothing but a roommate, a foreign friend who had nowhere else to go, perhaps even gay.

"Why is it wrong to have a male roommate?" I asked disingenuously.

"I don't think it is wrong. But in our community everyone talks about everyone else, and it is considered not the proper thing for a single woman to live with her boyfriend." Again the stab. "Pak has a double standard, like most Korean men. He has affairs with American girls but he thinks Korean girls should be pure before their marriage. I mean, I am no girl anymore — look at me!"

"He's probably jealous. He's probably still in love with you." I was teasing her but really talking about my own disappointment.

"Oh, no, he was never in love with me," Osao said, quite firmly.

"And the man you're living with — is he American?"

"No, he's Korean."

"Oh." I watched her finish off the meal preparations. I felt I had nothing more to say; the major purpose of the evening was defeated. I had to find a way to get through the rest of the visit without too much bitterness. So there would be no lovemaking after all, no trip to Korea, no violinist daughter. It began to embarrass me that I should lose all interest in Osao just because I discovered she was "taken," when a half hour before I had been trying to decipher everything about her. Why couldn't I still figure out the mysteries of her personality by paying close attention? Her hands were squeezing the dumpling dough with strong shapely fingers, capable and quick and a little plump.

"You have very nice hands," I said, feeling good that I could pay her a compliment even after the chase was lost.

"Really? I think they're common. No, you are the one who has beautiful hands," said Osao, looking down at mine as if I had paid her a compliment only to have one returned. "See? You have long sensitive fingers. Mine are ugly." She held hers up to the light matter-of-factly.

"I can't agree," I said. She gave me a look that stated I didn't know what I was talking about; she had made a study of the subject. And now that she had raised the point, I did think my hands were nicer than hers.

Just then we heard some stirring from the inner rooms.

"That must be Father," she said.

She led me into the dining room to meet him. A thin elderly man stood at the end of the table waiting for us to come toward him. He was not very tall; he had thin lips and badly broken teeth and the fiercely staring eyes of someone who is fresh-wakened from sleep, and he was wearing a dark green drip-dry suit jacket over a white shirt with a thin olive tie. The dominant impression he gave was of severity, but there was a bit of the artist-dandy in him: one could see he thought highly of himself. Osao spoke to him in Korean, and his face immediately relaxed into a leathery smile and he shook my hand.

"I am Woo," he said.

"I am Lopate." I turned to Osao. "He speaks English?"

"He speaks a little English," she said. Her father said something to her in Korean, looking at me, and I asked her to translate. "He thanks you very much for the translations, and he would like to invite you to the opening."

He nodded at the end.

I tried to react with surprise and delight, though Osao had already invited me.

Her father began looking over the dinner table with a grumbling, severe expression.

"I think he wants his beer. My father always has one beer in the evening," she explained. She asked him in Korean, and he nodded concisely. "I will be back in a minute."

Now we were left alone. The old man regarded me with steady curiosity. Apparently it was not considered rude in his culture to stare at someone in this way, or else it was a prerogative earned by age. After a while his focus relaxed, and he lit a cigarette and looked away, as though I were not in the room. I thought this as good a way as any of handling the awkward situation.

Osao returned with two bottles of Kirin, then she left me alone with him again. The old man poured the beer into his glass, filling it only halfway with the liquid, drank precisely half of that, and set the glass down.

I thought I would try a conversation. "Is this the first time you have been to America?" I asked slowly.

His lips formed a tired smile, and he shrugged to indicate either that he hadn't understood — or if he had, what was the point of starting so exhausting an effort?

We stared past each other into the middle distance, like travelers on opposite sides of a train platform.

The dining table took up almost all of the room. There was a bookcase behind me filled with Osao's sociology classics, a typewriter table, a mirror, and a picture of the Mona Lisa. The incongruous cliché of that image in this household made me want to laugh, until I realized that it was the exact counterpart of my Utamaro calendar, a tribute to the opposite culture's icon.

The old man had taken his wire-rimmed spectacles out

of his pocket and now he put them on; an act of sociability, I thought. Actually, he was not so old, only about seventy, and seemed to be in strong physical and mental condition. He must have known quite a bit about life, and about art. Too bad, I thought, that I understood so little about calligraphy, or I would be able to tell whether he was a skillful, cautious, middle-of-the-road practitioner, still worthy of respect, of course, or a giant in the field, a master. What did they call them in Japan? "A living national treasure."

I told myself I was sitting across the table from a living national treasure.

He began picking his teeth. A cockroach darted across the tablecloth. He looked at it, stern and a little sad. I remembered that I was supposed to close my eyes when I saw one. The calligrapher stared toward the kitchen with a reproachful, grizzled look. This was one of those relentless cockroaches that insist on exploring each check of the tablecloth. I banged my knee against the table leg to make him go away before Osao returned. Nothing happened. It was definitely bad manners to kill a cockroach in another person's home. At last he scurried off at a much bigger noise: the door had opened, and I turned and saw the man of the house.

The guilt I felt at that moment for having had designs on his woman made me want to stammer out an explanatory introduction that I was "only so-and-so," only this minor person not to be taken seriously. Osao came from the kitchen in her apron and put her arms around him, and I looked away.

She introduced me flatteringly. I rose to shake his hand.

"I am Jhun," he said, motioning me to sit. He joined us unceremoniously, taking a chair at the foot of the table. "Tired!" he exclaimed. He had a sympathetic, frank, workman's face, a face I trusted immediately, and he wore the standard white shirt with sleeves rolled up in a tight buckled square above the elbow. I was struck by his massive forearms.

Dishes began appearing on the table. There was clear noodle soup, shrimps, asparagus, beans, dumplings, broiled fish, rice, cabbage. Jhun ate with the rapid shoveling motions of exhausted laborers everywhere, lifting his face from time to time with a good-humored, inclusive grin of appetite. Now I noticed that Osao's father was refusing to look toward Jhun's side of the table, as though he did not approve of the man's eating habits or the man himself. Jhun winked at me. As formal as the old calligrapher was, Jhun seemed to be informal.

"Hot!" he warned, as I reached for the cabbage.

I took some in my mouth, and tried it gingerly, then reached for my glass of beer.

Jhun laughed and clapped his hands. "Too hot! I told you." Then he shared the joke with his "father-in-law," who grinned reluctantly also; and I went along with it, fanning myself. I was providing the Occidental comic relief. Jhun laughed till there were tears in his eyes. "Hot! Be careful!" Osao, who had finally allowed herself to join us, laughed too, but in a smoothing-over way, as though to mute the barking edge of her lover's voice. I sensed that she was a little ashamed of him. Jhun spoke in an urgent guttural Korean, almost buffoonishly emphatic, and yet there was a shrewdness in his eyes. I liked him. I could not guess exactly how old he was; his face was boyish but his hair was grey.

"Tired?" I asked him.

"Tired! I thought I get away sooner. But — trouble in the store."

"Jhun runs a clothing store in Harlem," Osao explained.

"You know — cheap bargain, garments." The word *garments* sounded strange in Jhun's Korean accent, since I heard it all my life with a Yiddish inflection.

"How do you like working in Harlem?" I asked.

"Harlem very bad." He shook his head. "Every day getting worse. Air bad. People fighting, killing. Even stabbing! Bad people up there." He continued to describe the life with sad, earnest disgust. It was a primitive analysis, one that I imagined Osao with her graduate training in social sciences must feel disdainful of, or at least superior to. She said nothing during his discourse, but began to clear away some dishes. I noticed that the father, our distinguished national treasure, was frowning more deeply than ever. I caught his gaze resting on me from behind the glasses on his narrow, austere face.

He asked his daughter something in Korean, and Osao went red with discomfort, while Jhun guffawed.

"What did he say?" I asked.

The calligrapher continued to demand answers in his curt, worldly voice, and Osao continued to protest, with obvious displeasure, at his line of questioning. They were arguing back and forth. Meanwhile Jhun was enjoying himself immensely, even winking at me to show there was nothing to worry about. (Though whether it was a good-humored wink or a nervous twitch I was no longer sure.)

"What is he saying?" I asked again. It was obvious they were talking about me, and I had to pull Osao's sleeve to get her to answer.

"Stupid things. For instance, he wants to know if you live at home with your family."

I laughed easily. "Did you tell him I didn't?"

"Yes. He is very curious about you. He asks all sorts of questions about your personal life. He is really being impossible tonight."

"Like what? Tell him I'll answer anything he wants to know."

"You mustn't encourage him," said Osao.

"No, tell him. I don't mind."

She translated the information. Her father cleared his throat, and spoke, looking at me.

"He wants to know if you are married."

"No."

He looked at me with great interest. Then he spoke to Osao.

"He wants to know why you are not married."

"Tell him I once was but am now divorced."

She shook her head, almost refusing to convey this dangerous information, but in the end translated. His eyes grew no wider. He turned to his daughter and began to lecture her. Jhun could barely keep from rolling on the floor.

"What's he saying?" I demanded. "What's he saying?"

"He says he does not understand why you don't go back and live with your family now. Or else, why you don't marry again. He says he does not understand my life either. You must excuse my father," Osao said. "He thinks he is the greatest because he fathered eleven children. All of them happy except me."

The father nodded in my direction and asked if I had any children. Now *I* was beginning to feel uncomfortable; I cast about for some way to take the heat off.

"He thinks you should get married again to have someone take care of you," said Osao, mechanically. "He thinks you must be lonely living this way."

"Why don't *you* two get married?" I asked Osao, to turn the spotlight on her. It was also the kind of coward's question one asks of a woman one would like to sleep with, when one is afraid to speak directly.

"Because. Korean men expect the women to be good housewives, to be home all the time, to keep everything clean. As you can see, I am not good at that." She turned to face the kitchen, ready to bolt if necessary.

"But do you expect that?" I asked Jhun.

"Oh, he is different," she answered for him. "He is not like most Korean men."

"Then why don't you get married?"

"Because she don't trust men," Jhun said, smiling bitterly.

"I don't trust *you*," said Osao.

"Me? What you know about me? You think you know me but you don't. You don't know what is inside me." Jhun actually smote his chest, pleased to be declaring this to her in front of everyone. "What you know about trust? You don't know what I would do," he muttered.

She looked around the room for something to deliver her from this conversation that, if nothing else, seemed to go against her sense of appropriate table talk. But Jhun was not willing to let her off so easily. He turned to me for confirmation. "We think we know what is inside another person? What we see? Cheap. A mask. China doll mask!" He snorted. "You don't know what I would do," he repeated boldly.

"Oh? Maybe I am wrong," said Osao.

"Maybe I am wrong, maybe I am wrong!" he said, mimicking her. "You will never find out, because you don't trust men enough. *All* men."

I felt sorry for Osao, and partly responsible for getting her into this. "Why don't you trust us?" I asked glibly, trying to make light of the situation, to turn it into a kind of parlor game.

"I have had too much experience with men," Osao answered, taking my lead. She had found the proper, generalized tone to get her out of her personal discomfit. "I know what men are like. All too well. And you think this one is any better? You should see what he thinks about women."

"Oh, that." Jhun held his head like a coconut, shaking

it from one side to the other. "She will start again. It's not true. I think women are pretty good."

"Yes, I know," said Osao, with a touch of jealousy. Then she left for the kitchen to replenish our beers.

"What you do?" Jhun asked me, point-blank but friendly.

"You mean for a living? I teach."

"I teach too. Martial Arts!" he proclaimed.

Looking at his brawny arms, I was not surprised. As he talked about giving lessons at a kung fu center, I began to see his relationship with Osao in a different light. I pictured them having a passionate and athletic, if combative, life in the bedroom. Perhaps only a muscleman like Jhun could satisfy her particular sensual needs — an idea that relieved me by offering an explanation for why I would never win Osao.

Jhun had many ancedotes about the funny Americans who wanted to learn kung fu, and who thought they could fly through the air because they had seen it in a Bruce Lee movie. Osao, who had returned from the kitchen, seemed entertained by these stories, chiming in from time to time, but her father was more bored than ever. He was obviously interested only in certain things close to him and, like a distinguished guest at a dinner party who is not allowed to show his stuff, became annoyed and hurt when the topic strayed too far from him. I though it was time to draw the old man back into the conversation.

"Tell your father I greatly admire the art of calligraphy," I said.

When Osao translated my comment, Woo's face brightened.

"But I know so little of it," I hastened to add.

"That's not true. I was amazed how much he knew about Eastern culture," she told Jhun, "probably more than either of us."

"Not so," I said. "Please — ask your father if he would tell me something about calligraphy."

She conveyed the wish, and he sat even straighter than was his wont, and talked for a moment or two, then waited for the translation.

"He says that all Oriental philosophy comes down to two essential things: Yin and Yang."

The father nodded happily. I had been hoping for something more heady than this, but tried to look the proper acolyte. He called for paper to be brought to him, and took out his fountain pen.

"He is drawing the symbols for Yin and Yang," Osao noted.

The calligrapher spoke again with sober ease, as though this were the reason he had been called to the United States — to make this explanation — and he was finally getting a chance to relieve himself of his mission. Osao translated concurrently: " 'All calligraphy must have a feeling of motion.' "

The old man began to draw. At first I could make little out of the characters, which seemed almost negligently sloppy notations filling the page. Then I began to see, not so much beauty, but motion. The old man stopped to grin at me. Then his hand began moving incredibly fast. Jhun was leaning forward, watching like a child at a fair. "He's fantastic, eh?" Jhun said proudly.

"What happens if you make a mistake?"

The old man did a gesture of crumpling up paper. With amusement he looked into my face for a reaction, waiting to see how I would take this iron law. Then he spoke again. Osao translated: "He says, 'Calligraphy is not just writing straight symbols like the alphabet, but is taking off from the original symbol by mental ideas — associations.' " When he gave a demonstration of how a commonplace character was transformed into something entirely different through a set of metaphorical associations, I saw that it was very close to the process of writing poetry.

"He says it is impossible to learn calligraphy unless you study with a master," Osao said. "You cannot learn it from a book. You must get it from a few people like him. . . . Now he is telling about his teacher, and his teacher's teacher. . . . The tradition he belongs to . . . goes back to the seventeen hundreds . . . the first great master of his school . . ." There followed a name I could not hope to remember. What a shame that I was the recipient of this teaching, since so much was lost on me, while another person, a student of calligraphy or one of those reverential American Buddhists, would have been in ecstasies every second. Nevertheless, what I got, I got.

"He says a master only takes a few pupils at a time. He is willing to take you as a student." The old man bowed formally. "My father is paying you a great compliment!" Osao explained. "He is not usually like this."

"I am very flattered. . . . Tell him that I would love to study with him, but I would have to move to Korea, and there isn't enough time for me to learn properly in the short time he's staying."

She translated this, and he nodded again. Then he made one more speech.

"What did he say?"

"He is inviting you to come to his show next week."

So the evening ended, with my third invitation to the exhibit.

The day of the opening came, and I was wavering back and forth about whether to attend. What business did I have dipping into their lives like a tourist? I would just feel out of place. In the end I went, perhaps to complete a loop in my own mind.

Not far from the door, past the table where one was supposed to hand in one's invitation card, Osao stood next to her father in a kind of receiving line, greeting guests. She looked stunning. Her beautiful gown of orange-and-black swirls, three-quarter length with black silk trousers underneath, suggested a traditional national costume at the same time that it seemed the height of Paris fashion. I was almost shy coming up to her, she looked so regal; her magnanimous black eyes glistened with quality. So she was a great beauty after all! The bracelets on her arms, the jewels in her ears, sent a secret pang to my heart. I waited for her to turn and notice me — she was talking to an otterish-looking young Korean whose television-blue shirt with white collar somehow rubbed me the wrong way — they were dallying like cousins. When she saw me she broke away, excusing herself to that pampered puppy, and received me with all graciousness. Her father, in a light blue seersucker suit, was standing so straight he appeared to be leaning backward. As I came up offering my hand he seemed happy and touched to see me, and opened his mouth wide in a great grin, his teeth just as broken as ever, the creases around his eyes lifted high in greeting. All the energy of his happiness at this encounter seemed to be ignited and spent in that wonderful smile, and I realized from the speed with which his eyes fixed on another guest that he had nothing to say to me. I had already performed my role simply by showing.

Osao, being the good hostess, quickly introduced me to an elderly Korean couple who happened to be standing next to me on the line, and made a few cementing remarks in an attempt to hitch us together — I was a writer who was interested in Oriental culture, this man was in the business of importing objects from Asia, we must have much to talk about. . . . The couple and I tried dutifully conversing, but I was conscious always of Osao, and eventually excused myself to visit the food tables, from where I could keep an eye on her and stuff myself. The affair had been admirably catered with hot stuffed dumplings, vegetable platters and light, dainty sweets; everything was delicious. No wonder that Korean who bribed American congressmen made such a splash with the parties he gave. This looked like the same crowd, well-off executives, diplomats, businessmen stationed comfortably in America with their begowned wives. I would have loved to eavesdrop, but no one was talking English. Nevertheless, one could imagine the talk from the stylized gaiety among the carefully coiffed women, pulling each other off to the side like bridesmaids, and the bluff heartiness among the men (learned here, perhaps), their shoulder-patting manner, fresh from the office, whiskey in hand. The language of property is everywhere the same. How did Osao fit in? If they were a cut or two above her in social standing, tonight she made her way through this crowd unapologetically. The artist's daughter, checking with her quick black eyes to see who was enjoying himself and who needed help, seemed everywhere at once, laughing, mixing. As the sole hostess of this sprawling, thickening reception, she was managing brilliantly — too brilliantly, in a way, for a high-school bookkeeping teacher.

Tired of spying on her, I began to apply myself to the art on the walls. It gave me a special pleasure to read underneath each scroll the neatly typed cards with our translations on them, and to remember some of the farfetched word choices. How unassailably orthodox they looked. Who would ever guess? As for Mr. Woo's calligraphy, I was honestly unable to judge. As I went from piece to piece, trying to detect the principles of connoisseurship behind these disciplined executions, I met an exclusion so total that I began to feel dizzy, and to fight this I forced myself to be more engrossed than ever, by setting the problem for myself of which scroll I would buy, if the price were right.

Osao was suddenly at my side. "How are you enjoying it?"

"Oh, I love your father's work. I was just thinking of buying one."

"No, you don't mean that."

"Yes. What are the prices? Are they very expensive?"

"They are not so bad. . . . And since you helped us — but we talk about that later. First meet Stephen. I think you and he must like each other, you have so much in common." She pulled me over to a lank, fastidiously tailored American in a three-piece suit who worked for a private foundation. It bothered me that she had lumped us together in her mind. "Stephen, this is the man I told you about, the poet who helped me do the translations." He shook my hand limply with as little apparent liking for me as I had for him. Osao left us alone together, and I asked him how he had come to know her. His responses were haughty and reluctant — and yet, didn't he see, we were the only two Americans, everyone else was jabbering in Korean. At last I steered him onto a subject that caught his enthusiasm, the ballet.

Just as he was about to loosen up, there was a request for silence. The ceremonial speechmaking began. Each of the dignitaries and honored guests was introduced, said a few words, received applause. Mr. Woo stood at attention throughout, severe, expressionless, as though at a military flag raising. I came alongside Osao and asked her, during a particularly long oration by a porcine man with a crew cut, what was being said.

"Oh — he is just telling the story of Father's life. That he studied with so-and-so who studied with such-and-such. . . . That he received all 'firsts' as a young man in school. . . .

That he was in the navy. . . ." She whispered in my ear, discreetly, so as not to attract attention. The orator's voice droned on, Mr. Woo stood alone with his fingers locked behind his back, isolated as the this-is-your-life encomiums rained down on his pointy head.

Then the artist himself came forward to speak, and was roundly applauded.

"What's he saying?" I whispered.

"The same thing as before," she answered with a dimpled smile. "It is mostly a — *regurgitation.* Did I say it wrong?"

"No, you said it right."

After the speechmaking had ended, I asked, "Where is Jhun?"

"He had to work late. He will probably come later." She seemed unconcerned.

Some emergency pulled her away, and I was again at a loss. Art openings are among the most difficult social situations to pierce. There are of course the "regulars" who know everyone in the gallery and need not give more than a five-second glance at the art before settling into serious, loud partying; but if one is not lucky enough to be in that crowd, one may have to join the "strollers," who wander around the wall edges like moths, pretending deep hypnotic attachment to this pattern or that texture.

I had imagined that we would all go out afterward for dinner at a little piano bar known only to Koreans, just the artist's private party. But it did not seem to be working out that way; the reception was breaking up into groups, the room was clearing, and I left before I could learn whether I would have received one of those last-minute whispered invitations accorded to the inner few.

There followed all the next week a series of telephone conversations, back and forth, about the scroll I had chosen.

Since I would not hear of taking it for free, it reverted to its original market price. Eventually, with Osao's coaxing, the artist knocked off a hundred and fifty dollars for me, so that I had the satisfaction of getting a bargain.

What was I doing buying this scroll in the first place? I did not collect art, nor was I in a financial position to start. The whole transaction was a mystery to me, one of those blind impulses I make myself follow in order to understand, in the end, what it was I was thinking about. Certainly I had in mind some way of prolonging a connection with Osao. Yet the scroll was more than a pretext to get to her: I wanted it. By owning some part of the old calligrapher, his daughter, and Jhun, perhaps I would find it easier to settle my accounts with them, and turn away.

On the phone Osao would become chatty, as if we were old friends. Just at the point when the business details had been completed, she would prolong the conversation, asking me about each of the different areas of my life. She seemed boundlessly curious about how I put the whole thing together, how I moved from part to part. I was not sure why she wanted this information, but I sensed her hunger to keep the conversation alive. "What have you been reading?" she would say, or "That sounds like you're having a good time!"

Jhun was a sincere, honest hunk, but she must have found him a limited conversationalist. How giddy she became on the phone! Sometimes she wanted so much to laugh that anything I said she interpreted as witty. Between us, through everything, I thought I saw the thin, hopeful strand of flirtation. No, I told myself, she just wanted more American friends, like that prune, Stephen. She was collecting American male aesthetes; or she was trying out her conversational skills with native speakers. Each time the phone rang and I heard Osao's voice, I asked myself, What is going on with her? Yet somewhere inside me I still hoped we would be thrown together as lovers — and I must have communicated that hope. Even when a woman has no intention of giving in to him, she may all the same want the one who has once desired her to remain under her gaze.

I had arranged with Osao to come by Saturday night and pick up my scroll, hand over the check, and have dinner. The old man had already flown back to Korea. Osao, that evening, seemed under a cloud. We had little opportunity to talk, because, as it turned out, several of Jhun's buddies joined us for dinner. They arrived in a noisy bunch, and began attacking the dishes Osao put in front of them with the same voracious hunger I had seen in Jhun. They were all Korean, and behaved toward each other with the joshing, boyish spirits of fraternity brothers. One lean-necked man was kidded incessantly, and he always laughed it off calmly. It turned out he had studied literature in his youth, a fact they thought immensely comical — they tried to get him to recite some poems. "He is also poet," Jhun said and nodded toward me. They offered me and the shy ex-literature student more and more liquor, to get us drunk enough to recite poems. They made many jokes about one another's capacities for drink and food.

Jhun was in his element, in the middle of all this noisy leg-pulling — a leader, in fact. But I no longer liked him as much as the first time we had met. Without the old man's disapproving formality to set him off, he seemed less striking.

I managed to learn that all except Jhun were employed in the garment district, mostly as crew managers. They made fun of the Puerto Ricans who worked under them. So this is how Koreans in the garment industry spend their Saturday nights, I mused. Watching them eat and laugh, trying to follow, however remotely, the line of discussion, I told myself it was an honor to be allowed to witness one of those hidden subcultures whose aggregate makes up New York City — so much of which will always be unknown, even to a native New Yorker like me.

At one point the discussion grew heated. I listened to the argument with the lost wonder of a man in a foreign port, at an outdoor café, surrounded by local bravos. But this was *my* city, damn it; I wasn't supposed to feel like a stranger. Jhun's voice became loud with skepticism and cynical experience. I wondered if they might be talking about Korean politics. Osao had left the room again — she had probably heard this a hundred times before. I turned to the man next to me, the tall bespectacled ex-poetry student, whose neck had been clipped so closely by the barber that its furrows appeared plucked clean.

"What are they saying?"

He answered that they were arguing about money. The fastest way to get it, the easiest way to lose it, the opportunities they had stupidly passed by, the ones they knew who pretended to be poorer than they were, but had actually socked away quite a pile . . .

For a while they would translate into English for me. But I got tired of asking them to translate; I didn't want to make a pest of myself. Now, there is some pleasure in watching people converse in a language unknown to you. The gestures, the tones of voice, become everything. And if the speakers are émigrés who are obliged to talk all week in a language not their own, it is wonderful to observe the sudden happy ease with which they explode into chatter. Yet, for this very reason, it is impossible ever to trust the sincerity of émigrés fully once you have seen them with their own kind. All that they can never share with you is suddenly quite exposed.

Osao returned with another six bottles of beer in her

hands, as she had been doing all night, and they took them without a word of thanks. The last time I had seen her, at the reception, she had had the look of an empress; tonight she could have been the barmaid. Her remoteness did not seem to bother anyone. From time to time she gave me a look that showed she realized it was not working out for me. But she had no idea what to do to make things better.

Eventually I said I had to go, pushing back my chair, a little drunk, clutching my wrapped framed scroll.

Osao followed me out.

"I am afraid this has been a dull evening for you," she said at the door.

This time I did not contradict her, as I smiled and took her hand to squeeze it goodbye.

"Think good thoughts and pursue them earnestly." The Confucian message on the scroll now hangs above the portal to my bedroom.

One day months later I received in the mail a snapshot of the gallery reception, in which I appeared next to Osao and her father. With a note: "You were the best-looking in this picture, so I couldn't resist sending it to you."

I had a very busy winter, working to meet deadlines, taking on new projects at school; I went back to my old girlfriend, or rather, she agreed to take me back, one last time; there were feuds in my family, the city underwent a budget crisis; in short, I forgot about Osao.

Not true. I didn't forget about her, but I saw no way to go forward with her. We didn't have enough intellectual interests in common to make a friendship, and besides, I had enough platonic friends in my life as it was. What I had wanted from her was a love affair. Once the sexual route was blocked, I made her over into a static figure of pathos, forever serving beer to Jhun's friends, and I sealed her in a chamber of my mind with those other fondly regretted would-be romances that were destined never to attain carnal form. She had become, to be frank, an episode in my memory that had rounded to a satisfactory closure.

At the end of May my phone rang.

"This is*****," a strange voice said.

"How are you?" I stalled, hoping the caller would give me a better clue in what she said next, while I tried to process the sounds through my memory bank. This time the caller saw through my scheme.

"It's Osao! Osao Woo. Don't you remember me anymore?"

"Osao, of course I remember you!"

"No wonder you forget. You are so busy, you never call me!" she said. "I think you must be leading a very exciting life to have forgotten poor Osao" — this in a theatrical pouting voice that was, like a geisha's, too teasing to be taken seriously. Was I supposed to call? She made it sound as though we were actually close friends and I had neglected her.

"I'm sorry. I *have* been busy."

"Never mind; I called to tell you I have moved. I have a new number. Do you want it?" she said suspiciously.

"Yes, certainly," I said. She gave it to me, and added that she had a house now in Queens. A whole house to herself. It was much prettier than that last place — she should have moved years ago. So, I thought, she made the leap to suburbia. Good for her.

"What are you doing with your life these days? Did you see the new Woody Allen movie?" she asked.

"Yes —"

"I thought it was very funny. Did you like it?"

"Yes, it was very good." Though I had deep reservations about the film, there was something so vulnerable in her voice, asking to be accepted into the club of knowingly neurotic New Yorkers, that I decided to praise it warmly. "I thought there were some very clever things in it —"

"I saw it twice. It reminded me of you, even, a bit."

"Really?" I said, stung. Did she think all Jewish New Yorkers were alike? "Oh, I don't think I'm like Woody Allen."

"No, just the sense of humor, you know."

"Perhaps. Oh, I keep running into your friend Pak," I said, "at the Xerox shop."

"Who? Oh, I don't see him anymore, now that I am all the way out here in Queens." Obviously she was not too interested in Pak. "What else has been keeping you busy?"

"This time I'm going to get that question in first. What are *you* doing with yourself these days?"

"Nothing. I am getting awfully lazy. I go to work and come home and eat. I have gotten terribly fat. You would not recognize me."

"I'm sure you still look pretty," I said, my courtier wits working slowly.

"No, it's true, there is nothing to do around here so I eat. I've gained lots of weight. It is nice out here — but boring!" She laughed, and I started laughing with her. There is something so infectiously comic at times about negativity. Besides, it was good to hear her voice; I remembered my fondness for Osao.

"Why don't you try exercise?" I said.

"I know, I thought of jogging but they would think I was a crazy person if I ran around the block. This is not the Upper West Side, you know. People are so proper and conventional here. Besides, it does not look nice, a middle-aged woman with too much weight running around in shorts!"

I wondered why she was trying to make herself sound so unattractive to me. "But at least you got away from the cockroaches."

"There were a few, but I got rid of them. It's very clean here. You should come see it."

"It must be a big change for you."

"Yes, at first it was, but now I am getting used to it. I think it was time for me to move," she added in an official voice.

"How is Jhun fitting in?"

A silence. "We do not live together anymore. I thought you knew."

"No, I had no idea. . . . Then are you taking the house by yourself?"

"Yes, I prefer to live alone. I am through with men. No more men!" she declared.

"That's hard to believe," I said, trying to sound light-hearted, though my throat was swelling up as at the presence of danger. "You're too young to enter a nunnery."

"No, I mean it. No more the other way. The only men I want in my life now is if they would be friend to me."

It sounded like an offer — perhaps the simple offer of friendship she had been making all along. Or was it a disguised invitation for more, now that Jhun was gone? Either way, I found myself weighing every word. What could I say? Whatever was meant, I did not have the heart to take her up on it. How could I admit that my fantasies about us were already used up? We were too different somehow, talking to each other was too awkward. Or maybe there was some defect in my character, some cowardice when I was faced with the possible love of a mature woman. Whatever, no matter, I knew I would never come through for her.

"How is school?" I asked.

"School is school. They are making me the treasurer because I have good head for figures, so I won't have to teach as many classes. But you don't want to hear about that."

"No, I do, that's why I asked."

"You are just being polite. So, well, what have you been doing? You must have gone to lots of plays, movies —"

"I *have* gone to a lot of movies. But at the moment I can't remember any of them."

"There is nothing around here. But I go into town sometimes . . ."

Again it seemed she was hinting. "Why don't we go to a ballet sometime?" I asked. "You said you liked the New York City Ballet."

"But how will we get tickets? They say it's very crowded this year, all sold out."

"No, I can get tickets. I can try to get tickets," I amended. "It's in my neighborhood. I can walk over and ask."

"You're so lucky!"

"So, how shall we — you want to call me and tell me the next time you'll be in Manhattan?"

"I can come anytime. It's up to you. You're the one with the busy exciting life!"

"Very funny. Okay, I'll call you when I find out about the availability of tickets."

We hung up. I never called her back. I knew I wouldn't, even while I was making the offer, and I think Osao understood it too. But I felt like a heel. Obliging on the surface, I was underneath just like her artist father, disapproving and aloof. Maybe that was what she wanted from me; maybe I hadn't disappointed her after all.

You see how tempted I am to thrash around in my own guilt and promote some sense of shame in lieu of a larger meaning. The truth of the matter is, Osao and I could never have worked out. There are those newly struck acquaintances that, for all the goodwill of both parties, peter out after a month. And there are those "bonsai loves" that, like the bonsai tree, perfect in its own limited way, are doomed to grow no higher than one's knee.

Part

Three

Summer Camps

NOWADAYS one sees parents going to stunning lengths to investigate the merits of this or that summer camp for their children. This camp has a tennis pro, another offers skiing in July, a third stresses classical quartets or has a professional potter in residence. There are long discussions around the dinner table about whether horseback riding, gymnastics or figure skating has more appeal for the youngster. For the parents, especially those who have recently ascended to the class that can afford such luxuries as riding camps and private schools, these searches must reawaken their own long-buried fantasies of an indulged childhood. And their children, if they play their cards right, will be invited to sleep-over holidays at ever more opulent estates by better-off children, some of whom already own their own horses and ski mountains, thus in the end obviating the need for summer camp itself. I see no harm in this. I am looking forward to a generation of the most extraordinarily well-rounded stable hands and ski instructors in American history.

However, *when I was a boy*, we had a very different approach to summer camps. My parents took what they could get. Being at the mercy of authorized charities, either the local newspaper's Fresh Air Fund or the neighborhood settlement house or the United Council of Philanthropies, Father and Mother simply sent my name in and prayed that there would be an opening. One day a letter would arrive in the mail, with directions about where my bus would leave, and my father or my mother would take me there along with a duffel bag that had all my things with name tags sewn on, and wave goodbye, not having the lamest notion to what sort of place I was being taken.

It could have been the castle of Count Dracula. I am not saying my folks were negligent, but their indifference to the personalities of these camps was at another, equally problematic extreme from the aforementioned middle-class parents, and led to some uncomfortable situations. For instance, one summer I ended up being the only white boy in an all-black YMCA camp, an experience I would prefer not to write about. Another summer I landed in a Christian Bible camp as the only Jew.

The Christian Bible camp presented me with an immediate dilemma, because of its Sunday church services, which all campers were required to attend. I was eleven at the time, a period in one's life when matters of conscience have a direct, powerful reality they so rarely do afterward. Was it a sin merely for me as a Jew to hear the services? How much more so if I participated? Praising J.C. didn't sit right with me. Supposing I read the words but didn't say them aloud? Supposing I pretended to say them but muttered something else under my breath, like "Pepsi-Cola hits the spot"? What if I kept sitting when everyone stood, would they get furious at me and beat me up? I had not had one of those ecumenical religious backgrounds where you are told that Jesus and the Buddha and Muhammad were all holy prophets — far from it! I was scared that something terrible would happen to my soul if I said a good word on Christ's behalf.

It would leak out to my parents, who would think me a traitor. Or I would instantly get an upturned nose and red hair and freckles and go around whining "Kathleen! Kath-*leen!*" like the goyish Irish kids with their starched green school uniforms whom my sister and I used to imitate among ourselves, doubling over with laughter.

I had gotten away with pretending to be sick the first Sunday, but that would never work twice in a row. I decided to ask my camp counselor, Chuck, for advice.

Our bunkhouse was situated at the top of the hill, sur-rounded by woods, and every morning we ran down to the mess hall for cocoa and pancakes, or whatever they had for breakfast. It was a pretty nice camp: all the activities — swimming, baseball, crafts, meals — seemed to take place on the field below, while the bunkhouses were notched into a steep wooded hill. Our cabin was actually a lean-to, with a roof but no supporting walls. At first I thought this a sign of the camp's extreme poverty, but afterward I came to like the way the night air would seep in, and the adventurous-ness of being practically out in the open. Once I lifted my head from my pillow in the early morning and saw a deer run by, through the mist around the lean-to. "No more than six feet away!" I kept telling everyone. Then they all pretended they had seen deer too.

The other boys had gone off to their first activity and I waited behind, knowing that Chuck would return to straighten up the bunk and inspect the beds. At least that's what we assumed he was doing — checking for contraband in our mattresses. He was probably just grabbing a few minutes by himself, to read a magazine. I had no sense of who Chuck was, other than that he had recently gotten out of the army. He had a crew cut and amazing biceps, which the kids liked to see wobble up and down like Popeye's, and which he would let them feel, with the greatest of patience, whenever they demanded it. He didn't tell horror stories like other counselors I had had. He just came off as a straight-forward honorable guy, with dark-framed glasses, which I associated then with intelligence, and a subtle look of amusement that made me think he might be more than just a muscleman.

Chuck was surprised to see me still in the bunkhouse. I told him that I had wanted to talk to him — about something that was bothering me. He immediately suggested we walk down to the lake and sit by the bank, where it was quiet and more private.

We sat on an incline along the bank, at a place where the tall grasses had been pressed down. So far none of us had ever been taken there; it was his secret retreat. Chuck listened to me explain my problem about prayer services. But instead of offering an immediate solution, he drew me out further: what else was on my mind? I found myself telling him that I did not feel close to any of the boys, but that I liked a few of them. He was interested to hear what I thought of each one. Then he wanted to know what I liked doing most, what I saw myself being in the future.

We entered a drifting state where we both let ourselves fantasize about what we would like to do with our lives. As we talked we looked out at the lake, and I experienced for the first time a country stillness. Odd that it should have come even then as a backdrop to a heart-to-heart talk — or was it our conversation that had now become the backdrop to the stillness? Being so far away from the others, hearing their noisy screams from a long distance off, flattened like the calls of painted Indians, affected us both with a sense of privileged peace. I savored every moment of it. How often does a child get a chance to talk this way with an adult? Not that there was any pretense of our being equals (although for a moment the boundaries between us in age almost dissolved, and I recognized someone who was also lonely for conversation); but my thoughts were listened to respectfully, as though I had the same right to speak as he did.

In the end he returned the conversation to the original problem, which by now had shrunk in my mind to practically nothing, and he told me that this place did unfortunately have a strict rule about church attendance, but that if I made a big enough stink about it with the camp director I could probably get out of going. On the other hand, that might make me stand out too much. He thought it might be better if I just went to the damned thing and didn't take it that seriously. I agreed with him. In fact, I no longer felt tense about Christianity one way or the other.

At church services I found myself not only reading but singing along lustily, until finally I was given a solo. Music can't be bad, I told myself. God is smart enough to understand the complexities of this situation. At the time I loved music more than anything else. Any song with a sad, minor-key melody would immediately win me over. I despised happy tunes that resolved themselves in a major key. The Jewish cantorial chants were in my blood, and some of these Sunday hymns had a namby-pamby victorious quality, not enough heartaches for me; but at least it was a chance to sing.

I kept waiting to see if Chuck would snub me, and if our closeness by the lake would prove a mirage. I understood that he could not single me out for favored attention, he had twelve other campers to take care of. So I purposely did not pester him, but from time to time I would come upon him when he was more or less alone and we would talk — if not as deeply as that other time, then certainly with easy friendliness. He liked me, I was sure of that now.

By this time I had also made friends with a few of the

guys in my bunk. My painful "differentness" began to be put into perspective. I was just another kid, and wanted it to stay that way.

One day we went on a hike, and all the boys were tired and we stopped and laid our walking sticks by the dusty road. We had been singing one marching song after another. Chuck asked if anyone knew another song that would be good to sing. I thought about the song I had written a few months before, when there had been a great songwriting fad in my family, a sort of competition among brothers and sisters. Finally I said boastfully, "I wrote a song." The other boys jeered, "Sure you did!" and even Chuck seemed, for the first time, not quite to believe me. I insisted I did. But I had been so shaken by their skepticism that when everyone quieted down to listen, the strangest thing happened: all I could think of was the opening line! I had completely forgotten the lyrics. As I stood there growing redder, I was not so much humiliated as surprised that my mind would play this strange trick on me, which it had never done before. But in retrospect I wonder if this blanking out was intended protectively, to keep me from revealing myself as too intellectually precocious. This way, the boys just laughed for a second at my expense, and Chuck suggested we hit the trail again. He put his arm around me momentarily to take away the sting of embarrassment.

Everything Chuck did that summer was kind, and helped me to grow normally. I would love to meet him now and thank him for all the strength I took from him. Every person probably encounters these "saints" again and again in his lifetime, without understanding their importance or being grateful. If I saw him now, the way he was then, I wonder if I would even appreciate Chuck. He was fresh out of the army, starting college on the GI Bill, had a cautious way of speaking, not much book culture. What hurts in all this is knowing that I probably would have condescended to someone like him at college, barely eight years after looking up to him as everything.

The last memory I have of him is rather amusing. One rainy afternoon, I came across him on his day off, typing something on a little portable. The dining room was deserted. "What's that ya doin'?" I asked, craning my neck at his paper. He ripped the page out of the machine and turned it face downward.

"What's it look like?" Chuck said. "Come on, scat."

"What are you writing?"

"A paper. For school."

"What kind of paper?"

"Something for my creative writing course. A story," he finally admitted. I knew it was a story because in the second I had looked over his shoulder I had seen some atmospheric writing about the streets of Chicago. I guessed I could even tell what kind of story it would be from those few glimpsed words — maybe a tough-guy detective, or something about lonely people in the city.

"Can I read it?"

"It's not finished."

"Can I read it when you're done?"

He looked at me with a patient grin, as if to say, You *are* a pest. "I don't think it would interest you."

"Oh yes it would."

"C'mon, scat!"

"Please, can I just read this first page you did? I won't say anything. I promise. I just want to know what it's like."

You could see he was struggling with the pros and cons; my persistence was starting to wear him down. On the other hand, did he want to entrust this eleven-year-old child with his fragile writer's ego? Then he looked up with happy clarity, as though the sun had come out over a rainy day, and said, "No." It was gentle but it was final. His refusal may have relieved me as much as it did him: these forays across the Maginot Line of childhood were getting out of hand.

Remembering Lionel Trilling

My first glimpse of Lionel Trilling came in 1960, during Freshman Orientation Week at Columbia College. This incredible ritual of beanies, upper-classmen's admonitions and chapel talks was capped with a closing lecture by Professor Trilling. We were all asked to prepare for this, our first academic lecture, by reading C. P. Snow's *Two Cultures and the Scientific Revolution*.

To my sixteen-year-old mind, the Snow essay was hot air, with one point about the unfortunate distance between scientific thinking and liberal-arts thinking stretched and padded to make a book. I was curious to see what the legendary liberal Lionel Trilling would do with this fatuous performance by the Tory Snow.

When Trilling walked to the podium of Wollman Auditorium, the entire freshman class rose as one. From the distance (I was sitting in the middle of the hall) he looked to be a delicate, slender man with thin, whitening hair and an egg-shaped head. He began speaking in a most civilized manner about "Sir Charles" and "Sir Charles's point," and I could not be sure whether Trilling liked the book or not. As the lecture wore on, I realized that he was not going to tell us. He kept reading imperturbably from a prepared paper, not pausing very often to look up at his young audience. He drew out several strands of the "modern dilemma," and held them aloft like intestines for us to inspect, at a fastidious distance from himself, and then tucked them neatly back in. The thrust of his talk escaped me. It dawned on me that Trilling was meeting Snow's book on precisely its terms: with a tone of cultured concern, a minimum of strain, and one or two insights.

Then he was gone. Before I quite understood that the talk was over, he had been taken offstage and led away. I had the sense that the university's crown jewels had been placed on display, and then put back in armored storage.

Certainly Trilling was the Columbia English department's very own crown jewel. He gave some legitimacy to the department's Oxonian pretensions. The Anglican reserve between faculty and students, the teas, and the subtle, bewildering code of manners seemed off-putting to students like me who were there on scholarships. During the early 1960s, this tweedy, formal atmosphere seemed just a bit ridiculous in a campus surrounded by Harlem. It would have looked even more ridiculous were it not for the very real prestige of Lionel Trilling, who had an international reputation for his essay collections, and was arguably the direct inheritor of Matthew Arnold's torch.

It gave me a nice, malicious satisfaction when I learned that Trilling was a Jew. People told of how he had been the first Jewish instructor in the English department to receive tenure. This seemed to explain the need for the mask of manners. At the time, I judged him harshly and incorrectly, thinking that, with that odd Alistair Cooke–flavored accent of his, he was trying to pass for Christian. Yet he made no secret of his religious background, as I later learned, and discussed it openly in his writing. Moreover, the "passer" tries to draw as little attention to himself as possible, whereas what Trilling did was to invent an exquisite, almost peacockish persona. Whatever models he was basing it on, he'd done such a fine job that he had gone them one better: he had more aristocratic gentility and refinement than the real English gentry. If I still thought him a bit of a poseur, I had to admire the sense in which he had turned the raw material of self into a work of art. And this knowledge of his humble New York Jewish youth, which had on first hearing the force of a scandal, in the end made me imagine what his fragility and isolation must have been, and drew me closer to him.

By the time I reached my junior year, I felt confident enough to take Trilling's modern literature course. Everyone else in my year seemed to have had the same idea. There were 150 to 200 students jammed into the steep-aisled lecture room, the biggest in Hamilton Hall. My experiences with this man, I thought, are destined to be mass ones.

Trilling proved to be a rather impressionistic lecturer. He would approach the day's text gingerly as though not to alarm its mystery. He might circle around it first with biographical detail or plot telling, but he would always work back in the course of the hour to an effort to capture the heart of the book. "There is this sense . . . this sense of . . ." he would say, looking for the key word to nail it. More than once, he would stare inconclusively out the window at "this sense of . . ." Thinking aloud seemed to be a toil. He did not have one of those shining deliveries that other popular professors enjoyed. Often he seemed puzzled as to why so many people had come to listen to him chase his thoughts. If he could not find the right adjective to describe a work, he would cast about for comparisons: the book would have "the noble quality of a *Don Quixote* . . . or *Middlemarch*" or else would have "none of the expansiveness of, say, *Tom Jones.*" It always seemed when he did that, that he would rather be talking about *those* books, any of those books, than the "crucial modern work" that he had been handed that day by the lottery of literary history and the inexorable logic of his own reading list. It was interesting to see which books he kept returning to in his analogies. They were not many. *Anna Karenina, Tom Jones,* Dickens's late novels, Jane Austen's works, Flaubert's, *Middlemarch, Don Quixote,* Keats, *The Iliad.* He seemed to have no desire to dazzle with erudite references, though of course he had read as much as anyone alive. His mind kept returning to meditate on those few mountain peaks. He was genuinely in awe of their achievement. This was one of his most endearing qualities. He left us with the feeling that it was not necessary to know many books, but to love a few deeply, and all one's life.

But it did seem that his mind, circling over certain of these mountain peaks with delicious deceleration, would sometimes go into hypnotic arrest. There was one curious afternoon when he started to say: "I am thinking of another book in connection with this." That was something he often said, so we waited. "Can anyone guess what other book I'm thinking of?" he asked, tilting his head capriciously. "*Tom Jones*?" "No, not *Tom Jones.* Though certainly as great a classic." Now there were quite a few hands; students called out different titles, all equally respectable, all off the mark. Here we were, grown young men, engaged in a twenty-questions quiz game: What Is in the Mind of Our Professor? He would give out another hint, and a few more volunteers would guess. The lesson had come to a complete stop, while we all went searching for this lost button.

Yet it was hard to get annoyed at Trilling for his classroom manner. He was too disarmingly gentle, and very vulnerable too, in his anxious desire that we all be gentle with each other. There was something about those large, sadly startled eyes of his. They began by looking very, very tired. Weariness was the dominant message of his physical presence. But then he might brighten up with almost naughty enthusiasm, particularly if he was taken away from his duty — which in this case was to pass on to us the meaning of modern literature. One day he gave over the last part of a lecture hour to telling us the life story of Eleanor Marx. He told it like a bit of juicy gossip that had just happened: Marx's daughter ran off with a bounder! Literary scholars notoriously take pleasure in collecting details about the misfortunes or loutishness of their subjects. But Trilling seemed particularly fascinated with domestic troubles and the relatives of titans. One has only to read his essay on Flaubert's *Bouvard and Pécuchet,* which devotes half its space to recounting how Flaubert's niece Caroline bled him dry.

In any case, such anecdotal digressions were holidays for us. I only wish he could have allowed himself more. But duty was always calling him back to the Text of the Week. This week *The Magic Mountain,* next week, *Swann's Way.*

I don't mean to imply that his discussions of the assigned books were useless. But often I would come away feeling undernourished. Here was this man who knew everything, and he could not manage to say it. Of the intelligence locked inside him, there could be no doubt. He reminded me of someone who had suffered a stroke, and whose struggles to employ his full vocabulary were painful to watch. Yet Trilling was then only fifty-eight; it seemed not a matter of physical illness, but of an insulation in the way he lived, which had become a burden to him as well. He seemed, for all his years of lecturing, shocked by the circumstance of finding himself talking to hundreds of strangers; wanting perhaps to make contact, but not knowing where to begin.

Occasionally he would abandon the lecture format and try to "get up" a discussion. The result would be more poignant than the lectures, because with all the goodwill in the world to have a town meeting, he clearly had little faith in democratic opinion, and the first gauche, stupid statement by someone in the room would throw him off. "But surely you don't think that . . ." he would say, embarrassed for the person. He was not like those professors who love to play Socrates, gleefully drawing out truth from a student's errors. Trilling, faced with the job of reforming human ignorance, would often as not retreat, or leave as is. Sometimes when he was in a chipper mood, he might try to sharpen these shapeless ventilations into a clash of ideas. But I always got the feeling that he didn't really believe in the value of such discussions, that he was throwing a sop to our strange, undergraduate desire for more "give and take" in class.

Naturally I participated in these discussions. I would raise my hand and talk to hear the sound of my voice, a bit more aggressively than was the style in that class. Others, some of the best students, prided themselves on never saying a word. They felt, after all, that they were there to listen to Lionel Trilling, not to Columbia juvenilia. Trilling, however, seemed grateful to the half-dozen students who spoke during class, and he would sometimes turn to us to get him out of a dull passage.

After the hour was up there would be a crush around the podium of those who wished to speak to Trilling personally. He inclined his ear attentively and politely to one at a time. I would listen at the perimeter of the group obsequiously surrounding him as he made his way to the door, and grit my teeth. It was strictly against my code to butter up the faculty. Eventually, though, I made up my mind one day to say something to him, after most of the others had gone away. He seemed to acknowledge me as an almost familiar face. "What is your name again?" "Lopate." "Oh yes. Didn't you write that story in *Columbia Review*, about the married couple?" I was flattered that he'd read it, and even more pleased when he said he liked it.

I found myself trying to multiply these moments of contact with him before and after class. Swallowing my pride, I would blurt out anything in his hearing about the books we were reading, hoping in that odd way to start a conversation. One day, while we were studying James Joyce, I told him in the doorway that I could not "get with" *Ulysses*. For all his technique, I said, Joyce seemed a sentimentalist. Trilling looked hurt and worried.

"But," he offered me, "don't you think the stories in *Dubliners* at least are very fine?" I was so touched by his concern, that he should bother to plead James Joyce's case with *me*, that I wanted to reassure him there was nothing to worry himself about; Joyce was obviously great and I would come around before long.

Nevertheless, what I said was something quite different. Perhaps because I had gotten a rise out of him in the first place by being contrary, I answered: "Even most of *Dubliners* I find corny, though better than the rest."

If Trilling was more stimulating before or after the lecture than during it, there were moments in class too when his personal strength burst forth. I remember his talk on *The Waste Land*, a poem that had previously seemed all too academic. Trilling read it in class, and more movingly than I had ever heard poetry read before. His voice reached out to grab the words so directly that no distance was left between the poem and him. When he came to the passage, "My nerves are bad tonight. Yes, bad. Stay with me," it was like an electric shock. Trilling had a genius for pathos. His reading quivered between lament and Eliot's irony. I learned more in that reading about timbre, poetic rhythm and point of view than I would have in a hundred exegeses.

Another time we were discussing *Women in Love,* and he came to D. H. Lawrence's idea about lovers plumbing the depths of each other's souls. He suddenly stopped and confessed, "I find something repellent about that notion." I raised my hand and asked him why, citing my hero Dostoevski and the drive for honesty. "I don't know. . . . Don't you find something destructive about all that delving into one another's depths?" he mused. "I should think lovers would want to keep some things mysterious. Hold a little bit off for a rainy day. What's left after it's all too known?"

It was just such moral asides that I loved in his teaching; nevertheless, I felt this one betrayed cowardice or self-protectiveness. But over the years, I kept thinking back to Trilling's sense of the need for privacy and separation; his viewpoint seemed to be working inside me, gentling me into giving up some of that rough curiosity that had made me approach everyone like a piñata to be shaken and opened.

His finest hour occurred at the end of the term. Trilling had assigned Albert Camus's *Rebel* as our final reading. He apologized on the last day, explaining that he had envisioned it as a culminating text, summing up all the issues of modernism we had discussed so far. He had not actually read it before assigning it, but he was planning to "bone up" on it the week before. Well, he said, he took the book out on the plane and started reading it. "I couldn't make head or tail of it! Everything was either so obvious that I didn't see why he needed to make the point, or else impenetrable . . . sheer nonsense. I read it from cover to cover, too. The whole thing must have gone right over my head!" And, if he couldn't find anything to say about it, he didn't see how he could lecture on it, or why we should be held responsible for it on the final — strike *The Rebel* from the reading list.

It was this honesty about the subjective sources of his taste that Trilling was quite free in admitting, even in paper-marking comments, that made him so likable and instructive as a teacher. He taught himself better than he taught any of the books. He was out of step with the times, but this in itself was educational. For instance, once he made a statement about the absence of love stories in the present era. I raised my hand and demanded (provoking a gasp, so rarely was Trilling directly challenged): "What about Godard or Truffaut or Antonioni?" He cupped his hand to his ear: "I'm sorry, I don't know those names."

"Antonioni? Truffaut? . . . They're film directors." I was amazed at this gap in his knowledge.

"Oh. Well — we rarely go to the cinema." He smiled. He said it frankly, straightforwardly, not with any haughtiness. We rarely go to the cinema. That was that. And I, who very rarely did anything else, had to accept it from him. I did, because what he gave me was much more valuable and rare than if he had stayed *au courant:* he gave me a glimpse of an older way of being.

Toward the end of the year I needed to approach Trilling on a different level. *Columbia Review*, the college literary magazine to which I and my friends contributed, had been seized in galleys and suppressed. Dean Calvin Lee's explanation was "that the language and sexual allusions of the poems, if published, would have brought administrative action — possibly loss of subsidy and individual probation."

The editors resigned, and set about looking for a sponsor to publish the banned issue. Meanwhile, I wrote letters to the campus newspapers and took around a petition to the faculty, asking for an impartial investigation into the censorship. I began with the English department faculty. My disappointment was quick. Everyone wanted the controversy just to go away. Some of the younger instructors, who I knew sympathized with us, begged off on the grounds that their position at the moment was delicate, while several older fossils roared their approval for the administrative action. "About time," they said. I decided to try Lionel Trilling.

I knocked on the door of his private office.

"Come in."

Trilling was in shadows, lit only by a pale overhead light from the highest of high ceilings. The office had the feeling of a personal study lined with books, though not so many as I had expected, and was furnished with plush red-leather chairs — smoking-room chairs, which gave it a warm tone. Trilling sat behind the desk, smoking, ready to receive the next appointment. Behind him was an oval window, which looked down onto the campus walk of trees and flagstones.

I quickly explained my business. I pushed the petition across the desk for him to read it. He apologized that he did not go in much for politics, but said he considered censorship a very grave business, and one close to his heart. Was I certain it was censorship — because if it was, he might certainly be inclined to take a stand against it. I assured him it was censorship pure and simple.

But, he said, wasn't it the right of the publisher to decide not to print something? And wasn't the university in a technical sense the publisher, since the funds for the magazine came from its budget? He had thought that censorship applied to governments and the press, not to individual publishers.

I argued that the university was in this sense very much a local government. Furthermore, I didn't think that the university could suddenly put itself forward in the role of publisher, when it hadn't acted in that function for decades at a time.

Trilling reverted to the distinction between governments and universities, and began talking about the Eastern European bloc, Czechoslovakia, the Soviet Union, in a very concerned and high-minded way that lost me. All I could gather was that something was troubling him about modern political states, as though he were mulling over his latest essay aloud. Then he took a step back from himself, apologized with charm for what he perceived to be a *non sequitur*, and asked me to fill him in again about the problem, from the beginning. I retold the events in sequence. He seemed to give my account some weight, and assured me that after he had heard the other side, had spoken to Dean Truman and Dean Lee, he would have more to say on the issue. In the meantime, he would not feel right about signing the petition, though he might very well after hearing all the facts. Perhaps we could meet again and talk further about this — say, in a week's time.

Though I did not expect much to come of it, I was happy to be getting as courteous and thorough an audience as this, and a chance to tell our side, after the brush-offs I had received from other professors.

We made a tentative appointment, and I assumed the conversation had ended. But Trilling was now in the mood for a chat. He asked me what I thought of the course so far. I said that on the whole I enjoyed it, and expressed some qualifications that didn't go very deep. But he seemed to want more criticisms. Evidently he had formed an erroneous idea of me as a young radical because of the petition. Finally he made it crystal clear. I remember him leaning forward casually, though with real earnestness, and asking: "But what is it you young people want?"

I was tempted to laugh at so vast a question, and at Trilling's almost guileless openness, his curiosity stirred into being to listen to the issues of this new generation. There could be no doubt of his desire to know, which even so had a bit of the exasperated ring of Freud's question, "What do these women want?"

I had no idea where to begin.

"You seem to be very upset about so many things. What are they? What are the areas of distress?" he prompted.

"I'm not upset. Do I seem upset to you?" I asked.

"No, of course I don't mean *you;* I mean you plural, young people, college students."

"Well — I'm not at all certain I can speak for the majority of young people."

"Yes, I know what you mean," he said sympathetically, leaning back and lighting another cigarette, with an approving inclusive gesture of his hand that I thought meant that we two could never quite stand for or speak for the great majority, we were a bit too superior. "But I'm interested in hearing your thoughts nevertheless."

I could not for the life of me muster any real discontent. Censorship was uppermost in my mind, and I could get indignant about that. But I was rather mechanical in conveying the rest of the party line. The truth was that I had never in my life felt *less* distressed and more agreeable than at this very moment when I was allowed to chatter confidentially with this man whom I so respected. All I wanted was to prolong the audience with him as much as possible. Yet in order to do so, I had to keep producing grievances.

I brought up the resentment about the college not allowing women to visit the dorms, which was a fiery issue of campus orators in 1963.

Trilling interrupted, "But surely you wouldn't want the dormitories to start looking like *brothels,* with women's nylons and girdles and things hanging from the doors." He smiled engagingly at me, a man-to-man, after-dinner smile.

Not only wouldn't I have minded women's undergarments floating around my room, my fantasies went quite a bit farther than that. Instead, I wondered what a strange man he was, to make an objection on those grounds — not to youthful promiscuity *per se,* but to the untidiness of the wash afterward. He seemed most repelled by the prospect of clotheslines taking over Alma Mater.

We saw this was an issue we would not agree on, and dropped it. We talked for several minutes then about literature, neither wanting to hurt the other's feelings with boorish insistence on differences of opinion. He seemed to savor the experience of chatting easily across generational lines as much as I did.

"Well, see you next week then. I enjoyed this," he said, as if surprised.

"I did, too," I said. I felt relieved and rewarded by his parting words.

The next week Trilling was ill; and by a week later the steam had gone out of the petition movement. I kept my appointment with Trilling anyway, out of curiosity. This was a shorter meeting.

Trilling told me that he had spoken to the dean of faculties, Jacques Barzun, at a dinner party and that Barzun had assured him that everything was aboveboard. The university had been more than justified in refusing to publish the *Review.*

What could I say? Anyone who could have taken on faith the reassurances of a character like Barzun, the Cardinal Richelieu of Columbia University, deserved to remain benighted. Barzun's hunger for machinations and power was a campus joke; and it had been rumored from the first that he was behind the magazine's censorship, disliking its avant-garde style even more than its occasional sexual references. We all knew that Trilling and Barzun had been close friends for years, and even taught a course together, but that friendship had always puzzled me. Now I saw it as a kind of deal, with clear complicity on Trilling's part. Barzun was his shadow, his worldly brother, who protected the senior faculty's interests with administrative cunning, leaving Trilling free to continue his detached scholarly life with periodic assurances from Barzun that everything was in order.

How much of this was true, how much invention or projection on my part, I don't know. To us, Lionel Trilling, Diana Trilling and Jacques Barzun were mythological beings, and we loved to play the game of making up dramas about their private lives.

Shortly after, the *Censored Review* appeared in mimeo form, selling for a quarter. Buyers were puzzled by the lack of racy material. Many were disappointed; it was just another experimental magazine. And so the episode fizzled out.

I joined the new *Review* staff to see what could be salvaged, and ended up being elected editor in chief. Now I was in a position to invite back the old editors, as well as publish those formerly excluded campus writers. I had in mind a greatly expanded *Columbia Review*. However, we would need a much larger subsidy from the university. I figured that the dean's office might increase our budget with "guilt money" to rectify their mischief of last year — if they could be convinced that we were going in the right direction.

I needed an *éminence grise*. I took our first issue to Professor Trilling and asked if he would review it. He accepted. On the day that the magazine appeared, *Columbia Spectator* ran Trilling's enthusiastic, long review. It was significantly titled "Out of Darkness," and I quote the beginning to show Trilling's handling of local political questions, as well as his amusing awareness that he was being used to proclaim "good news":

It is pleasant to be able to report that The Columbia Review under the guidance of its new editorial board has emerged from its troubled and darkened existence of last year into a new and remarkably bright life.

Among the merits of the Review's Winter issue the one that should be spoken of first is its size. It runs to a solid 64 pages and includes the work of no less than twelve undergraduate writers. I give priority to the gross quantitative observation because the objection was made to last year's Review that it was unduly exclusive, that it did not represent the literary activity of the College in anything like an adequate way. The justice of this objection would seem to be sustained by the achievement of the present editorial board, which has found it possible to present the work of what is indeed a considerable number of undergraduate writers and to do so quite without any relaxation of standards.

But "without any relaxation of standards" puts the case much too mildly. For there can be no question but that the work brought together in this issue of the Review is of a very impressive kind. I can recall no constellation of Columbia College writing within recent years that has been both so accomplished and so interesting.

Trilling went on to discuss the language of each undergraduate writer, praising, characterizing, demurring, in such a tone that the material under discussion could not help gaining in prestige. I was uneasy that he had lost no time using us to "prove" that a change was in order, while sidestepping the censorship principle. But perhaps this time both sides had exploited each other successfully. With

Trilling's review in hand, I went before the appropriations committee, got the budget expanded, and we put out a 128-page double issue.

That spring, 1964, I graduated from Columbia. I decided to make myself into a novelist. I began work on a book that had no more of a preliminary plan than that it would include everyone I knew, and all the interesting bits I had collected in my journals.

Taking odd jobs to support the book, working in unaccustomed isolation (compared to college) and knowing that no one was waiting for this novel at the finish line, I began to seem to myself a ghost, without even the shadow of an effect on the world.

During this time I had my first Lionel Trilling dream. In this dream (which he might have enjoyed, being a student of psychoanalysis), Lionel Trilling appeared to me in a brown morning robe, and told me that I was to be "the next Dostoevski."

I awoke from this dream with an indescribable sensation of bliss. I immediately thought of the wonderful incident about the young Dostoevski when he had just completed his first novel, *Poor Folk*. While he was sleeping, his friends took the manuscript to the great liberal critic Belinsky. Belinsky declared on finishing it that the author of this novella would someday be a great Russian master. Only a great critic, it seemed, could, like the prophet Samuel, discover and anoint the next in line.

I had been anxious for days until this dream came and reassured me; naturally I allowed myself to take the dream as a literal prediction! The other association I made about the dream was between Lionel Trilling and my father. My father in certain ways resembles Trilling: he is also thin, now frail, well-read, intelligent, gentle, withdrawn. But my father is a clerk in a textile house. Here I was "improving" on my father by investing him with all the magisterial authority and power that Lionel Trilling had; and specifically, the one power I needed from my father that he did not seem to be able to give — that of welcoming me into adult life. One has to be confident and secure in one's own life, in one's own achievement, to be able to reassure a son or daughter that he or she has the right of succession.

The connection between Lionel Trilling and my need for an approving father persisted over the years, as Trilling made other appearances in my dream life, eventually becoming something of a regular. Always he imparted a benign influence, and always he came only so close, as though separated from me by fog — like the already dead in Homer's Hades.

My fantasies of fame came to circle more and more around Trilling's endorsement. I decided to apply to the Eugene Saxton Trust for needy young writers, and wrote to Professor Trilling asking him to be one of my sponsors. I began by saying that he probably didn't remember me, tried to remind him with a few details, and apologized for the imposition. His reply was brief and handwritten. It came a week later, on stationery that read "The Colony of Wellfleet" with a red-inked logo of a seahorse on the letterhead. Like the few other letters I received from him, this one was on bone-yellow notepaper.

22 August 1966

Dear Mr. Lopate

It was a pleasure to hear from you and to have your news of your writing. I'll be happy to support your application to the Saxton Trust. Probably I have enough to go on without my seeing a piece of your novel, but supporting letters are always stronger if they can be at all specific and it might be a good thing if you were to send me something to reach me after September 6.

Yours sincerely,

LIONEL TRILLING

I preferred delivering it personally to his apartment on Claremont Avenue, rather than trusting my one extra copy to the mail. No one was home, no building personnel were about; I went skulking around the basement and found a wooden bookcase where the packages and mail for each tenant were left. I slipped it in his shelf and ran.

Less than three weeks later I got another letter from Trilling, this one rather long.

DEPARTMENT OF ENGLISH AND
COMPARATIVE LITERATURE

October 3, 1966

Dear Phillip Lopate:

I am sorry that I had to wait so long to get to your manuscript — do forgive my delay. I read it with great interest and involvement and with the sense that the value of these opening chapters would be even greater when thought about in their relation to the developing story. The reference to *A Sentimental Education* that you make in your letter seems to me to be much to the point in describing the technique you are using, that of patient accumulation of minute detail. You must, of course, be prepared for some resistance to this method — there are people for whom *A Sentimental Education* is a boring and detestable book! But it is one of my favorites and I respond to your own use of the minutiae of utterance with a sense of considerable involvement.

I think that the conversations are now and then open to

the criticism of being rather more toneless or spiritless than they need be. The scene of Eddie and Alex with the drawings comes off best: one has the sense of something going on *beneath* their conversational moves. I understand, I think, the state of essential muteness that, at certain times in their lives, overtakes young people, but beneath their torpor something is struggling to exist in the way of personal assertion. This is quite apparent in the drawings scene and at moments in other scenes, but I think that it needs to be made more manifest. Perhaps it will illustrate my point if I say that the moment in which Jeannie stands at the door as "mousie" (it is delightful) made me wonder why *she* should have such vivacious powers of humor, or self-dramatization, or whatever, and the others not.

Do you want the boys to sound quite as prissy as they do sound? Do they really speak with quotation marks around colloquial and slang expressions? — "under the weather" (p. 6), "take" (p. 13). Do they really use phrases like "more than I have power to express" (p. 13)? Is "prophylactic" a word they would really use? I have never heard the word in colloquial speech. (I take it that their designating the critics by initials is a temporary measure, but it adds to the effect of their cautiousness.) I wonder whether we ought not have a somewhat stronger sense of the characters' personal appearance. I am not wholly sure about this. Any moves in this direction will, of course, establish the existence of the observer-author and you may not want to do this: it must have the effect of "distancing" the characters, at least a little. I am inclined to think that this would be a good effect.

The manuscript is on its way to you. I take it that I don't have to do anything about your application until I am written to.

With all good wishes,

Sincerely,

Lionel Trilling

To understand how heartbreakingly kind Trilling's letter was, it would be necessary to read that first fledgling novel, which was never published, and never will be, and which I now cringe at having shown him. What tact, to have taken me so seriously and diplomatically at my own grandiose level of intention (*Sentimental Education*, no less!). The Saxton Trust was not as impressed.

Meanwhile, I began to be intrigued by Trilling's own career, and would go to the library to browse through his books. Sitting in the library, I could give in to that curiosity, that lovely spying feeling of learning the secrets of someone you know only slightly, by reading his or her thoughts in print.

Systematically reading through Trilling's essays years after taking his course, I was pleased to hear, even more musically than in his fiction, his full natural voice pour forth. It came through without any of the lectern hesitations, and sounded relaxed, acute, elegant, personal, self-doubting, self-reflecting — so much so that I could read it as a kind of confessional fiction. I don't mean that Trilling spoke of his own life circumstances in the essays; they were usually chaste in that regard. But his narrative persona had an almost fictive consistency: Lionel Trilling, knight of the mind, venturing into regretted, quixotic but unavoidable "quarrels with the culture" (his phrase).

Very characteristic are two essays, with almost identical arguments, in which Trilling set about wondering why modern readers shun Wordsworth and turn up their noses at William Dean Howells. He was not talking about lip service or university specialists; Trilling had a clear-eyed, marketplace sense of the true attraction that various classical "goods" still held for contemporary readers. His awareness of how rapidly literary texts stopped meaning anything to the modern mind prompted him to become an archaeologist of the near-present, looking at the source of the contemporary bias that prevented people from seeing the old vitality. In the case of both Howells and Wordsworth, he pointed to their moderate, mild, sunny dispositions, their love of the commonplace, and more damaging, their "deficient sense of evil." Wordsworth's "incapacity for tragedy" is seen as his fatal commercial flaw, especially in a time when "the word 'tragic' should be used as the ultimate recommendation of a sense of life." We have lost the ability to describe normal family life in fiction, says Trilling. "The extreme has become the commonplace of our day. . . . Why do we believe, as we do believe, that evil is of the very essence of reality?"

Trilling may have reproached the modern reader's smugly "tragic vision," but always in a way that implicated himself, using the first person plural: we, our. He recognized the lure of the apocalyptic. Yet it still made sense, he insisted, to celebrate in literature the simple daily rituals and the ordinary hearth pleasures and pains. This was a religious attitude — "normal mysticism," he called it — that had nothing to do with capacity for militant suffering, or heroics of any kind; it was not a willed overcoming of one's nature, but an acquiescence to the rocklike, healing commonplace. In a sense Trilling was the ideal bourgeois spokesman, with the added catch that he had to witness the fashionable defection of his own class from a faith in their traditional virtues, and their embrace of every kind of adrenalated aesthetic stimulant. The irony was that Trilling, who objected to the idealization of every schizophrenic-criminal-outcast, felt more and more an outcast himself in his defense of normal life.

But I understood what he was talking about; and more than that, I needed to hear it. Trilling seemed to be approving from afar my choice of subject matter: friendships, marriages, children, jobs. I had always felt uneasy with the writing of Beckett, Genet, Burroughs, and the whole "abyss" tendency. Whether it had been his intention or not, I took from his essays an encouragement to continue my direction as a writer.

Years passed. I wrote a novella about an émigré family in Mexico, called *In Coyoacan*. It was published in 1970, and I sent him a copy. This time he wrote back a letter that was like the dream come true: corroboration from the highest source, whose frightening impact can be felt so deeply, I think, only once in one's lifetime.

Dear Mr. Lopate:
    It gave me great pleasure to hear from you, to have the very kind inscription on the fly-leaf of your story, and — not least — to read the story, which seems to me in every way most successful. The first thing to say about it, of course, is that it is deeply moving. The "simple story," the history of unremarkable lives lived out almost wholly in family relationships, isn't fashionable these days, but I have an abiding predilection for it when it is told as well as yours is. The tone of the narration seems to me quite perfect, without ever a false note. Just what the idiom of the presumed narrator is I'm not perfectly sure — would it be that of a Mexican of Jewish origin? — but it makes a beautifully appropriate medium. I found the situation of Geraldo heartbreaking — one knows these largely inexplicable failures of family intention which the family tries not to realize, those children who somehow do not get formed, who seem to be affectless, often because the storms of their feeling can be given no shape. I think the most affecting

aspect of the situation as you describe it is the family's determination not to see the full of the boy's alienation, from himself and from them.

If you should be near Hamilton Hall in the course of the coming year, do come in to say hello. Meanwhile I send you my warmest good wishes for the success of your work.

Sincerely,

Lionel Trilling

I was too bashful to take him up on his offer right away, without any pretext other than just "to say hello." Finally, about nine months later I did come in for a visit — for what I suspected even then would be our last chat. He was growing old now. I had been warned beforehand by some people that I would find him, as the horrible expression goes, "a shadow of his former self." Columbia had passed through the troubles of 1968. From the point of view of all my friends in the Movement, Trilling had shown his true colors as a reactionary and had angered a large portion of the student body. I had been busy during the Columbia strike trying to raise bail funds for the arrested students and instructors; but though I found myself in the opposite camp from Trilling, nothing he was reported to have done seemed particularly reprehensible to me. I felt he had acted in character, in a manner consistent with his beliefs and his fears. He had protected his *home*, the university, from the threat of what he, if not I, saw as "apocalyptic" forces.

I sat on the wooden bench outside his office, as in the old days. Soon an undergraduate came out, and I stuck my head in the office door to tell him I was there. He recognized me immediately.

"Well!" he said, greeting me warmly. He seemed in very good spirits. He looked not much older than the last time I had seen him, six years before, but his hair was completely white. There was still that famous inquiring face, part owl, part lamb, with a little of the hawk's sharpness when roused to fight.

Trilling offered me a seat and began the conversation by telling me how fond he had been of my story, and how rare a thing it was in general for a young writer to be interested in those materials. We spoke about other generational novels, like *Buddenbrooks*; the rendering of order and continuity in a narrative, and why this had become so difficult in contemporary literature from a technical standpoint. Then he asked me what I was doing these days. Like him, I had become a teacher. I told him that I was teaching children to write poetry and make films and plays, and that I was very happy about it. He wanted to know what sort of methods were used to elicit poetry from children. The look on his forehead was clearly dubious, and I could already imagine the sort of objections that were forming behind it. When I mentioned the words *open classroom* he stopped me and said: "But could you explain this term, 'open classroom,' to me? I've heard several people refer to it in the last weeks." Again he was playing the foreigner in his own country, and I had to smile. I was determined not to arouse his anti-anarchistic prejudices. I purposely gave an explanation that emphasized the aspects of decentralized space and materials in the open classroom, though I did say that this would give the students more opportunity for individual study, with less dependence on the teacher lecturing all of them from the front of the room. He said, "I'm not sure I would go along with that. I'm rather old-fashioned when it comes to pedagogy. But go on." He seemed much more ready to label himself "old-fashioned." I sensed that the ideological battles of 1968 had made him defensive about anything even remotely approaching politics, and more apt to confess his platform right off, to avoid misunderstanding or disappointment in him.

I gave a fast rundown of the theory behind open education. I endeavored to put him at ease on this point, since I had no desire for Trilling to see me, his returning student, as a centurion bearing the new creed that would extinguish him. Besides, I was convinced that we were much closer than most people in what we valued as beautiful. And as soon as we had glided back to the safer subject of literature, we were again in enchanted conversational territory. We got onto the question of how few fiction writers had managed to capture New York City in their prose; and I mentioned Delmore Schwartz's *World Is a Wedding* and Howells's *Hazard of New Fortunes*. He seemed amazed that someone else had read these books. Of course, I was also playing the good son — knowing his tastes so well, it was easy for me, even subconsciously, to offer titles to him that would draw out his agreement. But even when that factor is taken into consideration, along with the influence he must have had in forming my literary prejudices, there was still a sympathy between our tastes, a *need* for the same kind of thing in literature.

"It's so *nice* to talk about these writers," he declared. "I don't often get a chance just to chat about good books!"

There was only one false note in the conversation. Knowing I had his confidence, I could not leave well enough alone, and asked if he knew where I might get a manuscript of my stories published. It was that old mania again. He turned toward the window, and said that I could send it to his publisher, Viking, but the president of Viking had just

been telling him that things were very tight right now; no
one seemed to be able to get books published anywhere, not
even famous names. He spoke so quietly and hesitantly that
I could have kicked myself. Now he would think I was just
out to use him, as so many other young opportunists must
have, time and again. But I had steeled myself to ask it, to
try to get something practical out of the interview. Besides,
that had been the original plan; I would have felt like a
coward not to have asked. I should have realized that what
Trilling had to give me, had already been giving me, was
something more special than a letter of introduction to the
czars of publishing. The curious part of it all was that, of
the two impulses, wanting him to do something for my
career and wanting Lionel Trilling to be friends with me,
I think at the time I was more ashamed of the latter. It felt
humiliating to want his goodwill so much and nothing else.

We managed to get back on a comfortable footing in our
talk, and, after an hour and fifteen minutes, it was time to
leave. Trilling turned off the lights in his office, put on his
navy blue overcoat, and said, locking up for the night,
"Well, you must come by again *soon* for a talk. I really
enjoyed that. And it's so nice hearing someone who likes
what he's doing! Most people these days are forever groan-
ing about their jobs. But tell me: I meant to ask you before.
Are you safe?" He stopped me, with a new concern in his
voice. "Do you have tenure?"

I came away touched by his concern, but also sorry for
him. That question, "Do you have tenure?," echoed in my
mind for days. He hadn't grasped that in the kind of work
I was doing, there was no such thing as seniority; there was
no guarantee even of funding from one year to the next. He
would have had a hard time picturing it. He seemed resigned, by the very height of his overview, and the symbolic

role he was asked (and had chosen) to play, to giving up a part of contact with life. It was as though only by keeping life at arm's length could he make it the subject of his nimble mental curiosity.

Yet perhaps the distance was also something I had insisted on from my end. Afterward I kept remembering him accompanying me across College Walk to the subway in his dark overcoat, a frail elderly Jew temporarily banishing the cold with conversation.

A year later, when I sent him a new story of mine that the *Paris Review* had published (again a family narrative), I was surprised to receive yet another letter from him, saying that I needn't have sent him the story because he had already read it in his copy of the *Paris Review*. He thought it better than the last. I was pleased most of all by the fact that he had read it on his own and remembered me. Almost as if he were following my career.

I had already gotten into the habit of sending him everything, so when my book about teaching, *Being with Children*, came out in 1975, my list of those who would receive complimentary copies was headed naturally by Lionel Trilling. I wrote on the title page how much his encouragement had sustained me through the years, fretted over the wording, and finally sent it. The next week I learned that he was very ill. He was so ill that the *New York Times* obituary editor, known in the corridors of that institution as "Mr. Bad News," had already assigned a reporter to pull together the threads of his life for a front-page notice. I prayed that the *Times* would be wrong this once. I thought, as in a fairy tale, that if I believed very hard, if I willed it from a different part of the city . . . Then I was distracted by other business, and while my attention slipped away, he died.

Of course it had nothing to do with me; he had terminal cancer and was scheduled to die. But I had to work my way into his death somehow. I even imagined my book on his night table, by the deathbed, his last reading! Anything to prolong the connection between us.

Trilling was dead. I felt very alone. I had lost the protector of my youth.

Newspapers

THE older I get, the more I like to read newspapers. At first it was only one newspaper; but now I like the feel of two morning newspapers wrapped in each other, the tabloid and the full-size, the populist conservative and the elitist liberal, each contradicting the other while being forced to cohabit. It seems to me that only by reading all the newspapers can one get the feeling of being *rained on* by history.

I have a friend, Richard, who likes newspapers even more than I do. Sometimes at night, just before we are about to say goodbye to each other, I will see him slowing down across the street from a newspaper kiosk, already preparing himself. "Wait a minute, I want to pick up a newspaper," he'll say, with that half-apologetic look of someone being caught in the pursuit of a vice. My friend Richard has beautiful manners, and dresses with elegant simplicity, like a European; and what a pleasure it is to see him in his topcoat and cashmere scarf and fine grey woolen gloves, standing at an oblique angle to the headlines, fishing in his pocket and folding the papers one inside the other, not even allowing himself a glance at the inside pages (he'll go over them later, in the privacy of his rooms). Around midnight, in the unpitying neon of the magazine stand, his eyes look tired, his face drained (he works so hard), but kind and sensitive as always: one would think that a man with such an intelligent face was going home to read *Orlando Furioso* in the Italian, not the *Daily News*. And all through this transaction with the news dealer, he is reassuring me with little sideways glances and statements that he did not mean to break the thread of the conversation. "Go on, I'm listening," he says, though how can I go on? It's as if I have just witnessed a man fall in love.

Certainly we both like to read newspapers, but Richard's is the real passion; he keeps it more hidden, and he reads them for different reasons than I do. For instance, he cares nothing about sports, which is the main reason I buy a daily newspaper. I try to get inside his skin and imagine what the excitement is. Perhaps it's like my own compulsion to look at stills under a movie marquee; but this itch is nothing compared with Richard's newspaper buying.

Once we went on a train journey together, and each time the train stopped for any length of time, he would pick up that region's newspapers. Sometimes he will even buy several editions of the same newspaper: the city, the late city, the seven-star final. Maybe he is looking to see how certain stories have been dropped, or given different play. I watch him reading. He follows the reporters' careers and their styles: "This is a big break for him," he will murmur, or "She's definitely a lightweight" — referring to someone who has botched a think piece. I try to get him to say what his eye sees. I feel sure he knows some connoisseur's secret that he won't tell me. I ask him point-blank: Is it the layout? Is it the ink itself, the rough feel of the newspaper stock? No, he laughs, he got over that long ago; when he was a teenager. . . . "I don't understand," I tell him, my mind stuck on that peculiar word *teenager,* trying to picture him an adolescent with unimaginable newspaper debauches. Then he'll say, "It's not worth discussing; give me a break," and turn the conversation to something else.

Flattery

THERE are people who love to feed our vanity, and others, like me, who enjoy receiving flattery. By no means is the first type more humble than the second. Some people flatter because it is sweet to do so. It is a leisurely sport, especially for people brought up with good manners (I was not one of them), and taught not to put themselves forward. With them, flattery not only brings the pleasure of imagining what the other person is like, but can be a discreet, displaced form of bragging. I am not speaking of the yes-man's base agreement or the flunky's insincerity, but of a flattery with the afflatus of charmed admiration, that takes off with a creative zaniness. How nice it is to be inspired by the winning complexities of a friend's person-ality, as though standing in front of a newly discovered Donatello — one that is, moreover, virgin territory from a critic's point of view. With each compliment the flatterer adds depth to his or her portrait of — not only the flattered one, me, for instance, but the mythical *balanced* human he or she dreams of becoming. They are dreaming. No wonder they become so animated when they form their compliments in bold strokes: their cheeks flare, they approach happiness, Eden; sometimes they go right past me in their convivial imaginings. I don't mind, I sit still and take it. Would you wake an ecstatic?

I once had a friend, Bruno, who was a maestro of flattery. Bruno's greatest pleasure in life was to praise me. But what gave him high joy was to compliment me for something *no one else could see.* Often it would be for involuntary little stuff that even I had not noticed, or else for some knack in an area in which I had become accustomed to thinking myself (rightly so) underdeveloped. So one day he went into raptures over my "feeling for nature," just because I had detached myself from the group and scuttled through some leaf piles. On another occasion he nearly convinced me that I had a strongly spiritual, mystical endowment — this in spite of my lifelong indifference to everything extrasensory and occult. And one afternoon, when I ran across town from my house to his, a distance of no more than two miles, he was astonished by my athletic energy! Bruno was forever discovering me to be the embodiment of all masculine roles: soldier, thinker, sportsman, lover, holy man, diplomat, ruthless truth-teller, delicate poet, man of the people, aristocrat, buffoon, Beau Brummell, Casanova, and St. Anthony. Of course I could see his point; I agree with every one of these characterizations! And when one of them seemed a little off, I figured it would come true eventually. No doubt Bruno had a prescience, could see things in me that were just about to blossom. If I put down people who went to gurus, Bruno was prepared to convince me that I was still on the spiritual path: I didn't need a guru, I was already a guru! Ah, what an imagination that boy had!

With all his talents for flattery he was also a master insulter, and could put people down as easily as he could raise them up. Maybe that was why I was always a little afraid of his enthusiasm for my every foible.

He knew well, too, the secret of good flattery: to mix it

with a little insight. Sometimes I have had to listen to ten minutes of dull compliments before something like a mini-perception about my character was aired; but I am ever on the alert for such information. This is the main sustenance, the real nourishment, of flattery. The rest is dextrose for high energy, burned off quickly. Flatteries are too often like sweet meringues that leave a slightly awful sugary grit on the teeth.

The flatteries of beautiful women are different, of course; they can be like the creation of the world. So the glamorous A. was talking all about my good qualities on the phone the other day, which she summarized by saying, "There's nothing like the combination of gentleness, generosity and power in a man." It gave me tingles to hear it. This is, by the way, a woman who has obstinately refused to sleep with me for seven years. Apparently she finds the combination, unique as it is, resistible.

The Brunch

I HAD been invited to a Sunday brunch by an old friend of mine — I should say ex-lover — Jan, who wanted me to meet some of her friends. They were mostly politically engaged men and women. The women were all professionals, running day-care centers or getting advanced degrees. Some of them knew each other from being in the same Upper West Side women's group. There was lots of good food — omelets and bagels and whitefish and fruit salad and coffee and wine. By noon everyone was mildly drunk. Some of the guests were dancing to a rock 'n' roll record. I sat on a couch talking to a woman named Betsy who was going to social-work school, who had brought her little daughter, and who incidentally, I knew, had been an off-and-on lover of the hostess, when my friend Jan had decided to take lovers of her own sex. I hadn't been very comfortable with that period in Jan's life; but I had to admit that I was more disturbed by the thought of Jan's changing than by the tangible person next to me, Betsy, who looked so trustworthy. Betsy clearly wanted to talk to me, and there was nothing in her manner that seemed hostile to men. She was very open, pretty in a maternal, buxom

way; and if I hadn't known she was otherwise inclined I
might have made a pass at her.

Her little daughter began climbing around her lap and
demanding her attention. Betsy ignored her at first, or
stroked her hair while trying to ignore her. I turned to the
kid to find out what she wanted. "Oh, that's right," said
Betsy, "you're very good with kids, aren't you?" The
thought that I had a reputation for being good with children, because I was a successful teacher, froze me. I found
myself having to overcome a distaste for this child. She was
whimpering about something, but basically had nothing to
say. Soon her mother went to the bathroom, leaving us
alone. "What grade are you in?" I asked her. "First," she
said. I began to play a kind of game with her, threatening
to cook her in a pot if she wasn't careful. She challenged
me to do it — she was delighted at the idea. "Cook me!"
she said. I grabbed her up and took her into the kitchen,
where Jan was clearing away a few things. "We're going to
put her in the stew," I said. "Oh, very good," said Jan,
immediately falling into step. "Where's the seasoning?"
"The spices are on the second shelf." I was still holding the
girl in my arms, and by this time I noticed she was becoming a bit frightened. I reached for the basil and sprinkled
a little on her stomach. "No!" she said, squirming to brush
it off. "How about some cinnamon?" I asked. I took down
the jar of cinnamon, and — this is the part I will never
understand about me — poured some on her face, even
though I guessed she would hate it. She began to cry. "Oh,
what's the *mat-ter?*" said Jan, taking the girl from me. "She
must have gotten some in her eye . . . I was aiming at her
nose," I said. "I know," said Jan; "some of it accidentally
must have gotten in her eye. Poor baby!" At this, the girl
began to cry twice as hard, and I thought to myself: Faker.
If she was a well-brought-up child, she would know to be

more stoical. She's just used to exploiting her mother's guilt as an only parent to get attention. We went back into the living room. "What happened?" asked her mother. "Oh, we were playing a game, and she started crying. . . . It's my fault," I said. Betsy apologized for her daughter and took her into the other room; and I thought it would be a long time before she said to me again, "You're so good with children."

The Second Marriage

In the second marriage they indulge themselves,
Give lots of dinner parties, entertain,
Knowing the price of too much symbiosis.
Weekends they "play," dress down; they share
The affectation of décolletage.
Her plunging tunic, his designer shirt,
Unbuttoned to the waist, grey hairs. And grass
On Sunday mornings, snacks in bed.
Demonstrative in public: on his lap
She rubs the curly hair behind his ear,
While they go right on talking to their friends.

All shortages of that first Puritan marriage
Straight out of college, serious and harsh,
Are now corrected Epicurean-style.
They buy each other fancy gifts (why not?
They both are pulling in good salaries):
Twin bicycles, cases of Beaujolais,
A brownstone where they can put up on visits
Their teenage children from first marriages.

These offspring do drift in so pallidly:
The boy's a vapid longhair into Rock,
The girl a homely tomboy, likes to hike.
They seem so unsure in this sensuous crowd;
Perhaps they both take after the dour parent
Who was left behind. The boy makes himself
Useful changing records, hides by the stereo,
He finds this joie de vivre *spectacle*
Revolting in a way, but thinks: "Maybe
they're right, they all have such conviction;
Maybe this time I'll get it if I watch. . . ."

And then, the invitation's always there
To take advantage of their generosity.
The private screenings of old Fred Astaires,
The crowd with dinner dishes on their laps
Applauding each dance climax. Between reels,
Wandering around, fingering the toys,
The Minnie Mouse collection on the mantel.
And afterward some coffee, chocolate mousse.
These people know exactly what they want.
The second marriage has to work.
It lasts till Death.

Bill and Walter

I HAD dinner with a gay couple: one, my friend Bill, about twenty-eight, a painter; the other, his lover Walter, a successful theater director, who is sixty-four. I felt honored in some way to be trusted enough to dine with them. I also felt that I was being asked to be a witness to — I'm not sure what exactly, to the two of them as a couple. They were both rather quiet. Walter had had a triumph the night before; his new play received strong reviews in all the newspapers. He was tired, but clearly pleased. He had that sitting-back curiosity that comes on someone when he has successfully mounted a long project. I did most of the talking, because I felt they wanted it that way. For some reason I talked about the 1930s and the Writers' Project, of which I'd just read a history. "Yes, those were great days," Walter said, his eyes sparkling. "You could see a play for fifty cents — well, in those days fifty cents was more like two dollars, but it was still cheap. I saw Orson Welles when he was running the Mercury Theater —" Walter turned in his chair to explain to Bill, who was suddenly made into the boy, the child, and Walter and I the same age. Bill of course knew all about Orson Welles and nodded briskly, to cut the explanation short. Then there was more talk, coffee, dividing up the check.

We left the Italian restaurant at eleven, and I shook hands with both of them, and they headed up Second Avenue by themselves. I saw them walking into the crowd — the two of them, Bill, tall, muscled, youthful, leather-jacketed, and Walter, with a white goatee, short and twice as old as his companion, a captain's cap on his head. I looked to see if they would put their arms around each other. But no, they respected the code of society, they walked a foot apart, and from a stranger's point of view they might not have been taken for lovers at all, but for father and son. But I myself was convinced for the first time that they were lovers. I thought there was something very fragile and dignified about the way they attended to each other. They stopped at the light, talking to each other, Bill leaning his head down to catch something Walter said, talking more freely now than they had in the restaurant with me. And I believed in their love. Even so, I felt the sadness underneath it. Maybe it was my knowing, from Bill's confidences, that their relationship was in trouble (because Walter did not take him seriously as a fellow artist), which gave their mutual attentiveness an air of poetry. It helped that it was a warm night for November, with fog and mist. I watched them until they were blocked from sight.

The Soap Opera

ONE afternoon, when I was on the road giving speeches and workshops, I had some time to kill. I went down to the lounge at the college where I was staying to see if I could scare up a conversation. The lounge was deserted. But the color TV set was on, mysteriously, so I sat down in front of it.

It was a soap opera. I was glad someone else had chosen the program instead of me, since I liked soap operas but would have felt slightly ashamed turning one on by myself.

A young, voluptuous woman in a flowered nightgown was getting out of bed, secretly, so as not to wake her companion, a middle-aged woman. Lesbian lovers? I didn't think it was possible on daytime television. More likely they were mother and daughter, or the younger woman was tending her sick aunt; that was why they were sleeping in the same bed. The young woman had long, wild hair — *wanton*, the code said. She dialed a number and whispered into the phone so quietly that even I couldn't understand her. Regular watchers would have. She got annoyed when she found out that the place would not be open later (pawnbroker? adoption agency?). Then she set down the phone soundlessly, and at that moment in a close-up, the older woman opened her eyes.

The wanton, voluptuous girl returned to the bed of her shriveled mother.

"Who are you calling so early in the morning?" asked Mother in an invalid's voice.

The girl had to wait a few seconds while she made up a lie. "Oh, it's the new job I'm starting next week. You're right, it is early. They weren't even open yet." Then she yawned, got under the covers, and turned her back to her mother to feign sleep.

The camera went to the dried-up, heavily powdered face, like a Kabuki actor's, of her suburban mother. There was a voice-over soliloquy on the close-up, as the older woman enacted thoughts traveling across her furrowed brow like ants. "She's gotten so secretive lately. I know she's hiding something from me. She wouldn't do anything that would get her into trouble, would she? . . . No, she wouldn't. Not after all those . . . Dear Lord" (and now the actress raised her eyes to the ceiling), "I know she's grown up, but sometimes I still see so much of the little girl in her. She takes risks without knowing what she's getting into. How will she ever learn all there is to protect her in this life? I can't do it for her anymore," she sighed, and the screen faded to a commercial.

I was moved, even as I sneered at the clichés. Maybe it was only my excitement at the body of this young woman at such an incongruous hour. She certainly looked great, but the older woman had gotten to me too. The virility of the genre is its power to establish its codes quickly and universally. This art is greater than mine, I thought with a twinge. But, since this is a thought I often have, it didn't hold me for long. There's nothing better than melodrama, I reflected instead. Why is "soap opera" such a pejorative term? Why do people who want to act sophisticated turn their nose up at melodrama? It probably tells the truth about life. Even if I am incapable of writing melodrama, at least I have the good taste to know that it is the most satisfying art. To give a story that tragic lift . . . The commercial was over, and I turned again to the program.

Different cameo, different characters. "We must talk this out, Julie." A man with a French accent was pleading with a woman to love him again. He was adorable, civilized, sympathetic, vulnerable; he had a charming French accent and a puppy-dog sweetness; he was eloquent, well dressed in a blue blazer and turtleneck sweater — no doubt a professional of some sort, a doctor maybe — but in the code of the show, he lacked some quality of animal maleness.

"I know you will always have a place in your heart," he said, "for Mark. But I am your husband! My love for you is — forever. You understand, it is a — different kind of love. To me you will always be the most beautiful woman in the world." Reaction shot of the woman to see how she was taking this. Her lip twitched a moment, her dimple flashed; she accepted the compliment, though still looking troubled, her judgment suspended.

He went on: "I have told you how I feel about you, though it is difficult to put into words. Now I want you to tell me if you still feel for me. Because I don't think you love me anymore!"

"I do love you! — in a very special way."

"That's not what I wanted to hear," he groaned. "I want to know if you *love* me."

"Oh, I've hurt you so much, Jean-Claude; I've been so awful to you. Tell me, Jean-Claude, what *is* love?" she asked, teasing behind her troubled air.

"If I tell you what love is, to me, it is trust. Love is ab-
solute trust — and beauty, yes; and it lasts . . . forever. Julie,
I want to make love to you tonight!" Quick reaction shots
of her panic, suggesting that their love life has not been all
that it should. There is even the suggestion in his urgency
that he has sometimes been impotent. "We will have a
candlelight dinner. With champagne, for just the two of us,
and afterward we will be man and wife again. What do you
say? Don't refuse!" He takes her hand. A close-up of her
face, bewitchingly confused — she also has loose strands of
hair curving onto her cheeks, identifying her as a potential
wanton. The "decent" women in the show all manage im-
peccable pillbox coiffures.

The next scene is between a third couple. The man is
drunk and pleading to be let in the door. The woman obviously wants to but says she is tired of being his "second
best." He has a rumpled, Elliott Gould disorderliness and,
standing in the doorway, manages to be desirably masculine
while unsteady on his feet. (Perhaps he is Mark? The one
whom the half-married Julie can never forget?) The lady in
this scene looks more proper. She decides that she can't send
him home in this state, so she will feed him dinner, and
then pack him off into the night. He must promise that he
will leave right after dinner, with no funny stuff. He
promises, smiling puckishly.

After a commercial we are back to the married couple
supping by candlelight. The Frenchman obviously feels he
is getting what he wanted, that things are going his way; the
woman, Julie, is as though in a trance, numbly carrying out
the agenda. He pours the champagne, supplies most of the
gallant, sparkling conversation. Finally, he stands up and
embraces her. They are kissing, but it is a kiss full of consolation and despair, his hands sliding over the back of her

silk blouse. And it is clear now what the problem is. As he has stood up and pulled her aloft with him, we see that he is a good two inches shorter than she is. There is not a woman in the audience who won't think: "This isn't going to work out. He's a shrimp!" By the iron law that governs love in soap operas, he will never make her happy.

The show is over. Besides, I have seen enough.

Renewing Sodom and Gomorrah

EVERY few years, on the front page of the *Times*, a plan is announced by a consortium of merchants and industrialists and bankers to transform Forty-second Street into a squeaky-clean thoroughfare. One recent proposal calls for glass-enclosed atriums (the Ford Foundation, sponsoring the project, is big on atriums), "bridges crisscrossing 42nd Street, and escalators moving through a complex set of spaces making up the display area," which would include "a ride that would simulate movement through the layers of a slice of New York from underground to a skyscraper top." They are also getting smarter: they are not going to knock down all the movie houses, just the less "historical" ones, and then turn those allowed to survive into what the planners genteelly term "legitimate playhouses" (a throwback to the old prejudice that Theater was the more respectable art, and Film the bastard).

Every time such an article appears my whole day is ruined. Because I think that if I ever get up the courage to marry and have a family, how will I be able to show my children Forty-second Street if there is no Forty-second Street? And if I lack the nerve and turn into a seedy old bachelor, then I will need Forty-second Street all the more, in those golden waning years.

All of Manhattan tilts toward that magnetic field of neon. Ever tried ambling through the streets of New York without any destination? I know that I am always pulled toward that glittering needle — at first into the triangle around Times Square, with the three-card-monte sharks and the Bible screamers and the sad-eyed camera stores bobbing me around until I wind up on *the* street, West Forty-second, between Seventh and Eighth avenues. Then I don't know where to start to turn my head and look. Heaven for a film lover is ten marquees that change bills every day. Forty-second Street comes close.

It was here I used to rush to at eleven in the morning, cutting classes in college to see *Rules of the Game* with my legs dangling over the Apollo balcony. And here I caught up with all the flicks that opened and closed fast and nobody else would show: with the last great Westerns of Raoul Walsh and Howard Hawks, with Otto Preminger's melo-dramas, like *Hurry Sundown* and *In Harm's Way*. And the show in the balcony was as interesting as the one on the screen. First you saw concessionaires hawking ice cream and caramel popcorn in between (and sometimes during) films, those sad sacks in white Good Humor uniforms climb-ing up the balcony steps; then the reefers would be passed around in back, along with criticism of the characters: "That girl is *dumb!*" "Why don't she just get out of there?" (This during a scene with a psychotic killer stalking a coed, what could be better?) The chorus in the audience started directing advice and taunts — "You better run, girl! I wouldn't stay in that house by myself, that's for damn sure."

Meanwhile some vagrant in the pit was snoring too loudly, having come into the theater only to escape the cold and rainy street, and was two-thirds through his second double bill with his head between his knees as an usher approached and rudely shook him awake. Shortly after, a fight would start between pit and balcony, the Guelfs and the Ghibellines, because some joker from on high had been throwing popcorn at the patrons below. All manner of threats were exchanged. Then someone tossed lit cigarettes from the balcony, each one a dying firecracker, drawing the attention of everyone in the theater. Meanwhile, the glories of late Hollywood-studio *auteur* style, outdoor night sequences all bluish black with just a few klieg highlights, tracking shots around corrals, men in white sheets, Jane Fonda making love to a saxophone, who can figure out what's going on? *"Shut up!"* someone yelled. It turned out to be me. I was appalled at myself and sank deeper into my seat. What a way to see a movie!

All that's changed, you'll say; I'm just being sentimental. The Apollo stopped showing art films years ago and now it's kung fu and sex from one end of the street to the other. Or as the article puts it, "violent or pornographic movies." But you know, even if I never walked into another Forty-second Street movie house again, which is highly unlikely, it would still do me good to take in the street periodically for health reasons, like a sauna. Such concentrated steaminess. Do planners know how hard it is to achieve a visual clutter so extreme that it makes the simple traversal of one city block as adventurous as running a gauntlet? Sure, there are hustlers, thieves, prostitutes, cripples, derelicts, winos, molesters, droolers, accosters — I'm not denying it. Would you prefer to cement over the whole beehive with a dipsy-doodle exhibition hall and kick out those people so they'll congregate on another block and make a new heaven and hell somewhere else, maybe not as bright and never as satisfyingly central?

The politics of such civil plans are transparent. What's

objected to here is not movie houses and pinball parlors but the people who go into them, who are the wrong class and the wrong color. No need to dwell on the racism and antagonism to down-and-out poor people that is the real message behind urgent appeals to "clean up" Times Square. But I wonder if this city knows how lucky it is to have a raunchy street so famous and so densely compacted. We are told that tourists can ride escalators in the new Forty-second Street and visit a gallery with an object or two on loan from each of the city museums; whoopee-do. Don't they know that tourists, even the straightest, come to New York City partly because they've heard that we've got a real Sodom and Gomorrah? They want to see something that they can go back home and tell their neighbors was "dis-*gust*ing! I mean — vermin!" Not that I see it that way, but it's nice to know that people who like to feel that way can go to a place and be shocked by it every time.

I remember once taking my then mother-in-law from out of town on a tour of New York City. She was very proper, and I wanted to protect her sensibilities — I was much younger then — so when we were within sight of that dangerous street I turned westward a block early. Imagine her disappointment as I took her down Forty-third Street, by the esteemed grey *New York Times* headquarters. Nothing but loading trucks and offices.

Supposing, though, that I *had* taken her on a tour of the strip — or, to leave my ex-mother-in-law out of it, supposing for purposes of this essay that we not evade the issue, but go into the topless bars and massage parlors, porno movies and bookstalls. I don't pretend to have an encyclopedic knowledge of these dens, but as an occasional imbiber, I will be happy to pass on what I know, in the interests of social science.

Stand outside any pornographic movie theater in a large city on a quiet afternoon, and watch who goes in. You will probably see a smattering of old men, widowers and inactive pensioners; some young blacks and Hispanics, mostly unemployed; a core of neatly dressed manual and clerical workers, black and white (the pornography parlor being one of our few models of racial integration); and a small number of middle-class businessmen.

Why do men go to pornography shows? The most obvious answer is that they are looking for a sexual satisfaction that is missing in their own lives. It is safe to say that the majority of people in this country, single or married, do not have happy sex lives. In lieu of the real thing many will accept images, experiences once removed.

The patrons of pornography may be divided into two types: occasional and regular. The occasional customer may approach pornography as an annual cleansing of the senses. Some unhappily married men use it as a kind of mental adultery; others may even be happily married or involved with someone, but feel the need from time to time to check into the Hotel of Erotic Dreams, to see what they have been missing. (Not always does pornography win out over real life; the man may run home to his wife or lover with a new sense of how lucky he is.) There are also inexperienced young men who look to pornography for education. If it implants false or, as the antipornography groups say, with some justice, "perverted" notions of sexuality, it also conveys demonstrations of a range of lovemaking possibilities — assuming, as marriage manuals have done, a teaching function that the society is too prudish to undertake.

However, the novice, the married man on moral holiday or the bachelor aesthete like me are all marginal. The industry would die on its feet if it had to rely on these occasional clients. What keeps pornography alive are the repeaters. The look they give as they approach the movie ticket-taker and slip five dollars across the booth opening is that of a pinched lab rat who has finally spotted a straight run of several hours within the maze. They are looking for mental space as much as for Eros.

Once inside, they take their seats quietly in the darkened hall (they are the most docile of spectators, and the most solitary) with as much seat and row distance as possible from other spectators. Very rarely do they venture a brotherly word to their neighbor. Each is there to be swept away in the great flood.

Men go to pornography for excitement, but also, I think, to be put in touch with their sadness. They know that before the experience is over, the connection between their own desire and the lusty bodies dangled before them will have been missed. Elegiac is the mood that often settles on a pornography audience. They go in search of something they don't have, that they half remember perhaps having had. The aged hero in Kawabata's novel *The House of Sleeping Beauties* is overtaken by sensual memories and regrets while contemplating the sleeping form of a young woman, in a brothel for men too old to do anything else. So the watchers of pornography often seem to be using the spectacle before them as a meditation screen from which to contemplate the missed opportunities of a lifetime. All the bodies in a film are as good as "asleep" in the sense that they cannot be roused to respond to us. Even when the entertainment is live, the convention that the performer herself cannot be made love to means that, for all the provocative come-ons of the artiste, the customer must remain as though in a stupor, interpreting but not interacting. At most, he may touch himself but not the other. This is the essential pathos behind all pornographic spectacle.

Some people have objected to the fact that these pornography parlors are "nothing more than masturbation halls." An *Equal Times* exposé reports that there are "naked women dancing in the peep show 'carousel' or performing 'live lesbian sex' on stage while men jerk off and the janitor comes around time and time again with the Lysol bucket." Is there something wrong with masturbation? Would it have been better not to use the Lysol? The problem cannot be that the customers are wrong to masturbate in public places, since everyone knows that these particular public places are employed for that purpose, and decent citizens need not go in there in the first place. The only thing these men can be faulted for is not having strong enough imaginations to produce erotic images on their own, so that they could jerk off at home and save some money.

No, I will be told, the objection is not that they are masturbating, but that they are masturbating off of women exploited as sexual objects.

Let us first ask who is being exploited. The woman on the film screen is certainly undisturbed by the jets of sperm her beauty has inspired. She contracted to do the film months ago. When the entertainment is live, the performer may indeed feel grossed out by some of her male customers' responses, but it is a job she chose, and if she quits there will be many others to take her place. The job may be horrible, or it may be like any other job, depending on the performer's point of view; in either case, the antiporn forces are not in the business of organizing female workers in the pornography industry to improve their conditions. No, their concern is not so much with the exploitation of the particular woman performing the simulated (or real) sex act, but with collective womanhood, all of whom are claimed to be affected by the reproduction of degraded images of females as sex objects.

There is much to be said for and against this argument.

Better polemicists than I have got their feet stuck in these bear traps, and I suspect that I would not be any more successful at disentangling the justice and logic on both sides. Feminists themselves are divided on these issues. On the one hand, the injustice and pain caused by sexual roles in our society merit angry opposition. On the other hand, there is the case for the defense of imagination, however barbaric. There are the rights of communities to set standards of decency, versus rights of minorities to seek private pleasures; the understandable desire of parents to control the intake of the young, balanced against the protection of free speech; the intuitive connection felt by many between pornography and violent crimes against women, and the lack of hard evidence to support this hypothesis. Finally, there is the pragmatic question: Is it practical to wage war against pornography, knowing that it will probably always be with us? What would you propose in its stead?

I confess I myself see nothing terribly wrong with pornography; but then, I have never felt myself to be victimized by it. I would only question, from the discredited (and hitherto largely ignored) standpoint of the pornography customer, whether the stuff is being accurately described in the first place.

For instance, regarding the matter of sex objects, it needs to be pointed out that men no less than women have shallow, thinglike personalities in pornographic presentations. There is precious little characterization of a novelistic sort in pornography. Part of the promise of pornography is that people can engage in pleasure without having to deal with each other's personalities. In such an arena, where there are no *dramatis personae,* only nerve ends receptive to pleasure, one could as easily say about the performers that, rather than being reduced to sexual objects, they have been elevated into embodiments of the physical life, like dancers. Everything personal has been extinguished, except during the minimal "frame" establishing a situation, the scant dues paid to narrative. With pornography at its purest — the loop — even the remotest suggestion of a story is removed and we are left with a continuously repeating reel of sex acts. All pornography follows, like Schnitzler's *Ronde*, a circular form. Its theatrical paraphernalia — the G-strings, the whips, the dildos, the boas — belong to a spectacle inherently repetitious.

Pornography is a sort of utopian kingdom, where the women are always ready and the men are always hard and they go at it for what seems like forever, and when they come they don't need to rest, they start again with someone else; and so they spend their lives screwing and have no worries about money or leaking radiators or family illnesses. Gone are psychological scars, fears of not impressing the other, needs for special treatment. There is no rejection in this utopia, no "He's not my type" or "She's too bland" or "I don't think he's intelligent enough for me." Everyone will do. No sooner met than made. Pornography transcends all of life's hesitations and doubts.

A milkman rings the doorbell and is met by a housewife in a negligee. She offers him a cup of coffee, the milk "accidentally" spills on her, she runs into the kitchen to wash off her slip, he peeks at her naked breasts through the doorway, she sees him staring and gives him a look of indignation that slides irresistibly into melting hunger. The next moment they are in the bedroom (oh, those sudden transitions of lowered resistance — you keep thinking you must have missed something), and the rest is — unmemorable.

Most pornography shows consist of what the trade calls

"sucking and fucking." To watch people going at these activities for any length of time is a numbing experience. At first one is titillated, then aroused, maybe even stirred, excited, at the edge of one's seat. Then the effect wears off. If pornography is a timeless world freed from social responsibilities, it is also a static one. The problem it has always faced as entertainment is how to build interest. The progression may go from a blow job to straight intercourse to lesbian sex to a threesome to an orgy or whatever, but the attempt to create an ascending curve of sexual stimulation will usually not keep up with the descending curve of involvement. The last scenes are generally anticlimactic, in more ways than one. Here the physiology of male arousal and pornographic spectacle may be at odds. The first close-up of genitals and penetration can be rapturous; by the tenth one feels as though one were taking a turkey-basting course.

It may be the nature of all utopias to be boring. But I am convinced that pornography is meant to be boring. Men bring to it their painfully aroused libidos in the hope not only that they will be turned on but that they will be turned off. Not enough has been made of pornography as a depressant and anti-aphrodisiac. The thoughtful, slugged look in the eyes of customers leaving such exhibitions shows that they have indeed rid themselves of some of their annoying sexual energy. For some of these men it is a way of looking the devil of unsatisfied sexual desire in the face and out-staring it, the reward for which is a hard-won indifference.

Not only is the stylized picture of sexuality represented in pornography unreal, but I would argue that those who frequent it *know* it is unreal. Pornography is like science fiction about a planet on which nothing can grow or develop because nothing important is at risk. The orgasm? It would be inappropriate to apply a Maileresque search for bigger and better orgasms to this more standardless, un-teleological planet. The orgasms in pornography are not graded, they are simply presented matter-of-factly in rough interchangeable sequence. Since there are no sexual dysfunc-tions that we are allowed to see, no failures to lubricate or premature ejaculations ("Cut! Take two!"), the sense of vulnerability and uniqueness in sexual communion is lost, which is perhaps why D. H. Lawrence hated pornography. There is nothing at stake. One watches it, like a slow base-ball game between two teams already eliminated from the pennant race, for a moment of awkward surprise.

In many ways, the experience of pornography resembles dream life. Both place us before a stream of images in which the normal laws of social reality are suspended. No sooner desire a thing than it begins to occur. Taboos of incest, class, color, age, gender, number, genus and species fall with a fluttering fluidity. All that has been repressed pops out. It is not surprising that hostility and violence also make their appearance; but as in dreams, they are only part of what happens, not the whole. As with dreams, too, the pornography watcher suspends criteria of quality, knowing that there will be a great deal of dross for every moment of magic.

To try to separate the broad stream of pornography into good and bad is a little like attempting to screen out un-interesting from interesting dreams, pleasant from horrible ones. That is why I think the effort to defend pornography by pointing to legitimate specimens of erotic art is mis-guided. As soon as the style becomes too brilliant it ceases to be pornography; it becomes "literature" or "art cinema." Pornography may be a sort of art-making activity too, but the sublimity that it does momentarily attain is never far from its sludgelike mediocrity. And it is this very medi-ocrity from which it draws its secret energy.

* * *

I don't want to leave this subject before reporting one final experience: a visit to a topless-bottomless bar. One night, in a benign mood, rounding out a pleasant evening with my older brother, I had suggested we stop in one of those clip joints on Eighth Avenue and Forty-second Street. It was a sort of long-delayed rite of whoring together, something we had never had the courage to do while growing up; and I knew it would go no farther this night than sitting at a bar being soaked for expensive drinks, which is essentially what happened, and staring at some female flesh. I expected to be disappointed; but it is in the nature of such ventures into the underworld that you want to know, *in what way* will I be disappointed?

It was a small, surly room, much like an off-off-Broadway theater between productions, perhaps because of the unfinished wooden flats used for dance platforms and the uncertain lighting. On one platform stood a young woman, completely naked, scratching her nose. She looked as though she had just stepped out of a bath and was trying to remember where she had put her glasses. From time to time she would remember to sway vaguely to the beat of the disco music, but mostly she just stood there like a figure model waiting to be told it was time to take a break.

She was a mildly pretty brunette with a ski-jump nose and Slavic features, and I imagined her growing up in one of those goulash-and-paprika restaurants in the East Eighties, where everyone spoke Magyar and the middle-aged men with thinning hair got dressed up on Sundays and told jokes to her chubby mother, who worked the espresso machine, and once a year they all went on a boat ride.

On the other platform, a black woman was shaking for all she was worth, definitely earning her salary. She did an odd trick, which was to put her fingers by her crotch and snap them as if igniting a match — a metaphor. She tried winking and talking sexy to the deadbeat customers, but they — we — were like lobotomy cases with blue stigmata of electroshock on our foreheads.

Crossing in front of her, a much more haggard woman with a see-through nightie and battle-scarred face and bony legs approached us at the bar and asked if we would buy her a drink, "for thirty dollars." We could drink it "inside" if we liked and have some fun. We declined and she went on to another customer.

At a table near the door, the manager (or was he the bouncer?), a heavyset man round like a bowling ball in a shiny black suit, was talking to another man about something he had in his eye. He lowered the skin under his eyelid and showed the other man — a boil or a sty. Then, oblivious to the black woman, who was shaking her hips and trying to maintain at least some semblance of erotic illusion, he got up on the same platform, standing with his back to the audience, to use the tall mirror behind her. He worried his eyelid this way and that, trying to see himself in the dim mirror light. "See, it's all red," he called over to his friend. "I told you it was swollen!"

The man with the carbuncle sharing the platform with the topless dancer was that intrusion of the mundane into the lewd that always strikes me as the essence of Forty-second Street. I don't find it dehumanizing, but rather, all too human. It depends on what your definition of human is.

Lives of the Poets

I̲N the poetry world (it becomes a world only when the business of writing poetry is done, and the isolates break out of their rooms for promiscuous socializing and career promotion), there are certain people you run across at book parties and readings who finally seem friends, although for years your whole contact with them is at social occasions. Pleased to see their warmer faces bob up in these crowded gatherings, you move toward them for what you know will be a generous greeting. Maybe the recognition signaled between you two is based on nothing more than a shared disdain for the same phonies, or pleasure at being alive in the same era. But there is always the potential to take the recognition further into a true friendship.

I had come to feel that way about Greg Cannon. He had an old-fashioned solid manliness and a gentle voice I found protective. One night I ran into Greg at a poetry reading in the East Village. This time we managed to latch onto each other long enough to get out for a beer afterward.

He had on a green-and-black-checkered camping shirt as an outer jacket, and an Indian band. The headband was a sort of joke, I assumed, left over from his hippie days, or a reminder that he was not a native New Yorker but had come originally from out west — Montana, I think. In the way he bounced his weight, up from his toes to his shoulders, in the fierce high cheekbones and black hair and alert eyes behind mild granny glasses, he might still have been stalking something in the woods, absurd as that seemed on Second Avenue. He took his cigarettes out of his left shirt pocket and offered me one.

"How is life treating you?"

"How's life treating me?" He laughed, curling his upper lip back like a wolf. "I'm falling apart. I'm at the point where my teeth have started deteriorating beyond redemption, and I've got lower back pains and the reflexes are slowing down just that extra step. It's downhill from here on in."

"You don't look so broken-down to me," I said. Greg was only thirty-three or so, but he loved to enunciate a philosophy of decline as a point of pride.

"I've been getting hints of my own mortality. I can feel Death laying his creepy fingers on my back."

A whole slew of poetry folk had joined us, taking over several adjoining tables in the bar, among them some younger acolytes fresh out of college. They were fans of Greg's and wrote poems that read like blurred third-carbon imitations of his. In the fast-moving generations of schools of poetry, Greg Cannon was already an Old Master. Maybe that was why he was feeling so old. He and I knew he had barely scratched the surface of his talent, but here they were, imitating him and trying to catch his eye. I was flattered Greg spent the whole time talking to me, especially because it was unusual for him to talk this much ever.

I remember when I first began going to these literary gatherings downtown, ten or fifteen years ago, I was amazed at how *nonverbal* the poets were. None more so than Greg Cannon. I would see him leaning against the wall with a beer in his hand, or politely passing a joint, silent and inward. A lank cowboy leaning against the fence rolling a cigarette. Later I got to know him better and hung out with him at parties, though I can't remember his ever coming uptown to see me.

None of the East Village poets liked to go much above Fourteenth Street. They would drive across the U.S.A. more easily than take a subway to the Upper West Side. Uptown was Mammon, the land of office jobs and straights. Some of it may have been laziness: they just hated to leave their neighborhood, their supportive poets' ghetto with its shared art-making and child-rearing and getting-stoned procedures. Sometimes they seemed like friars who had taken the vows of poverty, dope, poetry, and family.

Coming from universities all over the country, the poets had settled in the broken-down Ukrainian–Puerto Rican neighborhood around St. Mark's Place in the early 1960s, lured by cheap rents, the ethnic streets and each other's company. For a while it was like a grand social experiment. They never made much of the fact that the area was a rather dangerous slum, as though, being from out of town and eager to roost in New York, they didn't seem to notice this. If anything, they regarded themselves as pioneers of some swank breakthrough — an attitude given mixed corroboration when the hippies, runaways, and national media followed their lead, flooding the place around 1967. There were free rock concerts, limos stolen off the street, a few killings. Most of the hippies had disappeared by 1972, but the poets stayed on, raising their families, shopping at the local bodegas, and joining the PTA — a tight community of veterans, older and somewhat grimmer.

I felt a bit out of place when I came down to their poetry readings, because of my steady job, my jacket and tie. I was on the lookout for snubs — once I even heard someone mutter, "Oh, here comes the uptown crowd" — but most of the poets greeted me cordially enough. Especially Greg. At moments he almost seemed to be reaching out to me for a friend. But so much separated us in the way we lived. Perhaps it was not life-styles at all but literary philosophies, he being an avant-gardist like everyone else down there, and I — well, a realist. For writers to be friends, they have to say bluntly what they think of each other's and everyone else's work, since literature is, in the long run, their deepest care. Greg, I am sure, held many secret reservations about my work, and I found it painful not to have the courage to say that many of his poems were incomprehensible to me. They were meant to be incomprehensible, no doubt; he had mastered that bleak modernist surface of echoes in the void. Flat tones, industrial objects, whimsical linguistic transformations and wistful stellar lyricism created a texture as cool, mysterious, passive and forlorn as outer space. I always wanted to ask him *why* he chose this free-fall construction that mocked one's hunger for meaning, but I never got around to it. Even more, I might have liked to ask him how he managed to stamp every blinking line — even the most irritatingly arbitrary — with the music and density of poetry.

But we never got to talking about the secrets of literature that night. Writers rarely let their hair down with each other about the real, fussy discoveries of craft and the specific problems emerging in their writing. Maybe the language doesn't exist for them to talk about it. In any case, Greg and I shot the breeze. He was in a good mood. The more fatalistically he spoke about his life, the more easygoing he became. I wondered why he seemed so expansive. When I asked him how his family was doing, he said his son, Benny, had an ear infection and his wife, Annie, had been "freaking out." I had to conclude that he was just happy to get out of the house.

As we left the cocktail lounge, he told me the reason for his good mood. He had bought himself a telescope. "Come on over to the house. I'll show it to you. It's a great night for it: we should be able to see Mars and Venus. We'll go up on the roof and set it up."

What did I have to lose? I had never had much interest in the stars, but maybe Greg could show me the way to appreciate them.

It was a December night, "unseasonably warm," as they say. We strode down Second Avenue, past Ratner's Cafeteria with its smell of onion rolls, and the boarded-up Fillmore East Theater. There were still some ragged descendants of flower children huddling in the lobby, probably exchanging drugs. A bum was trying to stand up and kept falling back on his seat and cursing. Greg stopped in the candy store to buy an early morning newspaper.

I saw a dead mouse on the sidewalk by the newsstand; its long grey tail I thought at first was a mop string. I thought of pointing it out to Greg when he came out. I thought of saying "dead mouse" or "Look, a dead mouse," but none of the combinations seemed to click, which plunged me into a *déjà vu* sensation of not being able to find the right words. By the time I was over it and ready to say something about the mouse, the moment had passed, we were already a block away.

We went by some Christmas trees on the sidewalk, and Greg told me that he was selling Christmas trees for a living. He and a friend had gotten a good price on sixty trees from an upstate lumberman, and now he was on the street every day, "accosting people like a lunatic."

"It sounds like it could be fun."

"Actually it is fun — when it's not utterly awful. I'm grateful for being pushed out of myself and forced to make deals and approach complete strangers in the street."

"Where do you store them?"

"In my partner's garage."

We were at his house, climbing the tenement stoop to the Cannons' apartment on the first floor. It faced the street, protected by steel window gates. The geranium window box must have been Annie Cannon's touch.

"Are there many robberies?" I asked him.

"We were broken into once. It's not a particularly violent scene . . . except for the Hell's Angels who gun their bikes all hours of the night. I'd like to wake up one morning and find their bikes totaled and their heads bashed in with a monkey wrench. In fact, I'd like to be the one to do it," he said with a swagger.

I had no doubt that Greg had a violent streak; on the other hand, I accepted the statement in the spirit of poetic license.

"Honey, we got company. I brought home Phil Lopate," Greg called as he pushed open the pockmarked metal-plated door with its police lock. A little black Scottie dog ran up to him. Greg pushed his muzzle this way and that, the dog loving it. "Anybody home?" he called.

"Oh, Greg, how could you bring someone home when you know this place is a horrible mess! . . . Sorry, Phil, I've been sick and *Greg* hasn't gotten around to cleaning it yet and the kids don't seem to understand that you can't live in a pigsty."

I stepped over the tricycle and Greg unlocked the wooden gate so that we could pass into the living room. The scissors gate was used to keep the little dog corralled, Greg told me, since he shit all over. But things had already gotten out of hand: jigsaw puzzle pieces were scattered on the linoleum floor next to newspapers with green urine stains; breakfast cups and wine bottles clogged the table.

The inner rooms were pitch-black. Greg switched on a bullet lamp, and orange shadows lit the walls. I jumped when I realized that Annie Cannon was lying on the couch in the dark. Her long blond hair was stringy and unwashed, her chin broken out in fever sores. Her grey-green eyes followed us with some resentment. She pulled the nubby flannel blanket over her jeans, for either modesty or warmth, and started involuntarily to turn toward the wall before thinking better of it and raising herself on one elbow.

"Hi. I thought we'd go up on the roof and let Phil look at the telescope."

"Greg, I'm feeling incredibly awful," Annie answered with a whiny quiver that sounded like trouble to me.

"How was your evening?" Greg asked ingenuously.

"I did nothing but watch television. And I put Corey to bed. She seemed very upset about missing her story."

"Was there anything good on TV?"

"Just 'Creature Feature.' It was *Curse of the Cat People* and I've seen it twice already. Greg, I've just been lying here all night with an incredible fever. It wasn't very considerate of you to stay out so late. The reading must have been over an hour and a half ago."

"How's Benny?"

"He seems all right. . . ."

"Did you get to sleep any?"

"No! I've been home alone with the kids all day and I'm really freaking out!"

"Sorry," Greg said with mild, long-suffering fortitude. "Are they asleep now?"

"*Yes*, they're asleep. I hope you enjoyed yourself while I've been running a high fever. Hi, Phil," she said, managing a pretty smile.

"Hi, Annie."

"I'd get up to say hello but I'm too weak."

"That's fine. I just came over for a quick visit." I looked to Greg for verification but he had already tiptoed silent-Indian-style into the children's room. "Hey, Benny," I heard him say softly. "How're you feeling?" The tenderness of his father voice sent shivers up my spine. Annie shifted her blanket moodily. I imagined she didn't like playing the shrew any more than he liked being at the receiving end. He had the good role: the comforter of his children, the stoical bearer of an outrageously nagging (or so people had begun to speak about her) wife's misplaced rage.

When he had retreated into the kitchen, her eyes went sarcastically up to the ceiling and then over my left shoulder to rest there. She might have been looking through me. We both listened to the noises he was making in the next room, bringing out the telescope from the closet.

"It would be nice if you could stop playing with that — toy for once and think about doing something for me! You care more about the telescope than you do about your wife."

"Maybe you should take some Empirins."

"I *took* three Empirins. What I need is something to drink. I'm dying of dehydration! . . . Did you bring home the ginger ale I asked for?"

"No. Forgot."

"Oh, Greg!" The disappointment made her eyes shine with tears. I began, ficklely, against my will, to shift my allegiance from him to her, like a child who can never decide which parent's side to be on.

"I knew there was some reason I made myself stop at that candy store. Right, Phil?"

"We did stop at the candy store," I confirmed.

"But what's the difference if you forgot?" Annie yelled.

"I'll go out and get it now," he said.

"There's nothing open now. It's too late!"

"The bodega's open."

"The bodega closes at eleven, you know that."

"But sometimes they stay open to play cards. Or else there's that twenty-four-hour place on West Houston Street."

"That's too far. Just forget it, all right?"

"I'm going," said Greg.

"Don't bother."

Now I thought she was being ridiculous. He was already heading toward the door.

"Greg!" she called tensely. He returned to the entrance of the living room with a greyish smile. "Do you have any money?"

"I've got over a dollar."

"I'll go with you," I said, with every intention of leaving.

"No, stay here. You can keep Annie company."

And he left. Too suddenly for me to object. I was not sure I wanted to be left behind with this upset, angry woman whom I barely knew.

I also had a funny tribal sense that he shouldn't have left me alone with his wife so easily, that he was taking her — us — too much for granted.

Some of the embarrassment must have filtered through to her in the silence, though she gave no sign of life except for her uneven breathing on the couch. I looked around the dark apartment to find something to compliment, or at least talk about. I had always found Annie Cannon somewhat sexy, or potentially very sexy, if she had done the least bit with herself. For the moment of course she looked wrung out. It was a look that many of the wives of the poets had: a haggardness from having to answer demanding children and prepare meals in a tiny apartment and stretch the budget while some large white abstracted goofy American male sat at his desk, investigating the experimental properties of language.

It was, if you will, a completely sexist society. The men went off together and played pool and basketball and poker, or read each other their new works; the women took turns baby-sitting for each other. The women were encouraged to pursue some little artistic expression of their own. They made small intriguing artworks, watercolors and collages that they gave out as Christmas presents, or designed clothes and tried to sell them through the local boutiques.

The men were reserved, tall, courtly and thin, like scholarly rock musicians, and they had all married women who were rather traditionally feminine and pretty — it seemed a necessity of this hard life to have a pretty wife, even if most of the time she looked drained. Once or twice a year everyone got all dolled up in satin to show they could still be royal or vampish if they tried, and went off to a fancy uptown soiree like the Gutmans' annual bash or to pose for one of the painters who were constantly doing portraits of avant-garde writers. These pop art–styled paintings invariably glamorized the poets and their wives, smoothed away blemishes or economic strains while turning them into vapid bohemian starlets, "beautiful people."

One such painting hung above the couch, a large study of Greg and Annie Cannon completely nude, in mock-soothing pastels, Adam-and-Eve-ish next to a long-stemmed snake plant. Greg's dong angled to the side like a waiting pencil; Annie had crossed her legs over her sex. Her breasts were very full and her blond hair fell in a single braid over one shoulder. The artist had denied them any expression, but one could imagine, from the way her head turned off to the side, that she was scoffing at the whole enterprise. Maybe not. I found the thing painful.

"That's a nice painting of you," I lied.

"I'm getting used to it," she said. "I used to hate it there; now I don't mind."

My eyes went from the voluptuous nude to the woman on the couch. Her hip curved sharply upward as she faced me, a dungareed odalisque. I wondered if she almost preferred to become one of the peasant women in black, or the bohemian variant of same, in her sadly bleached peasant blouse and embroidered jeans — to ward off complications and temptations. Something about her expressive face with its sour, rebellious spirit gave the lie to resignation. I would have liked to draw her out. Now I was pleased to have been left behind with her, because she suddenly seemed the more vital, the more unpredictable of the two of them.

Just as I was trying to figure out some way to open the whole can of worms, she cleared her throat with determination.

"You must think I'm a real bitch jumping on Greg the moment he comes in the door."

"I figure you had your reasons."

"Usually I let him come and go as he pleases. I don't keep a leash on him. He takes off when he wants to, like tonight. It's just that I hate being alone when I'm sick."

"How long have you had this?"

"Since last week. I must have caught it from Benny. He's been sick."

"And how are things otherwise?"

"Oh, I've been freaking out," she said matter-of-factly, as if they had both come to an agreement to speak of her in these terms. "I was pretty bad a month ago. They were even thinking of putting me in the hospital. Then I stopped climbing walls and now things are back to 'normal.' Greg's got what he wants, a wife to minister to his domestic and sexual needs and take care of his children. He doesn't have to bother with the ordinary hassles so his mind can be free to write poetry. He's starting to make a name for himself . . . but I don't have anything. After ten years I'm still at the same place I started. What's in it for me, you know?"

"What would you like to do?"

"At this point, anything except be a Poet's Wife. The way people treat you! — I don't mean you, Phil. You know, I used to write poetry myself when Greg and I met. And some people said I was even better than Greg." She let that sink in. "That's right. I had talent. I'm not saying I was the greatest poet who ever lived, but in the New School workshop Greg and I were considered the two best. We were considered about equal. Some people even preferred my work. I had poems printed in the original *G Magazine*. Then we fell in love and got married and the next thing I knew he was the poet and I was the wife."

"Still, why didn't you keep writing poems?" I asked.

"Someone had to bring in the rent money! Greg doesn't worry about those worldly things. I *tried* not to let it bother me either. But eventually the anxiety got to me, and in that situation whoever cracks first is the one who loses. And brother, I cracked. I went out and got a job typing in an office from nine to five. When I got home I wasn't in exactly a poetic mood. Then we had Corey and Benjy and since then I've been stuck taking care of the kids and cleaning up after all three of them."

"I agree, it sounds like you got a rotten deal. But didn't you also — help make the situation what it is by accepting those conditions?"

"I know what you think," she said bitterly. "It isn't always a question of masochistic complicity. Sometimes there's just simply a struggle between two people over who's the stronger. I ended up being weaker so I had to give up my life."

Her conviction got the better of my skepticism for the moment, and I dropped the question about past responsibility, which was fruitless anyway. "But it doesn't have to stay that way," I said.

"Oh, they'll let me do a few things on my own. This spring I'm taking a course in modern literature up at Columbia. That should keep me from going crazy."

"Why don't you try writing poems again?"

"This family doesn't need writers. And the truth is that I don't feel like writing anymore. But I'd like to use my *brain* again: read hard books, take exams, anything to get me out of this nonintellectual rut."

"That sounds like a good idea."

"The other thing bothering me is just that I'm tired of being so poor. I don't want us to live in a slum all our lives. This isn't the way I pictured it, believe me. I was brought up in a nice, comfortable home. . . . I'm not saying we all have to go back to being upper middle class like my parents; but when you're raised poor, you know how to make do with little money. I don't. When Greg won a CAPS grant last year, that helped a little. But then he bought me a washing machine and that telescope and coats for the kids, paid off some debts, and pretty soon the money was gone and we were back where we started. At the bottom."

"He's bringing in money now, though, isn't he?"

"Selling Christmas trees," she said scornfully. "That's not serious. Oh, he tries. I don't say he doesn't. He's been pretty considerate lately. But most of the time he's just not here. He's either away at the job or he's sitting in a chair and his mind is on — Mars."

"He told me he hasn't been writing that much lately."

"Don't believe it. Greg writes all the time. *All the time.*" She underlined it. "No, the trouble is he's waiting for some kind of breakthrough and it just hasn't happened yet."

"What is his new stuff like?"

"I don't know, he doesn't show me. I wouldn't be surprised if he hasn't written a really good poem in a long time. He used to write wonderful poems. But some of the poems in his last book I didn't care for. They were like a brick wall to me. Why can't he write poems that move people, poems about humanity and feelings?"

I was stunned to hear her say this and yet I dared not agree; suddenly I seemed to be on very treacherous ground. "I think he would say that the humanist-realistic tradition has been exhausted, that it was sentimental and manipulative," I said cautiously.

"Maybe it is sentimental, but . . . and you don't find what he does with language manipulative? I can't give him advice about his poems; he won't take it," she said, breaking off. "Greg doesn't care about anyone's opinion of him. For a long time I mistook his independence for personal coldness. I didn't know how to get him to like me. He seemed so unapproachable. Now I know he's a warm person and a caring person, but he has these definite limits . . ."

"Like what?"

"You just can't push him. Most of the time I don't know what he's thinking. He'll tell his friends, he'll tell you, Phil, probably before he'll tell me. And I hate to keep nagging him to confide in me. Because he's the kind of person you just can't pressure."

"Why not?"

"Either he gets very sick or he explodes."

"Maybe he can take more than you think," I said, sounding to myself uncomfortably like a therapist, and yet wanting to give her strength to stand up to him. This whole "pressure" business sounded like another alibi.

"I know what he can take. I've pushed him and I've seen him when he reached his limit. I don't want to see him hurt like that ever again."

"But you can't go around on tiptoes and swallow your anger. Greg's not made of glass. You've got to tell him. He can take it," I said, carried away with my family-adviser role. That she seemed to have had no shyness about badgering him just a while ago slipped my consciousness. I was acting out the fantasy drama so dear to my own life, of what would happen if people had the courage to tell the truth.

"I can't," she said calmly, with a finality that piqued me.

"Why not?"

"Because, Greg's an epileptic. You know that."

"No, I didn't. I swear . . ."

"He has seizures. The last one was over two, three years ago; but still, the danger is always over our heads."

I had nothing to say now. It did seem that she had reason to feel trapped.

Annie began playing with the split ends of her hair. Then she cleared her throat, as though making a formal speech. "I never knew anyone like Greg. Greg arrived from another world. Even children in that world knew that when you fall there's no one to pick you up. You go off alone. Trust no one. Greg has that reserved fatalism of western towns. Birching kids early and too much silence in the company of ignorant bastards." So she rolled out her idea of Greg, as if in a trance. I stopped listening at one point, fascinated by the flow of words and the monotonous fullness of her analysis. This was her poem. She had been working on it for years. For all her criticisms of him, I understood that she was just as much in love with Greg as when she had first met him; that she had been hypnotized by him and now was obsessed by him. He had stolen her spirit, and the problem of her life had become to live with this secret of having been overwhelmed by and still adoring a man who remained as remote as a deer that came and went through the window.

If it was any consolation to Annie, I would have bet that Greg loved her as deeply. Amazing. A couple whose passionate love had lasted ten years, camouflaged by domestic bickering. Or maybe I was going off the deep end again.

We heard the key in the lock. Annie stopped talking.

"Hi. Everything was closed. I had to go down to the other end of Houston Street. Here, I got you some oranges too," Greg said proudly. He seemed buoyant as he went into the kitchen for a glass and poured her the ginger ale.

She began coughing violently.

"What's the matter?"

"It must have gone down the wrong pipe. I can't drink any more," she said, pushing the glass away. "Here, Greg, put the rest back in the refrigerator."

"All right. . . . What you been doing while I was gone?"

"Just talking."

"We had a good talk, Annie and I."

"Hey, Frank! Get off my desk. That dog gets into more trouble," said Greg, stroking him behind the ears. "We're going to go up now and look at the stars."

"Don't take too long," said Annie.

"See you." I waved goodbye. "Feel better." She nodded tiredly. I followed Greg, grateful to be getting out of that claustrophobic apartment, but wishing I had found some better way to assure her that our talk had meant something to me. Oh well; she could figure that out for herself.

We went up on the roof. It was a sharp, clear night — clear for New York, that is. Yet when I looked down at the city there was an intervening layer of white smog, warm and fetid, like steam from a ubiquitous Chinese laundry, and it lit up the darkness no less than the neon signs and street-lights did. I realized that New York was a place where night never totally fell. We who lived here all our lives, with our white nights, never knew the elemental power or tragedy of the dark; and in exchange we got the comforting sur-round of neighborly pathos, the skeptical half-night.

Greg had set up the tripod and was cocking the eye of the telescope. "Mars is closer to Earth than at any time in years," he said.

"Let me look."

"One more minute."

I wanted to have the first look. Dexterous and gentle as always, he showed me how to crouch and adjust the focus. As he leaned himself lightly against my back to show me, I suddenly remembered how an older man had once taught me to line up a rifle and fire it when I was thirteen. The same respect for the apparatus, the same calm faith that I could do it, despite my instant of panic that I was the only one in the world who couldn't. "See it?"

"Uh-huh."

Then we tried it with a different lens that brought the body closer. Now the orange blazed. I wanted to look at some stars. I panned with the telescope across a swatch of sky, frustratingly empty and black. I was moving too fast, Greg told me; I had temporarily lost the knack of seeing through the eyepiece. I surrendered it back to Greg. He wanted to train the telescope on Venus, his favorite. "You can't get the gas ring around her as much as usual. Let me try the first lens." He fidgeted a bit with the controls and I stood there, hands in pockets, waiting to have a look.

Greg held the instrument steady as I squatted on my

hams. Seeing Venus all shimmery gave me a rush. "She's sexy!" I said inanely.

"Damn right. Why do you think they gave her that name?" Greg peered through the scope for what seemed like an interminable time at Venus, as though at a sepia photo of a lost love. What a strange mind he must have. I thought of one of my favorite poems of his, with its references to wandering stars and Vivaldi. It was written quite a while before he bought the telescope.

I kept staring at the stars and wondering what the true significance of all this was. Millions of miles away, blinking lights — and so what? I wanted to pick out a lone star from the blanket and he showed me how to bring it in. For the first time it hit me that stars come in all colors, they aren't necessarily white. That was a discovery at least. Then I turned the telescope over to Greg. He was going after remoter bodies. I stood behind him to give him a pure, nonhuman field of vision. He continued to sight one constellation after another. The longer he stayed on the roof, with its sloppy tar foundation and chimney like the mast of a ship, breathing in the cool night air, the more he seemed to find his natural center. Happy. He was happy. His black hair fell in thick wild clumps over the upturned collar of his green hunting shirt; and the odd thing was that he managed to seem absolutely material and absolutely insubstantial. I would have liked to hug him around his plaid woolen shirt, if only to have some human connection to him, but the shirt was more real than he was; he would vanish like a spirit into air without it.

Looking at first tentatively over the edge of the roof, my eyes began to hunger for anything but stars — other tarred roofs, Fourteenth Street, the pool hall, fire escapes. How lovely and interesting this supposedly ugly world looked.

Thank God I lived here and not on Uranus. We had been sighting the stars nearly forty minutes. His wife must be really aggravated by now. I began to picture her downstairs, getting more annoyed by the second, while we stood on her head.

"Let's go down soon. I'm getting chilly."

"Okay. Few minutes more," said Greg.

I walked away for a minute, then pulled at his sleeve. "What would happen if we trained it on that big neon sign with the clock?"

"You want to look at that? It's pretty damn weird. I usually end up by staring at that thing. It's like bringing you down to Burroughs's Nova City in one crunch."

The clock in the display sign had Day-Glo pink markings: I was able to watch the second hand hop from one tingling ridge to the next. It was excruciatingly beautiful, fascinating. I realized that if I had a telescope, earthbound fool that I was, I would train it on these very streets, to see what I knew by heart already with enormous magnification.

Greg unscrewed the tripod legs and the telescope collapsed into smaller parts. "All set?"

"Yes. Let's go down."

He took a final lingering look at the sky. "Funny," he said, "this is the longest I've spent with the telescope since I bought it."

Part

Four

My Early Years at School

IN the first grade I was in a bit of a fog. All I remember is running outside at three o'clock with the others to fill the safety zone in front of the school building, where we whirled around with our bookbags, hitting as many proximate bodies as possible. The whirling dervishes of Kabul could not have been more ecstatic than we with our thwacking book satchels.

But as for the rest of school, I was paying so little attention that, once, when I stayed home sick, and my mother had to write a letter of excuse to the teacher, she asked me what her name was and I said I did not know. "You must know what your teacher's name is." I took a stab at it. "Mrs. . . . Latka?" I said, *latka* being the Jewish word for potato pancakes (this was around the time of Hanukkah celebrations). My mother laughed incredulously, and compromised with the salutation "Dear Teacher." As I learned soon after, my teacher's name was actually Mrs. Bobka, equally improbable. She wore her red hair rolled under a hairnet and had a glass eye, which I once saw her taking out in a luncheonette and showing to her neighbor, while I watched from a nearby table with my chocolate milk. Now, can it be possible that she really had a glass eye? Probably not; but why is it that every time I think of Mrs. Bobka my mind strays to that association? She had a hairnet and a very large nose, of that we can be sure, and seemed to have attained middle age. This teacher paid no attention to me whatsoever, which was the kindest thing she could have done to me. She had her favorite, Rookie, who collected papers and handed out pencils — Rookie, that little monster with the middy blouse and dangling curls, real name Rochelle. "Teacher's Pet!" we would yell at her.

Yet secretly I was attracted to Rookie, and admired the way she passed out supplies, as well as the attention she got.

Otherwise, I was so much in a daze, that once I got sent on an errand to a classroom on the third floor, and by the time I hit the stairwell I had already forgotten which room it was. Afterward, Mrs. Bobka never used me as her monitor.

The school itself was a wreck from Walt Whitman's day, with rotting floorboards, due to be condemned in a year or two; already the new annex that was to replace it was rising on the adjoining lot. But in a funny way, we loved the old school better. The boys' bathroom had zinc urinals with a common trough; the fixtures were green with rust, the toilet stalls doorless. In the Hadean basement where we went for our hot lunches, an overweight black woman would dish out tomato soup. Every day tomato soup, with a skim. Sometimes, when the basement flooded, we walked across a plank single file to get to the food counter. And that ends my memories from first grade.

In the second grade I had another teacher, Mrs. Seligman, whose only pleasure was to gossip with her teacher pals during lineups in the hall and fire drills (when *we* were supposed to be silent). Such joy came over her when another teacher entered our classroom — she was so bored with the exclusive company of children, poor woman, and lived for these visits.

By second grade, I had been anonymous long enough. One day we were doing show-and-tell, wherein each child bragged how he or she had been to the beach or had on a new pair of tap shoes. My parents had just taken me to see the movie *Les Misérables*, and Robert Newton as the tenacious gum-baring Inspector had made a great impression on me. Besides, I knew the story backwards and forwards, because I had also read the Classics Illustrated comic book version. As I stood up in front of the class, something possessed me to elaborate a little and bend the truth.

"Mrs. Seligman, I read a book called *Les Misérables* . . ."

She seemed ready to laugh in my face. "Oh? Who is it by?"

"Victor Hugo." I stood my ground. There must have been something in my plausible, shy, four-eyed manner that shook her. Her timing was momentarily upset; she asked me to sit down. Later, when there was a lull in the activity, she called me over to her desk.

"Now tell me, did you honestly read *Les Misérables*? Don't be afraid to tell the truth."

"Yes! it's about this man named Jean Valjean who . . ." and I proceeded to tell half the plot — no doubt getting the order confused, but still close enough to the original to give this old war-horse pause. She knew deep down in her professional soul that a child my age did not have the vocabulary or the comprehension to get through a book of that order of complexity. But she wanted to believe, I felt. If I stumbled she would dismiss me in a second, and I would probably burst into tears. Yet even then I knew (children know it better than adults) that in telling a lie, fidelity is everything. They can never be absolutely sure if you keep denying and insisting.

Just then one of her teacher pals came in, the awesome Mrs. McGonigle, who squeezed bad boys into wastebaskets.

"Do you know what? Phillip here says that he read Victor Hugo's *Les Misérables*."

"Really!" cried her friend archly. "And you believe him?"

"I don't know."

"What's it about? *I've* never read it. He must be very smart if he read it and I haven't."

"Tell Mrs. McGonigle the story."

"It's about this man named Jean Valjean who stole a loaf of bread," I began, my heart beating as I recounted his crime, aware that I myself was committing a parallel one. By this time I had gotten more than the attention I wanted and would have done anything to return to my seat. Mrs. McGonigle was scrutinizing me sarcastically with her bifocals, and I was much more afraid of her seeing through my deception than Mrs. Seligman. But it came to me in a dim haze of surprise that Mrs. Seligman seemed to be taking my side; she was nodding, and shushing the other woman's objections. Perhaps nothing so exciting had happened to her as a teacher for months, even years! Here was her chance to flaunt a child prodigy in her own classroom before the other teachers. I told the story as passionately as I could, seeing the movie unroll scene by scene in my mind's eye, a foot away from the desk.

"There's only one way to find out," interrupted Mrs. McGonigle. "We will take him down to the library and see if he can read the book."

My teacher could not wait to try this out. She rose and took my arm. "Now, class, I'm leaving you alone for a few minutes. You are to remain quiet and in your seats!" So they marched me over to the school library. I was praying that the school had no such volume on its shelves. But the librarian produced Victor Hugo's masterpiece with dispatch — as luck would have it, a sort of abridged version for young adults. I knew enough how to sound out words so that I was able to stumble through the first page; fortunately, Mrs. Seligman snatched the book away from me: "See? I told you he was telling the truth." Her mocker was silenced. And Seligman was so proud of me that she began petting my head — I, who had never received more than distracted frowns from her all year long.

But it wasn't enough; she wanted more. She and I would triumph together. I was to be testimony to her special reading program. Now she conceived a new plan: she would take me around from class to class, and tell everyone about my accomplishment, and have me read passages from the book.

I begged her not to do this. Not that I had any argument to offer against it, but I gave her to understand, by turning dangerously pale, that I had had enough excitement for the day. Everyone knows that those who are capable of great mental feats are also susceptible to faints and dizzy spells. Insensitive as she was, she got the point, and returned me regretfully to the classroom.

Every day afterward I lived in fear of being exhibited before each class and made to recount the deed that I had not done. I dreaded the truth coming out. Though my teacher did not ask me to "perform" *Les Misérables* anymore, nevertheless she pointed me out to any adult who visited the classroom, including the parents of other children. I heard them whispering about me. I bowed my head in shame, pretending that modesty or absorption in schoolwork made me turn red at the notoriety gathering around me.

So my career as genius and child prodigy began.

"Victor Hugo, *hélas!*" Gide said, when asked to name the greatest poet in the French language. I say "Victor

Hugo, *hélas!*" for another reason. My guilt is such that every time I hear that worthy giant's name I cringe. Afterward, I was never able to read *Les Misérables*. In fact, irrationally or not, I have shunned his entire oeuvre.

Once, a Woman Who Had
Started to Go Out with Me ...

ONCE, a woman who had started to go out with me decided to do some research. She was a feminist and she wanted to know where to place me on the scale of "consciousness." She asked around town about me at bookstores, parties, asked her friends, and came back with a report that I had a clean bill of health; that is, I was not a male chauvinist. Somehow this miffed me a bit, because I know in my heart of hearts that I am a male chauvinist, and because there was something in this clean bill of health that suggested a eunuch. I must be giving off the wrong signal. Or maybe the women she had asked were not attractive to me; I had probably been understanding and polite with them while not making a pass — my sexual lack of interest had been misinterpreted as raised consciousness. On the other hand, I was pleased that they thought me all right.

Her report from the men she had asked was less flattering. Someone in a bookstore whom I hardly knew told her I was "arrogant." In fact, it turned out I had a general reputation for arrogance. It pleased me to hear this too, since it meant I was throwing people off the scent; I know perfectly well how modest I am.

My modesty is something not to be questioned. It is not even modesty, but a correct evaluation of my talents. As a writer, for instance, I will never be a Tolstoy, a Shakespeare, a Thomas Mann. Even Kafka I won't come close to touching. If I work like a dog all my life I will have written twenty books with some nice passages in them that will interest mainly graduate students, the way certain Creole dialect novelists of the nineteenth century are now being studied. Professors whose business it is to know everything about postbankrupt New York City will have to consult my texts. My luckiest stroke would be if, after I die, some discerning editorial intelligence, a Malcolm Cowley or Edward Seidensticker, were to put out an anthology, excerpting passages from the novels, with a few letters and poems thrown in, and pointing out that, while the books as a whole do not stand up, and "he never learned to shape his material, or to cut," nevertheless a sensibility is at work here that is "interesting," or at least characteristic of his time.

Really, the goal of my whole life is one of these Portable anthologies, the Best of So-and-So, remaindered at Marboro Bookshops. So how can you call a man like that arrogant?

Book Titles

M y friend A. wanted advice on naming her book of poems. "How about *Striking Out?*" she asked coyly. "I rather like the double pun: striking out on one's own, and also failing to connect."

"Too self-pejorative. And whatever you do, don't make it a gerund," I counseled. I explained to her my theory of the gerund title. During the early 1970s, when women's books were first having an impact, gerund titles predominated, possibly because of a feminist notion that women were more process oriented than men. "So you had titles like *Changing, Becoming, Emerging, Breaking Loose, Breaking Open, Breaking Up, Getting Off, Slouching Toward —*"

"Enough! Enough. But now the men have started to use gerunds." And she pointed to *Shrinking, Soda-Jerking, Shooting Up* and *Slowing Down.*

"True, the men have finally caught up with the gerunds just when their market value is seriously depleted. It's interesting that the men give their gerunds a guilt-ridden, downbeat turn. The women have begun to move on to two-word abstractions that have an air of mystery and cliché, with a sprinkle of communications lingo: *Loose Connections, Static Signals, On Hold,* and so on. The success of

Final Payments will bring a spate of merchandising contractual titles. And I predict a turn toward the disenchanted in both men's and women's titles; soon we'll be seeing *Sour Hopes, Disappointing Vacations, Queasy Dreams, Unpleasant Mothers* and all the rest of it. Meanwhile, a counter-reaction — euphoria — only partly protected by irony, will make a run for it: *Happy Families, Domestic Tranquillity, Cloud Nine.*"

"How depressing!" said my friend. "Maybe I should start thinking along those lines, since it is the wave of the present and foreseeable future."

"No, don't. I'll never speak to you again."

"You make it very hard on a struggling authoress, you know. What kind of titles *do* you like?"

"I like titles with pieces of clothing or physical descriptions in them. Like: *The White Linen Dress, The Red Flannel Shirt, The Blue Pants, The Gold-rimmed Spectacles, The Girl with One Green Eye, The Man with the Braid, The Dog with the Goiter, The Fat Woman in the Dotted Swiss Housedress* . . ." I would have gone on, but my friend had already put on her coat and left.

For Coffee

The editor invited me for coffee
after his magazine took one of my poems.
He lived in one of those rambling West End apart-
  ments
that doubled back on itself, with double doors
and stacks of complimentary books unopened,
bills on the dining room table.

He'd just shown me in when the phone rang.
"Excuse me," he said and went into the next room.
I snooped around his bookcase. Under
some journals was a personal letter and I could
just barely make out: "Words are useless
at a time like this. . . . Please call if there is something
we can do." I almost moved the pile to read the rest,
but it was clear enough, someone had died.
That might explain his voice each time we'd spoken
on the phone: heavy and tired, deep-piled
with meaning beyond the simple business words.
              "Sorry to keep you waiting,"
he said, steering me into the kitchen
where he ground coffee in a French machine.

"My children will be home soon.
I've got to start their dinner — my wife died recently."

                                        I nodded.
That it was no surprise to me seemed rude.
Yet I did not want to make more of it;
after all, I'd only just met him: he looked no more
than forty, an intellectual, it must have
hit him hard.
                        "What of?" I asked.
"Cancer." And he laughed (what was the joke?).
" 'Cancer,' said the man, lighting a cigarette,"
he mocked himself,
                        shaking the flame out of the match.
"How old was she?"
"Thirty-eight. She was an artist. Sculptor.
Actually more a potter," he emended
uneasily, as though to falsify her after death
in any way was bad luck.
"She laughed a lot. We all knew it was coming.
But still, no matter how much you prepare —"

I shook my head. It all
seemed possible and true.
I looked around the kitchen at the children's artwork
pinned on the refrigerator with magnetic bars:
colored sailboats, a purple horse,
stick figures of a family held in place,
nothing unusual; and on the other wall,
a large rough valentine on drawing paper —
"We love you Mommy!
To the best Mommy in the whole wide world" —
lettered a bit more desperately than usual.

Bachelorhood and
Its Literature

BACHELORHOOD is like the educational system: everyone passes through it at one time or another, however briefly, so that even those who have long ago left that state still consider themselves experts. Yet the figure of the bachelor continues to be blurred by stereotypes, both positive and negative; little is known about the terms of this arrangement with life. Underneath the bachelor's comings and goings, I think you can often find that a deal has been made — a trade-off between certain rewards and deprivations. Even the bachelor may not know how conscious or how final this arrangement is. But for some beginning insights, I have looked to the records of those bachelor writers who dealt systematically with these problems and this terrain.

For a long time I have been interested in a certain point of view in literature, which might be called that of a bachelor narrator. It is particularly prevalent in personal essays, memoirs and diaries, but crops up from time to time in fiction — for example, in the characters of Nick in *The Great Gatsby*, Conrad's Marlow, Kerouac's Sal or Turgenev's "I" in *The Hunting Sketches*. The Turgenev model is the classic type of roaming bachelor narrator who is permitted to

peek into the lives of neighbors and strangers for one long revealing moment, before their self-absorption and his own
queasiness force him to quit the scene. So we are dealing here
with a hit-and-run personality. That may be putting the matter too harshly, too soon. In any case, it seems to me that this
type can be found in the literature of widely different nation-
alities and eras, which leads me to believe that the condition
of bachelorhood encourages certain stylistic adaptations and
perceptions about life, above and beyond local conditions.

For the pure type of bachelor writer, I look not to the
Giants who happened to be unmarried — Balzac, Chekhov,
Stendhal, Proust, and so on — and whose very prominence
overflows the boundaries of the category, but to belletrists
and storytellers of narrower focus. Though they may seem
far removed from one another, I have found much common
ground in the nineteenth-century British essayists Charles
Lamb and William Hazlitt, the modern Italian novelist
Cesare Pavese, the tenth-century Japanese court diarist Sei
Shonagon and her latter-day countryman Kafū Nagai, the
German critic Walter Benjamin, the French essayist Roland
Barthes, and the Chinese short-story writer Lu Hsun.* Of
course the danger in looking at their commonalities divorced from time and place is that of achieving a false synthesis, and concocting a genre for the purposes of hanging
together a number of random insights. Still, I think it worth
this risk to search for a common pattern beneath historical
variations, establishing the perimeters of the bachelor narrator's existence.

There is a difference between the bachelor narrator as a
literary convention or subject, and the bachelorhood of the
individual writers. Inevitably the two may get confused at

---

* I am well aware that Benjamin, Kafū and Hazlitt were married for a
time (Hazlitt twice); but the alliances were short-lived and did little to alter
the essentially bachelor sensibilities of these writers.

some points, but I am more concerned with the former. The type is basically a masculine one, or has been until recently; hence, most of my examples are men (the one exception being the sharp-tongued court lady from Japan, Sei Shonagon). Besides, I feel more comfortable writing about the masculine point of view, since much of what follows will inevitably be an exercise in projection.

We come to the question of motives. Why am I doing this? I suppose it is a search for the self in other texts — a selfish undertaking but a common reason for reading. I also want to share these favorite authors of mine. I identify with this line of writers and, just in terms of crass ambition, would love to see myself annexed to their tradition. They are my sources, my friends when I have wanted company.

The first thing to be noted about the bachelor-narrator style is its liking for the first person. An "I" sets about to establish immediate contact with the reader, through a voice that is personal, conversational, quirky, revealing and opinionated. It is on the whole a trustworthy "I" — oh, games may be played on the borders of the antisocial, and a reader's mistrust courted momentarily, for the fun of it, but there is the rock-bottom reassurance that, while the narrator may not always be nice, may even be obnoxious at times, he is of a whole, and the same person from one page to the next. This solidity of self is offered as the main achievement, lesson and reward of the life described.

The first-person bachelor narrator loves irony, seemingly cannot do without it, because he trusts irony to correct his own misperceptions and prejudices, like eyeglasses for astigmatism. The aim is always truth-telling, clear sight. One may even speak of a *vanity of honesty* in relation to these writers. Irony also comes in handy in drawing a distinction between narrator and writer — a distinction that, as scrupulous professionals, they are bound to make. Charles Lamb goes so far as to set up a quasi-fictional persona, his "Elia"; but the tendency with the rest is to disdain to pretend to any nominal identity other than that on the title page (just as Henry Miller's main character is called "Henry Miller" in his novels). Shamelessly autobiographical, pressing their friends and restaurants into print, they assume that their main strengths as writers lie in analyzing and faithfully recording their life experiences, rather than in trying to concoct imaginary worlds; it is often not even worth the bother to them to make one of those transparent conversions so dear to the modern novelist, like changing the central character's occupation from writer to composer, architect or lawyer. No: if, as I say, some distinction can be felt between writer and narrator, it is not because the writer wishes to disguise the fact that the narrator is based on him, or is speaking his opinions, but because the narrator is inevitably less than the writer.

Irony comes into use both as a playful flavoring and as a confession of the bachelor self's limitations and lack of universality. The bachelor narrator is ever conscious of himself as idiosyncratic, singular. Sometimes this awareness causes pain, but at other times it is a point of pride, a reward for the solitary life.

"It is difficult," wrote the novelist Cesare Pavese in his diaries, "to transform oneself into a Dantesque 'I,' a symbolic Ego, when one's own problems are the product of such an individual experience as the 'city-countryside' and when all figurations lead only to personal and psychological meanings."

Sei Shonagon expressed some surprise at the approbation her "pillow book" journals received when they were uncovered, since "I am the sort of person who approves of what others abhor and detests the things they like."

William Hazlitt wrote, "I am not in the ordinary acceptance of the term, a *good-natured man*, that is, many things
annoy me besides what interferes with my own ease and
interest."

Tastes are no small matter to writers of this type. Their
involvement with the world of art inevitably leads them
into "pronouncements, denouncements and confessions"
(Hazlitt's phrase) of every kind. They have a heightened,
touchy moral sensibility, and are fierce observers of manners, quick to draw the distinction between the considerate
action and the hollow show. But, while in the realm of manners one may speak of their ethical alertness, and in the
realm of aesthetics one may call it taste, in other areas of life
their views come closer to simple *prejudices*. Hazlitt de-
nounces Methodists and small noses; Lamb declares himself
against coast towns and Scotsmen (claims they have no sense
of irony); Shonagon is an encyclopedia of dislikes, from
lovers who dress in a hurry to oxen with large foreheads;
and Kafū Nagai begins his short-story masterpiece, "A
Strange Tale from East of the River," with the ominous
words (for a modern story) "I almost never go to see a
moving picture." Most of the time these admissions of *bêtes
noires*, however silly or slight, are carried by the charm of
honesty; the reader, knowing he has prejudices too, is relieved to find someone else admitting his. Occasionally they
do give offense, as when Lamb goes down the list of peoples
whom he cannot seem to like (Scots, Jews, Negroes, and so
on) and one's own group is lightly satirized. Yet even in this
essay, "Imperfect Sympathies," the point Lamb makes is that
one does not want to be thrown together too much with those
who are not one's kind — a perfectly understandable senti-
ment. The bachelor narrator, generous and in favor of humanity on many occasions, is also scrupulous about delineat-
ing the limits, the imperfections, of his sympathy. His horror

of being considered a nice sweet guy who loves everybody causes him sometimes to exaggerate his rancor against popular love objects, "children and dogs," in a W. C. Fieldsian manner.

The master of this art of insisted-upon spite was William Hazlitt. One of his greatest and juiciest essays is "On the Pleasure of Hating." He gives most attention to friendship (that obsessional area of potential disappointment for the bachelor narrator):

Old friendships are like meats served up repeatedly, cold, comfortless and distasteful. The stomach turns against them. Either constant intercourse and familiarity breed weariness and contempt; or if we meet again after an interval of absence, we appear no longer the same. One is too wise, another too foolish for us; and we wonder we did not find this out before. We are disconcerted and kept in a state of continual alarm by the wit of one, or tired to death of the dullness of the other. . . . The most amusing or instructive companion is at best like a favourite volume, that we wish after a time to *lay upon the shelf;* but as our friends are not willing to be laid there, this produces a misunderstanding and ill-blood between us. . . .

We may try to tamper with the wounds or patch up the carcass of departed friendship, but the one will hardly bear the handling, and the other is not worth the trouble of embalming! The only way to be reconciled with old friends is to part with them for good: at a distance we may chance to be thrown back (in a waking dream) upon old times and old feelings: or at any rate, we should not think of renewing our intimacy, till we have fairly *spit our spite,* or said, thought, and felt all the ill we can of each other.

Hazlitt seems to be having such fun writing this essay that you cannot help coming away from it with a good feeling. The pleased relief he takes in airing his experiences of animosity and negativity shows an unbounded faith in the cauterizing power of telling the truth, which in itself is healthy and positive.

The testy bachelor writer prefers to be known in all his uncomfortable complexities, and doesn't mind at all contributing a little *dirt* to the picture of himself. The obligation he takes on himself to oppose, in a spirit of perversity, some of the ethical assumptions, fashions and received attitudes of the day is a testing of the reader's friendship. He would rather be disliked on the basis of negative information he has furnished himself, than loved right away by others while there is still some doubt in his own mind about having withheld damaging evidence from the scales. "Do not understand me too quickly" (Gide) might be his motto.

It is almost as though he were afraid of receiving that simple, doting, partial, uncomplicated "mother's love" from others, and has armored himself against it with hard-to-take confessions and distinctions of taste. Perhaps all writers are edgy about the public's acceptance of their oddities, wanting but resisting love for the uneasy separateness that drove them to write in the first place. Certainly the parading of idiosyncrasies can draw one closer to others, in a universal conclave of eccentrics. It can also hold people at a distance. Intimacy and marriage can be successfully avoided if one insists that he is too singular ever to be understood.

Pavese says something interesting about this in his journals: "If it is true that a man marries, for preference, his opposite (the 'law of life'), that is because we have an instinctive horror of being tied to someone who displays the same defects and idiosyncrasies as ourselves. The reason is obviously that defects and idiosyncrasies, discovered in someone near to us, rob us of the illusion — which we formerly fostered — that in ourselves they would be eccentricities, excusable because of their originality." *Single* and *singular* seem very close from this perspective, each appearing to hinge on the other.

The perfect format for this temperament in literature is the personal essay, which tolerates large doses of quirkiness and to which bachelor writers have made a disproportionate contribution. Two of them, Charles Lamb and William Hazlitt, were not only friends (off and on) but wrote their best work for the same periodical, *London Magazine*, and in the same years, around 1820. It makes me giddy to think of receiving such a magazine today in the mail, with a fresh essay apiece by Hazlitt and Lamb. Though they have often been contrasted and their differences made much of — Lamb was the more gentle, avuncular, even-tempered and facetious, with a partiality for antiquarian language, while Hazlitt was more controversial, energetic and fierce, and favored a colloquially direct style — the fact is that they shared a remarkable number of strategies and themes. Together they forced the English essay to take a leap forward and become more personal and rapid. Freed from the Johnsonian syntax, its prose was able to catch everything, small and large, of London daily life. The essay became the meeting point for poetry and the short story. It was poetic in the sense that it could make associational leaps and respond to the immediate without excuse — a fast form, like watercolor. At the same time these essays had a strong fictive coloration, due partly to the presence of a powerful character, the narrator, with all his vocal shadings, and partly to the anecdotal subject matter. Many of Hazlitt's and Lamb's pieces — their descriptions of street encounters, their character portrayals of high and low life, beggars, actors, poets — veer from the essayistic toward perfect little short stories.* The essay form seems to offer a protective base from which to make forays into poetry and fiction, without requiring a commitment to the formal architecture of either.

A conversational, warmly opinionated style naturally falls into digressions. It is the hallmark of this style that it loves to wander off the topic. The charm is found in the surprise of unexpected "organic" connections that await the writer who will let himself discourse uninhibitedly. The other gravitational pull on this type of writer is toward the episodic, off-the-cuff diary entry. He has great confidence in conveying the meaning of things by a report of their surfaces. He believes in the concreteness of social reality; and his penchant for commentary and satire on manners has much to do with the way he has trained his senses to note externals. He puts his money on his eyes and ears. The anecdote of the social encounter — justly recorded, without sparing himself or the other person — is often all he needs to portray character. Not for him the empathetic interior monologue, the stream-of-consciousness burrowing into different characters in a story. That would seem almost a presumptuous breach of another's privacy.

Faith in the anecdote well told rests on the confidence that experience itself has form. To put it another way, memories have structures that are akin to the structures in art, and if you as a writer work patiently with them, you may be lucky enough to excavate the organic shape of each. You need to *tell* what happened thoroughly, though, and in the telling will discover the structure underneath the recollection.

* In this, they were like their predecessors Addison and Steele, who also invariably used bachelor narrators and protagonists to get their whimsical impressions across.

Of course there are dangers to this approach; the digressive and anecdotally personal may be paid for by a weakness in overall architecture. There is an inability to see ahead, to "plot," in certain writers of this type, and when, like Kafū Nagai, they try their hand at long fiction, they are unable to pull it off; the novels read like strings of episodes and commentaries that do not build. Even Cesare Pavese, who seemed to care a great deal about literary structure, produced novels that usually leave an impression of disconnected, if engrossing, rambles through fond or alien landscapes.

Why do these bachelor writers have such a negligent or underdeveloped feeling for large, sweeping plots? Can it be that *action* in the traditional plot-fashioning sense is connected to building a family? Certainly one kind of long novel is based on this personally accumulated knowledge: the chronicle of successive generations, like *Buddenbrooks*, showing the tragic alteration of family life. The most important experience of growth that life has to offer may finally be having children and watching them grow up; the bachelor, denied or self-denied this central experience, has a more static relation to the world.

Perhaps there is some truth to Roland Barthes's notion that all narrative is based on the Oedipal complex and marriage:

The relation to Narrative (to representation, to *mimesis*) has something to do with the Oedipal complex, as we know. But it also has something to do, in our mass societies, with marriage. Even more than the number of plays and films of which adultery is the subject, I see the sign of this in that (painful) moment of a TV interview: the actor J.D. is being questioned, "roasted," as to his relations with his wife (herself an actress); the interviewer *wants* the good husband to be unfaithful; this excites him, he *demands* an ambiguous phrase, the seed of a story. Thus marriage affords great collective excitations: if we managed to suppress the Oedipus complex and marriage, what would be left for us to *tell?*

The bachelor writer tries to answer this challenge partly by working with material that, in a sense, can be seen as Oedipally derived, but also partly by taking for himself the smaller and more neglected details of daily life. His pileup of minutiae sometimes becomes a suspenseful tease, like the prolongation of a shaggy-dog story that in the end has no particular point. Sei Shonagon takes the process of recording circumstantial perceptions and rescuing the detritus of daily life quite far. In *The Pillow Book*, shards of episodes are included that seem to have no other point than that they happened; narratives break off easily into lyrical prose poems and lists. Shonagon is an inveterate compiler of lists: there are lists of embarrassing things, things that one is in a hurry to see or hear, things that fall from the sky, squalid things, things that give one a clean feeling, and so on. Nothing is too mundane to escape her commentary: "I cannot stand a woman who wears sleeves of unequal width," she writes. Her attitude toward realistic detail may be seen in this list of "Things Without Merit," which surprisingly trails off after only two entries:

"An ugly person without character.

"Rice starch that has become mixed with water. . . . I know that this is a very vulgar item and everyone will dislike my mentioning it. But that should not stop me. In fact I must feel free to include everything, even tongs used for parting-fires. After all, these objects do exist in our world."

A pride in the "trivial" can be found in many of these writers, especially Charles Lamb, whose discourses cover subjects such as china dishes, roast pig, ears, grace before meals, and whist. Hazlitt poured some of his best writing into descriptions of a prizefight, Indian jugglers, clocks and newspapers. Walter Benjamin was a great collector of curios and old toys. Experts at nonattachment in the romantic sphere, they nevertheless developed a "collector's mentality" that attached itself to curious objects and rare old things. This collecting impulse seems to fulfill a need for ritual and domestic order not otherwise available.

Rituals of another sort have to do with the collecting of cultural experiences and spectacles. What is remarkable at first glance is the richness of resources and amusements that the bachelor narrator maintains close at hand. Theaters, variety halls, restaurants, friends' homes, books, the streets and all the distractions of big-city life fill his leisure hours. The bachelor narrator is an urban creature: first, because only in the city are all these bail-out diversions within easy reach; second, because the city offers him a perceptual field uncannily suited to his quick-scanning temperament; and third, because the city gives him freedom to pursue his fantasies of meeting love just around the corner, a limitless potential for erotic adventures that usually don't material-ize. Walter Benjamin, that student of modern cities, showed he understood this well in analyzing Baudelaire's sonnet about the strolling poet and the beautiful passerby: "Far from eluding the erotic in the crowd, the apparition which fascinates him is brought to him by this very crowd. The delight of the city-dweller is not so much love at first sight as love at last sight." The bachelor narrator, with his psycho-logical investment in remaining single, is addicted to "love at last sight" — needing hope to be revived daily, in the form of beautiful strangers, and needing to see that hope disappear. If for no reason other than the loss of this con-stant visual supply of possible-impossible loves that torture and tantalize him, he could not afford to leave the city.

No writer had a more intimate relationship to his city

than Kafū Nagai to Tokyo. In Kafū's lifetime (1879–1959) he published many novels and collections of essays and short stories; and the nickname he gave himself, Kafū the Scribbler, speaks of both his uncontrollable itch to write and a sense of his own literary stature. Even Kafū's most partisan defenders would stop short of arguing that he was a great writer; he created no rounded, memorable characters except himself, or the thinly veiled narrator who is obviously Kafū — unless you count Tokyo as a character. In some of his tales of romantic entanglements, Kafū's descriptions of the city are so tender — indeed, more caring sometimes than his feelings for the women themselves — that he appears to have transferred his erotic regard onto the very paving stones and night stalls. One could draw maps from the precise street information given in his stories. "And now," he writes, "since it is something I have recently learned, let me play the connoisseur and describe the history of the district" — which he does, in a manner not far from that of Charles Lamb's little "history lessons" about London.

Cities have influenced the prose rhythms and obviously the wandering movement of the peripatetic bachelor writer's style. Baudelaire characterized the supple poetic prose that formed the ideal of such writers' dreams as an urban phenomenon: "This obsessive ideal is above all a child of the experience of giant cities, of the intersecting of their myriad relations." All these writers are great walkers — some very proud of the fact, like Walter Benjamin, or Cesare Pavese, whose city was Turin. The bachelor observer abandons himself in the crowd, which "permeates him blissfully like a narcotic that can compensate for many humiliations" (Benjamin). Walking provides not only an anonymous and vicarious participation in mass life, but also a kind of elongated proscenium. The streets are a huge stage set for the incitement of imagination. Lamb makes this very connection between theater and sidewalk in his essay on city beggars: "When they come with their counterfeit looks, and mumping tones, think them players. You pay your money to see a comedian feign these things."

Think them players. The main point is to be entertained. This type of bachelor (I extrapolate from myself) is an opportunist. If he has nothing on the immediate horizon to take him out of himself, then he will gladly play the melancholy stoic. But such is his fickleness toward suffering that as soon as something entertaining begins to tantalize, he will let himself be dragged off to a show at the drop of a hat. I would like to think it is not necessarily a matter of shallowness, but of being so sure of one's sadness that one has no fear of losing it, knowing it can always be picked up again on returning to isolation. This rapid flip-flop, from bon vivant in company to disenchanted misanthrope the moment one closes the door to be alone, is one of the more alarming tricks of the bachelor personality.

The word *opportunist* may imply a happy-go-lucky fellow who goes around plucking good fortune while others are suffering. But that would be unfair to the race of opportunists: most of us spend the greatest part of our time disappointed, skeptical and watchful. Because a practiced opportunist, who is ready to spring into appreciation given half a chance, knows how rare the real opportunities are and how many turn out to be false leads, he is ever on the *qui vive* to exploit each moment's potential for allure — so much so that he wears himself out. Vulgar prejudice denigrates the opportunist. His is actually a trying métier.

Books are one of the most dependable diversions and companions of this life. It is touching how the writers come forward to testify to their gratitude for books — not only for the pleasure of reading, but for the sacred, sensuous character of the objects themselves. Lamb speaks lovingly about "the sullied leaves, and worn-out appearance, nay, the very odour . . . of an old 'Circulating Library' Tom Jones." Kafū makes a ritual out of airing his books: "Airing my books in the sun of early fall, and burning leaves on an early winter afternoon, were among the chief pleasures of my solitary life." Benjamin devotes a beautiful essay to "Unpacking My Library": "Now I am on the last half-emptied case and it is way past midnight. Other thoughts fill me. . . . Memories of the cities in which I found so many things. . . . O bliss of the collector, bliss of the man of leisure! Of no one has less been expected, and no one has a greater sense of well-being than the man who has been able to carry on his disreputable existence in the mask of Spitzweg's 'Bookworm.' "

As he walks, so he reads; the bachelor writer is a *flâneur* of the bookshelves. "When I am not walking, I am reading; I cannot sit and think. Books think for me," notes Lamb; "I bless my stars for a taste so catholic, so unexcluding." Yet this very catholicity, as Lamb admitted, led in his case to a knowledge that was spotty and disorganized. Such writers make poor Hegelians, or followers of any intellectual system. The same voracious, roaming eye that takes in the streets will wander through the volumes of a library, staying with one field just so long as it charms or diverts. Even Walter Benjamin, the closest to a disciplined intellectual among these writers, appalled his fellow Marxists by the way he was pulled hither and yon by each new reading interest. The intellectual "systems" that writers like Lamb and Shonagon do devise turn out to be largely improvised on disconnected preferences. Their mental strengths lie in being open to contradictory impressions and enthusiasms.

Underneath these enthusiasms for books, cities or the theater is the search for the animating spark, that thing that Hazlitt (and unfortunately Schlitz beer) called "gusto."

This is the holy ark of the bachelor writer's religion. "The problem is to find a new vivacity," wrote Pavese. The bachelor writer generously expresses gratitude to any hobby that will divert him and fill him with the vitality that is necessary to continue writing and living.

At times, there is a conscious admission that the diversions are not enough — are in fact an evasion. Such is this crucial statement, or lament, by Hazlitt: "So have I loitered my life away, reading books, looking at pictures, going to plays, hearing, thinking, writing on what pleases me best. I have wanted only one thing to make me happy; but wanting that, have wanted everything!" Even here, you can read between the lines a certain ambivalent satisfaction; it doesn't sound like such a bad life. Not everyone can get away with "writing on what pleases me best." And actually, Hazlitt records happier feelings about the whole of his life in another text: "I have had nothing to do all my life but think, and I have enjoyed the objects of thought, the sense of truth and beauty, in perfect integrity of soul. No one has said to me, *Believe this, do this, say what we would have you;* no one has come between me and my free-will; I have breathed the very air of truth and independence. Compared with unbiased, uncontrolled possession of the universe of thought and nature, what I have wanted is light in the balance, and hardly claims the tribute of a sigh."

This statement reveals a great deal about the literary bachelor temperament. Again, mention is made of the thing "wanted," or missed, without its being specifically named (I assume it is love). There is a kind of *deal* hinted at here, in which one will agree to forfeit claims on a loving life companion and a family, in return for "possession of the universe of thought and nature." When Hazlitt writes that "no one has come between me and my free-will," he may be referring to publishers and bosses, but I cannot help also thinking of that very creature whose absence occasions a sigh.

The bachelor writer's being in the world, and *having* the world, in the sense of perceptual possession, seems to rest on an act of renunciation of the dyadic focus. It is as though we were superstitiously convinced, however irrational this may appear to others, that the very fact of seeing clearly is contingent on remaining single. The bargain has been struck — a devil's contract, perhaps, burning and chafing; yet the idea persists that the perceptual apparatus will become clouded if the writer spectator enters into a marriage union. What is the basis for this conviction? Is it merely that, having developed clarity and literary powers in a bachelor state, one is afraid to risk changing the formula? Or is this conviction based on an accurate assessment of personal limits?

Whatever the reason, the bachelor writer has achieved an *intactness of self*, at a cost of effort and early family struggle one can only surmise, and will fight anything that poses a threat to that delicate synthesis. Hence his caution before embarking on any liaison that might unbalance his observer role. Flexible as few are in response to the varieties of humanity, art and ideas, he becomes inflexible the moment his means of exploring the world — his detached writer's eye — is threatened. I should make clear that it is a (perhaps antiquated) conviction of this type that one *can* see clearly, that the world *is* fairly knowable in an objective sense — at least so long as he is allowed to follow his method of peripatetic experiencing and collecting everyday objects and impressions.

A bachelor's clinging to the minutiae of daily life has something puzzling and poignant about it, especially in view of his being locked out of what society regards as the heart of the quotidian: family life. It is almost as if we were saying, We who are excluded from what you consider the central axis of social existence, the nursery and the conjugal hearth, will make a life out of the ephemeral impressions and bric-a-brac that chance throws our way. This is not too far removed from some homosexuals' setting up of decorator shops — collections of camp nostalgia and wryly superfluous items of domesticity, where each object is given a faintly sarcastic and, I might even say, subversive twist. On the other hand, the bachelor (as do many homosexuals) often has a more conventionally pious attitude toward domesticity than most married people. "Bachelors regard matrimony more seriously than married people do," noted Pavese, who also observed in a diary entry that he did not understand "the craze so many people have to break away from the bourgeois mentality."

In short, the bachelor narrator does not see himself as an "outlaw" against bourgeois society. From an objective point of view, a bachelor's way of life may well be a threat against the established social order, but he himself does not experience it that way. Quite the contrary; he prefers to play the role of the honored dinner guest — like Henry James, who confessed to accepting 107 dinner-party invitations over one winter. The bachelor narrator's antagonism toward married, settled society is kept under close wraps, and checked always by irony (a vigilance against "sour grapes"). For the most part one expresses pleasure at being invited as a spectator into people's homes, to witness the sport of marriage and all the other diversions of family life, to lend a hand or put in a helpful word during domestic troubles, and then to go away again, back to the bachelor quarters, and think about what one has just seen.

Sometimes a bachelor's pride may be roughed up a bit at the hands of insensitive happily married people. I have had times when I made it a rule to stay away from married folk as much as possible. There is a delicious essay of Lamb's, "A Bachelor's Complaint of the Behavior of Married People," that begins: "As a single man, I have spent a good deal of my time in noting down the infirmities of Married People, to console myself for those superior pleasures, which they tell me I have lost by remaining as I am." Lamb proceeds to complain of their embarrassing demonstrations of affection in front of him; of the wife's complacent looks that tell you "that her lot is disposed of in this world: that *you* can have no hopes for her"; of being silenced on matters of cooking and marketing as an "incompetent" old bachelor; and of being called on to adore their children indiscriminately, "to love all the pretty dears, because children are so engaging."

Yet, in spite of the pain that Lamb's essay touches upon, it is surprising, finally, for its lack of venom. The condemnation is light, and the author seems grateful, all in all, to be included in the domestic lives of others. Sometimes, though, one's alienation around married people is not to be denied. Roland Barthes, whose sense of exile from the communal scene may have been heightened by his being a homosexual, wrote compellingly of this: "A man of paradox, like any writer, I am indeed *behind the door*; certainly I should like to pass through, certainly I should like to see what is being said, I too participate in the communal scene; I am constantly listening to what I am excluded from; I am in a stunned state, dazed, cut off from the popularity of language."

He (writing of himself in the third person) comes across a wedding:

Walking through the Church of Saint-Sulpice and happening to witness the end of a wedding, he has a feeling of exclusion. Now, why this faltering, produced under the effect of the silliest of spectacles: ceremonial, religious, conjugal, and petit bourgeois (it was not a large wedding)? Chance had produced that rare moment in which the whole *symbolic* accumulates and forces the body to yield. He had received in a single gust all the divisions of which he is the object, as if, suddenly, it was the very *being* of exclusion with which he had been bludgeoned: dense and hard. For to the simple exclusions which this episode represented to him was added a final alienation: that of his language: he could not assume his distress in the very code of distress, i.e. *express it:* he felt more than excluded: *detached:* forever assigned the role of the witness whose discourse can only be, of course, subject to codes of detachment: either narrative, or explicative, or challenging, or ironic: never *lyrical,* never homogenous with the pathos outside of which he must seek his place.

In this passage Barthes provides an explanation of the detached, ironic bachelor-narrator style by rooting it in the terms of bachelorhood, which calls on one to be a witness. His statement that this posture forbids lyricism is a curious one, since it would seem to me that the personal essay often relies on the lyrical — or the mock-lyrical — to get things going. But Barthes is using the word *lyrical* in the sense of merging with or belonging to the scene of pathos being described, and in that sense he is correct. The distinction might be that the bachelor narrator's mode is not lyrical but elegiac.

He rhapsodizes the routines of daily life; consequently he is driven into elegy, since to celebrate the quotidian is to grasp at the fugitive. This was certainly true of Charles Lamb, many of whose best descriptions were given over to old neighborhoods, since modernized, to old practices, now deceased. As Hazlitt wrote about his friend: "Mr. Lamb has a distaste to new faces, to new books, to new buildings, to new customs. . . . He evades the present, he mocks the future. His affections revert to, and settle on the past, but then, even this must have something personal and local in it to interest him deeply and thoroughly." The same was true for Hazlitt. "If there is anything which delights me in Hazlitt," noted Robert Louis Stevenson, "it is the loving and tender way in which he returns again to the memory of the past. . . . The imaginary landscapes and visions of the most ecstatic dreamer can never rival such recollections, told simply perhaps, but still told (as they could not fail to be) with precision, delicacy and evident delight." Kafū Nagai could not stop regretting the coarsening of everything in the modern world compared to the way it had once been. And Walter Benjamin was another who believed that "the amount of meaning is in exact proportion to . . . the dead occurrences of the past which are euphemistically known as experience."

Perhaps in childhood resides the lost order, "the deep-seated memory of an underlying harmony, the sense of which haunts life," as John Dewey put it. The bachelor narrator has carried more than a little of the equipment of childhood with him, in his love of miniatures, toys, spectacles and sacred objects, whimsy and holidays, and in his avoidance of certain responsibilities traditionally associated with adulthood, such as raising a family. Lamb put it beautifully when he made this discerning comment about Elia, his stand-in narrator: "He was too much of the boy-man. The *toga virilis* never sat gracefully on his shoulders. The impressions of infancy had burnt into him, and he resented the impertinence of manhood."

Pavese was quick to say, "There is nothing fine about being a child; it is fine, when we are old, to look back to when we were children." Yet his insistence that children are miserable should not be taken necessarily as a retreat from looking back. Declaring your childhood unhappy is one of the surest ways of binding yourself to it. In fact, one reason why the bachelor narrator may not be able to make real for himself the "ashes" of a childless old age that his relatives keep predicting for him is that he is so close to his childhood phantoms that he cannot imagine losing that tie with the young.

The emotional conservatism of the authors in question, and their tendency to locate themselves in the past, should not be taken to mean that they supported reactionary politics. On the contrary, Pavese and Benjamin and Lu Hsun all came close to joining the Communist party, and Hazlitt was certainly a defender of progressive causes. In Pavese's case, what he called the "profession of moral politics, contact with the masses," represented a dream of "inner well-being" and simplicity, and perhaps an escape from bachelor's bad conscience. But a pattern can be seen in the way that Benjamin, Pavese and Lu Hsun all flirted with joining the Communist party and then shied away from tying the knot. On one level, the independence of thought that Hazlitt prized so highly makes these writers tend fiercely to resist party discipline; on another level, there is a very real terror of becoming "engaged," in a sense that couples both meanings of the word: *engagé* and *fiancé*.

Lu Hsun (1881–1936) is an interesting case because he examined political questions and wrote polemical articles more readily than the others. Yet his favorite narrator, a solitary first-person bachelor observer obsessed with the past, is brother to Hazlitt, Kafū and Lamb. Lu Hsun shared with them a liking for personal essays, prose poems and childhood vignettes. He was also, like them, a fundamental skeptic, who disdained "writing under other people's orders" and mocked the concept of "revolutionary literature" (notwithstanding which, Mao had him named posthumously as commander of China's Cultural Revolution, and his collected works are in massive reprints today). Lu Hsun also scoffed at the idea of "revolutionary love." "I think there is only non-revolutionary love," he wrote in a letter. "With sex as with food, there can be temporary selection but no personal involvement." Here the old bachelor voice asserts itself from within the political ideologue.

Sympathetic as he was to the peasants, Lu Hsun wrote many more stories about the distresses of his own class, the straitened lower-middle-class intelligentsia. These were the trained humanities scholars who, after graduating with ambitious idealism, found themselves, like many present-day counterparts, economically superfluous. In one such story, the delicate "In the Wine Shop," Lu Hsun's bachelor narrator returns to his hometown and runs into a destitute ex-classmate, listens to the scholar's meandering confession of sinking into mediocrity, and then wanders off alone, "refreshed" by the sight of "the white, shifting web of thick snow." Poetic perception is regained by dipping into, without taking on, someone else's misery.

In terms of class, many of the men of letters discussed here made their livings at the margins of the journalistic world, and were intertwined both psychologically and economically with that free-lance existence. Walter Benjamin, in his magnificent unfinished study, *Charles Baudelaire: A Lyric Poet in the Era of High Capitalism*, connects the economic development of the early nineteenth century with the rise of *feuilleton* journalism and the emergence of the *flâneur*. The *flâneur* was one who strolled the boulevards, affecting idleness, observing all; the literary expression of this type filled the periodicals' back pages with "Talk of the Town" snippets of city life. The public showed an increasing appetite for light essays, genre and character sketches, anecdotes and verbal panoramas. It took a specialized eye to satisfy this market, "the gaze of the *flâneur*, whose way of living still bestowed a conciliatory gleam over the growing destitution of men in the great city" (Benjamin). The *flâneur* was situated between the powerful bourgeois class and the poor, at home with neither, but able by his special viewpoint to reconcile each to each. He could render beggars in the streets picturesque and therefore part of the eternal landscape, as in Lamb's essay on beggars. Benjamin saw these writers as spokesmen for "the petty bourgeoisie, which . . . was only at the beginning of its decline. Inevitably, one day many of its members had to become aware of the commodity nature of their labour power. But this day had not yet come; until that day they were permitted, if one may put it that way, to pass their time. The very fact that their share could at best be enjoyment, but never power, made the period which history gave them a space for passing time."

Benjamin's insight into these men of letters' historical impotence, which turns them into butterfly men flitting from one entertainment to another, is chilling but well taken. I am reminded of Hazlitt's earlier-quoted statement: "So have I loitered my life away, reading books, looking at pictures, going to plays. . . ." It makes me wonder if the bachelor-narrator style itself implies a politics, above and beyond its practitioners' stated political views. The prose style of the bachelor narrator is idiosyncratic, digressive, skeptical, observing, unhortatory. Such a voice seems to imply that it is not for its owner to take power or change the world, but at best to watch and enjoy the life into which he has been thrust, and at worst to endure it. As for whiling away large units of time, what better way has ever been devised than writing?

The reward for solitude is work. As the bachelor writer grows older, his love of work becomes a major reason for keeping marriage at a distance. An author creates in his writing the loved object and the undisappointing respondent, who will give back to him understanding and charity. It is no exaggeration to speak of a writer's having an amorous relationship with the act of writing, which indeed may be his primary love relationship. (The trite comparison between finishing a book and giving birth applies here as well.) Elizabeth Hardwick once made a strange but understandable comment: "I think all writing is profoundly unmarried." The seclusion that writing necessitates must be arranged for by married writers through the offices of an understanding mate, whereas with bachelor writers it is virtually guaranteed from the start.

In discussing Walter Benjamin's melancholic stance in the world, Susan Sontag addressed this problem:

The need to be solitary — along with the bitterness over one's loneliness — is characteristic of the melancholic. To get work done, one must be solitary — or, at least, not bound to any permanent relationship. Benjamin's negative feelings about marriage are clear in his essay on Goethe's *Elective Affinities*. His heroes — Kierkegaard, Baudelaire, Proust, Kafka, Kraus — never married; and Scholem reports that Benjamin came to regard his own marriage (he was married in 1917, estranged from his wife after 1921, and divorced in 1930) "as fatal to himself." . . . For the melancholic, the natural, in the form of family ties, . . . is a drain on the will, on one's independence; on one's freedom to concentrate on work. It also represents a challenge to one's humanity to which the melancholic knows, in advance, he will be inadequate.

Part of the guilt in being a bachelor has to do with the suspicion, amounting to an abstract judgment on the part of the world and sometimes the bachelor himself, that he has been "inadequate" to meet "a challenge to one's humanity."

Yet the tension of bachelorhood, as far as I can see it, is that one can never be sure whether one is finally a human failure at this business of being able to love, and so be it, or whether one has simply not had the "good luck" to run across a suitable mate. There is always the chance that love or marriage will enter in the final hours, as it did for those old bachelors Balzac, Chekhov and Kafka. It is impossible for the bachelor — except one absolutely determined to remain so — to know for himself whether he is evading a call to love, or making himself ready to answer one. Given the passivity and the waiting, and the tentativeness of the identity of "bachelor" (which only hardens into a certainty when the eyelids are closed), bachelorhood seems to be a state almost structurally guaranteed to produce rationalizations.

It is not always easy for a bachelor himself to locate a moment when some "challenge" was sidestepped — a questionable judgment in itself. Such judgments presume that love is readily available and that anyone who does not choose a loving partner is being obstinate, selfish or perverse. However, hindsight helps. There may be the figure of a "lost love" in the shadows of one's personal history, like Elia's Alice, whose disappointing choice of someone else after a long courtship becomes mythologized into the reason for a life of bachelorhood. Often, as in Lu Hsun's story "Regret for the Past," the youthful love is sentimentalized retrospectively as a crossroads, or crucial test, which the bachelor narrator now sees himself as having failed: if only he had been less demanding, less choosy, he would not have rejected the love of this good devoted woman and would now be happy.

These incidents almost have a religious function for the writer: they "testify" to that crucial negating incapacity to get over the hump, like Kierkegaard's untaken "leap of faith" regarding Regina, which leaves a taste of mystery and awe in the mouth of the failed leaper. The failure itself is equivocal; he has, on the one hand, been unable to embrace trust in another, but has succeeded passionately, on the other hand, in embracing his solitude for the future.

If the rewards of solitude are work and self-definition, its drawbacks are loneliness, self-pity and temptations to suicide. There comes a time when the bachelor is alone with himself, can no longer be diverted by entertainment or work; when he is thrown back on his irreducible isolation. It is a dangerous time, though it is also perhaps the base, the necessary emptiness from which all productivity arises. No one wrote as candidly about living alone as Kafū Nagai, especially in his later years as a grumpy old bachelor. The unapologetically forlorn tone may be gathered from this passage from his short story "Quiet Rain":

There were times, after I fell victim to an intestinal ailment and on cold nights would have to light a fire to warm my medicine, when I wished some kind lady were around to take care of me; but I did not then, as I do now, look upon my solitude as a trial. Indeed, its quiet, melancholy music was an inexhaustible spring of poetry. . . . As long as there is poetry, the life of solitude need not be a life of loneliness. . . . But the poetic urge is a strange, mysterious affair. It does not come when you beckon or answer when you call. In your solitude you seek the promptings of poetry and they fail to come, and for the first time solitude moves from melancholy to sheer wretchedness. And the solitary pleasure in which the poet so prides himself, the pleasure of reminiscence and reverie, becomes a source of regrets and descends to womanish complaining.

By "poetry," I think it is fair to assume that Kafū is not speaking only of verse, but of that luminous effusion the world gives off to the properly receptive, intoxicated spectator. But this slant, this trick of the mind, is impossible to hold on to: "If it rains for three days the stomach cramps invariably come back, and I find myself sunk in truly dyspeptic thoughts." Kafū has another story called "Getting a Cold." Illness, however minor, can become a life crisis for the bachelor. The headaches and "rheums" these writers often complain of, just short of hypochondria, seem to be an opportunity for dramatizing the pathos of their isolation, a theatrical reproach to the world. Such occasions also offer the opportunity to indulge and mother oneself, as in Lamb's essay "The Convalescent": "He makes the most of himself; dividing himself, by allowable fiction, into as many distinct individuals as he hath sore and sorrowing members. Sometimes he meditates — as of a thing apart from him — upon his poor aching head. . . . Or he pities his long, clammy, attenuated fingers. He compassionates himself all over; and his bed is a very discipline of humanity, and tender heart . . . world-thoughts excluded — the man a world unto himself — his own theater — *What a speck is he dwindled into!*"

If Lamb mocks the bachelor convalescent's self-involvement, gleefully turning him into a kind of incredible shrinking narcissist, Kafū conveys the raw side of illness. Indeed, Kafū's writings could almost be read as a cautionary tale of what happens to the bachelor in old age. Yet, he reserves a little ironic affirmation up his sleeve: "A person need not despair while he still has the spirit to grumble."

To move from Kafū to Cesare Pavese is to descend from grumbling to something grimmer: a suicidal temperament trying both to stave off and embrace the final act. In the complicated equation of the bachelor writer's life, suicide is a temptation to be warded off at all costs by ritual enjoyments and daily preoccupations — or else succumbed to, as with Pavese and Walter Benjamin. To the bachelor incompletely reconciled to living alone, suicide may present itself as the avoided but secretly wished-for marriage, contact, merging; and death may seem to bring peace, or a relaxation of the severe discipline of self. However, the very idiosyncrasies of the bachelor character are usually marshaled successfully as life defenses.

It is only when we come to someone like Pavese that we see this system of defenses breaking down. Here is one of the many balance sheets of his bachelor life that Pavese draws up in the diaries: "Every man has a woman, a human body, peace. But have you? . . . You are alone. Having a woman to talk to is nothing. All that counts is the press of body against body. Why, why are you without that? 'You will never have it.' *Everything has its price"* (my italics).

What makes Pavese different from the others is that he seems to think he is the only one who lives alone; he does not recognize the society of bachelorhood, with all its shared eccentric and mundane elements; he assumes, instead, that his situation is purely deviational, a personal psychological quandary that he must rack his brains to solve. There is none of that cheerful understanding of Lamb, who says, in effect, I am a boy-man and that's the way it is. Pavese is not interested in the humorous side of this question; rather, he pits himself in Promethean struggle against his own isolation. Having certain programmatic notions about the nature of nobility and maturity, a strong picture in his head of moral wisdom and its commandment to break out of self-centeredness, he is tortured, both by how far short of this stage of development he falls, and by a petulant inner demand that his needs for a woman be filled, *now*. On the one hand he is pulled toward resignation and stoicism; on the other hand, toward an almost juvenile rage at being "cheated." I don't mean to criticize Pavese; most bachelors have felt the same way, when they have allowed themselves to.

Pavese's prose aches with lack. Whereas Lamb joshes about the happiness of married couples and Hazlitt stops just short of naming the minus in his life, Pavese crosses the line and intentionally embraces self-pity. It is no less self-pity for having a tone of astringent, dry self-criticism. But this is Pavese's strength and uniqueness as a writer — his drive to question the mystery of loneliness, his refusal to take it for granted. Here he tries to puzzle it out:

The greatest misfortune is loneliness. So true is this that the highest form of consolation — religion — lies in finding a friend who will never let you down — God. Prayer is giving vent to one's thoughts, as with a friend. Work is an equivalent to prayer, since ideally it puts you in contact with something that will not take advantage of you.

The whole problem of life, then, is this: how to break out of one's loneliness, how to communicate with others. That explains the persistence of marriage, fatherhood, friendship, since they might bring happiness! But why it should be better to be in communication with another than to be alone, is a mystery. Perhaps it is only an illusion, for one can be perfectly happy alone, most of the time. It is pleasant now and then to have a boon companion to drink with, provided that what we ask of others we already possess within ourselves. The mystery is why it is not enough to drink and fathom our own individuality alone; why we should have to repossess ourselves through others.

The possibility of *self-sufficiency* is like a standard Edenic myth for all bachelors. In Pavese's case it was never a serious option; he still needed people to launch his solitude. "Now P — ," he noted wryly about himself in a letter, "who is clearly a solitary, is the living martyr of his own opposed needs. He wants to be alone — and he is alone — but he wants to be alone in a circle of friends aware of his loneliness."

Sometimes Pavese achieved the self-sufficiency he dreamed of. At the end of a long writing day he could relax into it. "You have started spending your evenings alone again, sitting in a corner of the little cinema, smoking, savoring life, and the end of the day, watching the film like a child, for the adventure, the brief pleasure of beauty or an awakened memory. And you enjoy it, you enjoy it immensely. It will be the same at seventy, if you live so long." But he did not; he committed suicide at forty-two, in 1950.

"Blood is always shed irrationally. . . . Your modernity lies wholly in your sense of the irrational," wrote Pavese. Most of the other bachelor writers discussed here have less "modernity" by these standards; they would shy away from the irrational or apocalyptic. They were considerably milder, more skeptical, amused and nonviolent in their habitual expressions. To a modernist taste, the work of a Lamb or a Kafū may seem to be lacking in *bite* and elemental terror. Perhaps that is a shortcoming, but it also must be understood that their strength lies elsewhere: the underlying meaning of the bachelor-narrator style is a dedication to the art of survival.

To the degree that the frustration of romantic and sexual needs constitutes, in an extreme case like Pavese's, a threat to survival, and, at the very least, a disturbance in the bachelor writer's psychic housekeeping, it seems understandable that he may welcome those moments when there is a cessation of desire. They restore one's freedom to observe ubiquitously and unenviously. This expanded freedom to watch, at the moment of relinquishing sexual intentions, comes across in Walter Benjamin's account of a drug experience, "Hashish in Marseilles": "My mood was free of all desire. It was amusing to see a young man with a girl in a white dress coming toward me and to be immediately obliged to think: 'She got away from him in there in her shift, and now he is fetching her back. Well, well.'"

Some of the same relief can be seen in Kafū Nagai's boast about being let into the backstage dressing rooms:

The place where I chose to pass my time was neither the star's room nor the singer's. It was rather the big room where the dancing girls lay sprawled about. There had been a warning from the police that men who had no business there were to be seen in the room under no circumstances. I alone had complete freedom of access. . . . There ought to be elaborate reasons that this should have been the case. . . . Perhaps it would be simplest to say that when I first visited the dressing room, I had reached what might be described as a most advanced age of discretion, and was therefore seen as one who no longer had the physical capacity to do damage to the public morals, in whatever numbers and whatever postures of abandon naked women might surround him.

Kafū in his old age in the crowded dressing room, watching under a tangle of arms and legs — not an unpleasant image of the bachelor narrator's fate to take away with us. As long as he still has the eyes to gather fresh impressions that can grow into commentary, he will feel reasonably satisfied. Perhaps all along this type has aspired more than anything to becoming an old man; as a student of survival, he looks forward to merging with the half-crochety, half-tolerant elderly spirit he has carried so long inside himself, practicing for the day.

It is not a paradox that the bachelor should have large doses of both young boy and old man inside him. Those are the two periods in life when he can be most socially and personally at peace. The pressure to procreate is off him; he rejoins the universal.

Has it been a good life? Some will find it enviable, others pathetic, and both may be right; for it would seem that a bachelor's way of being in the world is both rich and arid, exciting and static. It is not for me to pass final judgment on the bachelor life. To assume that single people of either sex are emotionally crippled because they have not formed a marital bond is, for one thing, to project onto the majority of married society a much more developed sense of maturity than has been demonstrated in real life. However, there is an equal danger now from the other direction: to be self-righteous about being single, as though bachelorhood were a contemporary virtue or a "vanguard" position. A loner should not be sneered at, nor should he be regarded as heroic or allowed to gloat. The understanding that, collectively, bachelor writers have conveyed about the limits and rewards of this solitary condition helps us to envision a possible balance between these two distortions. For one who finds himself in such a position, the best that can be wished is that advice which Nietzsche gave himself — *amor fati,* to love one's fate — and I would add, without necessarily wishing it on anyone else.

The Greek Coffee Shop

W E bachelors are moved to eat often in cafés and restaurants. The proximity of warm bodies and loud conversation seems reassuring, while the act of being served hot food simulates the family scene. I take my place at the communal table, asking both to be ignored and to be fussed over, waited on. A bachelor is, in a sense, one who has never stopped being a Son — a favorite son, perhaps, though not always; in any case, one is certainly not the father. I return to the restaurant to reclaim my filial prerogative, that of the working grown-up son who should be served no matter what hour he comes in.

The waitresses are my sisters and my mother. Sometimes, in the way I look them over as they travel toward me and away, they become, too, a sort of harem of potential lovers. But for the most part, my shyness and the quasi-incest taboo combine to place the waitresses off limits. I eavesdrop on their private conversations, think — or imagine — I know their hopes and dreams, and in the end leave them alone. Usually I am content with the perfect fantasies of "love at last sight" that reality offers me as its shadow.

The real world affects me so thoroughly as a concluded

composition that I am sometimes loath to intrude myself and disturb it. It is my bachelor observer's vanity that I can make myself a totally invisible, noninterfering presence in these places. I frequent restaurants not to meet people but to experience myself in crowds. This is the same "solitude-in-crowds" that has become such a cliché criticism of life in big cities, but that the experienced urbanite finds a light enough burden for the pleasures of being given a ringside seat.

I like to go to a Greek coffee shop around the corner, which has become very popular — too popular lately. Although I like to think I am getting to know the regulars, I always take along a newspaper or book so that no one will talk to me. On some nights I become so irritably antisocial that it disturbs me if people are talking at a nearby table and I am forced to hear their conversation while eating. I will even change tables if the food hasn't arrived, just to get away from some garrulous dumbbells. This changing of tables can become a mania with me, as I search the whole place, rejecting one because it is too near a draft, another because it abuts the kitchen's swinging doors, until I find the most remote red formica top. Then there are nights when I welcome a nearby discussion. What I like best is to have some quiet conversation a table behind me, which I can listen in on if I sharpen my ears — preferably a tense, repressed conversation between two people in which each statement is a grudging revelation.

I also like to sit catty-corner from a woman eating alone, a table in front of me. She needn't be attractive. In fact, if she is too beautiful the meal is spoiled. I keep feeling throughout the dinner that I should act, introduce myself. Best on the digestion is a woman in between ugly and pretty, who is unaware that I am stealing glances at her.

She could be reading a book, and I could be straining my eyes to make out the title. Sometimes, halfway through the meal, a friend joins her, just as I was getting bored, and she looks up with a mixture of reproach and relief, and I get to imagine what their relationship is like.

You can find me here often after a long workday, sitting in a window booth if I'm lucky enough to get one. I know as well as anyone that the food isn't very good. It's bad nourishment, and unimaginatively cooked. "That's why you get so many colds," says my friend Emily. "You shouldn't eat in those restaurants so much." Well, I'll learn how to cook someday. As a matter of fact — but I'm getting off the point. I come here to the Athens to think; to sink into the formica.

It's the same with cabs. I love to take cabs when I'm zonked out, and huddle in the backseat with supreme weariness. This coffee shop is like a big yellow cab for me. A cab going nowhere. Or it is like those diners that resemble railroad cars that have suddenly stopped, slid off the tracks, and settled awhile to think things over. I like to stare out the window on a foggy night, my bacon cheeseburger deluxe on the fire, with maybe a cup of pea soup and crackers already started.

As soon as the temperature drops, the fog comes in. The lampposts seem to be drawing mists like darting mosquitoes around their bulbs. The late-night walkers stroll in their raincoats. And the soupy steam plunges out of the steam pipes, whose heads are bent like periscopes looking up from the construction site, the street an open gash, as it gets to be eleven o'clock, in front of the lit Athens coffee shop.

Who goes into the coffee shop at this late hour? A few too busy to have taken their dinners earlier sit at single tables barely watching the food they put in their mouths. In the larger booths are spillouts from exercise classes, rehearsals, discussion groups, meditation centers; the group spirit is high, they are all chewing on the same experience. For those who went to the activity really only to socialize, to meet a man or woman, the coffee shop where they repair afterward is the whole point of the evening.

Here begins the fancy come-on, or the soft modest Ping-Pong of "What did you think of the class tonight?" and "Well, this is only my first time. . . ." "I like all kinds of music. Classical. Light-classical. Rock." "I like jazz myself." "Oh, of course, jazz. . . ." Tastes are weighed against facial expressions, looks. Sensitivity is important, but must not shade into moroseness, or they will say, "She's very attractive but she always seems to have this cloud of despair above her head." These tables are happiest when they order.

At the counter is a different set: more old-timers, bearded ladies, loners; an occasional drunk, talking to himself in a mushy undertone and facing straight ahead, so that it looks as though he's addressing the large flat crumb cake with square sections cut out of it. "I can't stand her freakin' mouth." The crumb cake, like a bartender, pretends to listen inside its plastic box.

Coffee is always being served, but it has a different meaning and a different taste when it's drunk at this hour. No longer the honest optimistic cup of coffee to wake you up and send you off to conquer, this is the fifth cup of the day, the cup of "so what?," a briny toast to insomnia, with a little of mother's-milk nurturance poured from the creamer. Half-hearted coffee! Even the creamer at this hour leaves spots of spoiled curd, like white phlegm. You can demand a new cup, or you can drink it and accept whatever else comes from the waiters' hands, imagining that these discontented Greeks — longing to go back to their native sunshine, telling you how much they hate this city with its cold and crowds and rain — are curly-headed instruments of the

Divine Will that sets a feast before you every moment. You take whatever passes in front of you and give it a light twist, send it spinning a few seconds like a top, then return it gently and gravely to its original position.